TEENAGE MUTANT NINJA TURTLES

CHANGE IS CONSTANT · VOL. 1

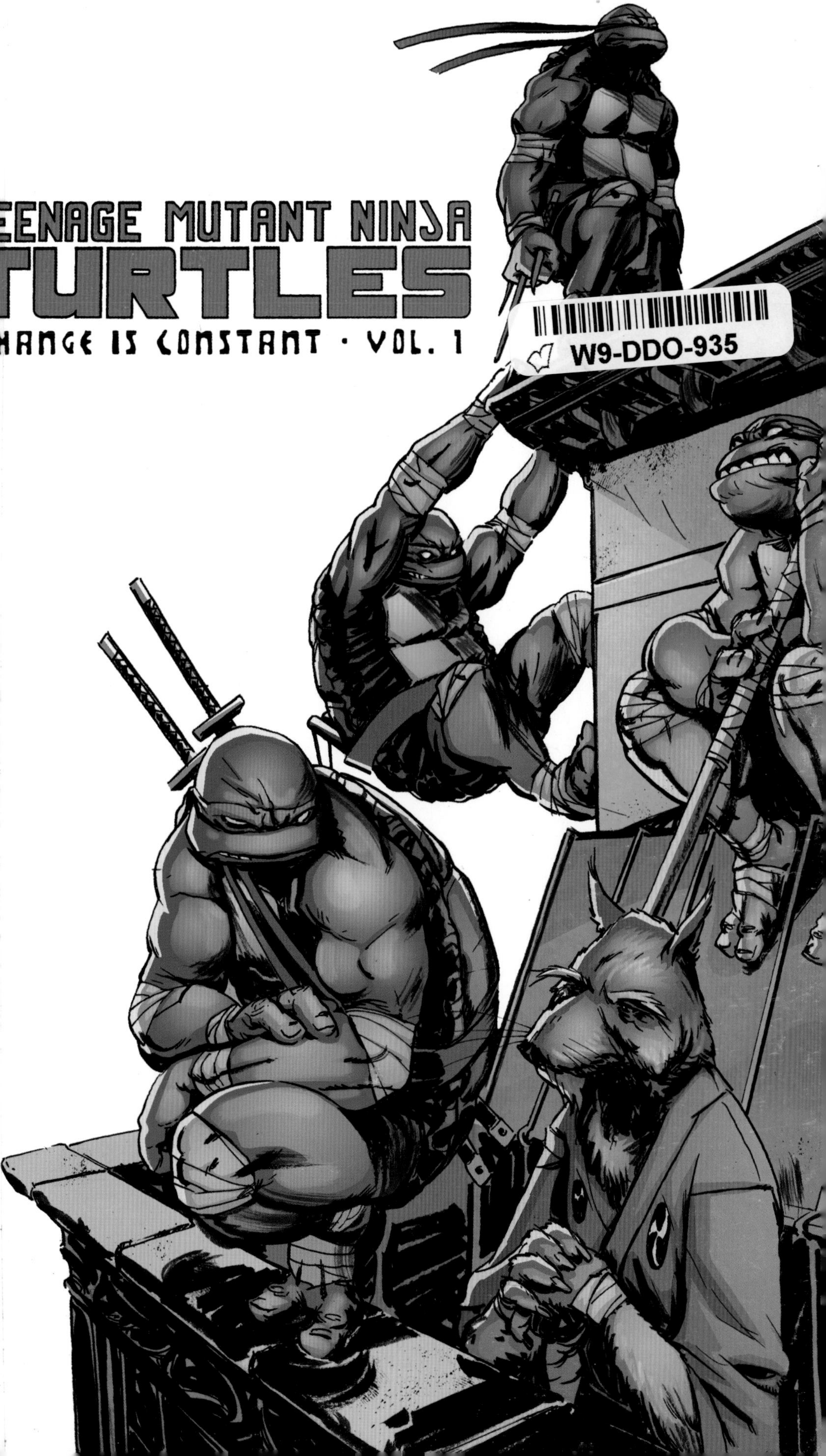

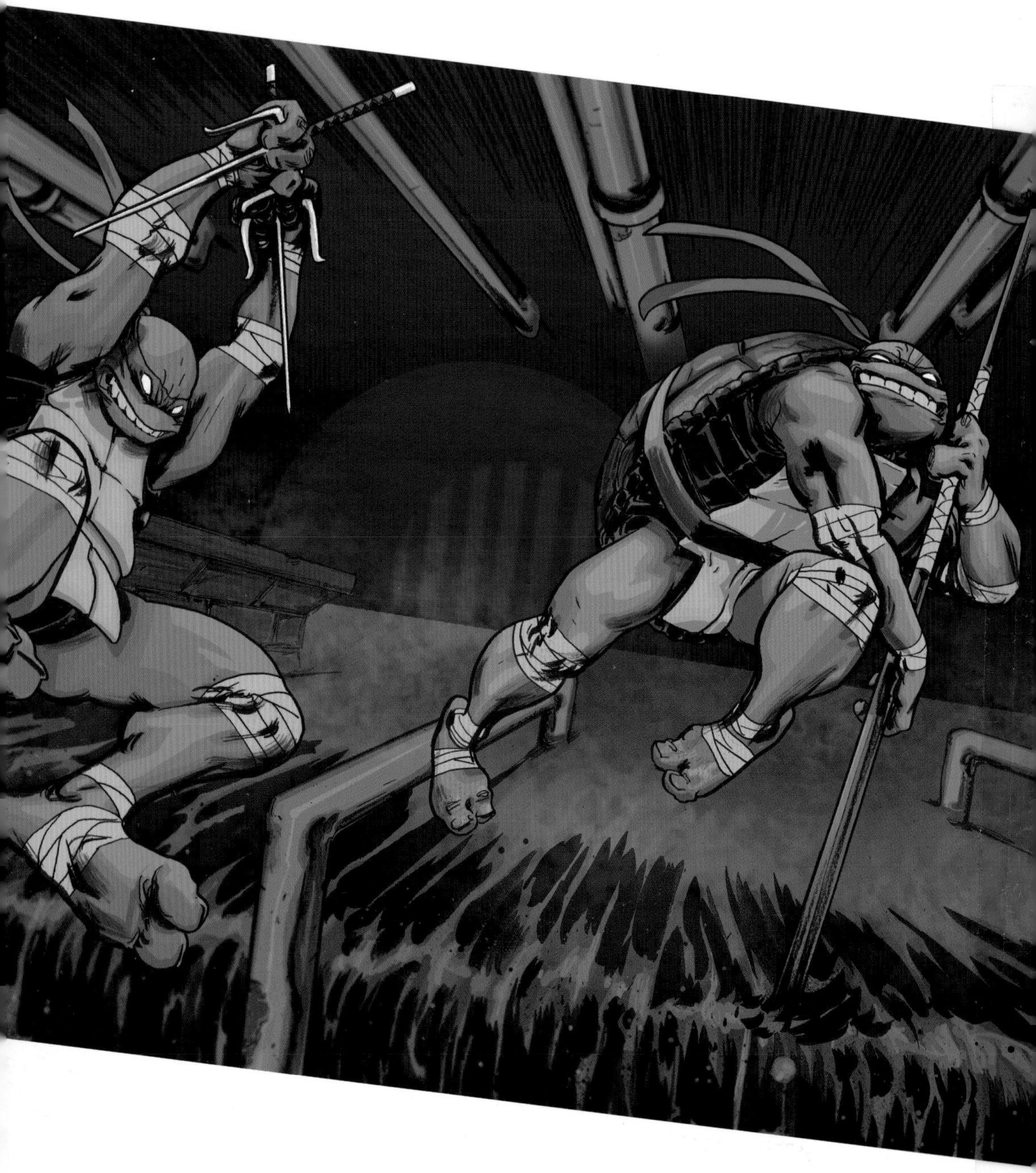

Special thanks to Joan Hilty, Brian Smith, Linda Lee, and Kat van Dam for their invaluable assistance.

nickelodeon™

IDW founded by Ted Adams, Alex Garner, Kris Oprisko, and Robbie Robbins

ISBN: 978-1-61377-139-6

16 15 14 13 5 6 7 8

IDW®

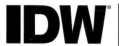

Ted Adams, CEO & Publisher
Greg Goldstein, Chief Operating Officer
Robbie Robbins, EVP/Sr. Graphic Artist
Chris Ryall, Chief Creative Officer/Editor-in-Chief
Matthew Ruzicka, CPA, Chief Financial Officer
Alan Payne, VP of Sales

Become our fan on Facebook **facebook.com/idwpublishing**
Follow us on Twitter **@idwpublishing**
Check us out on YouTube **youtube.com/idwpublishing**
www.IDWPUBLISHING.com

Originally published as TEENAGE MUTANT NINJA TURTLES Issues #1–4.

Story by Kevin Eastman & Tom Waltz • Script by Tom Waltz • Layouts by Kevin Eastman • Art by Dan Duncan
Colors by Ronda Pattison • Letters by Robbie Robbins • Series Edits by Scott Dunbier & Bobby Curnow

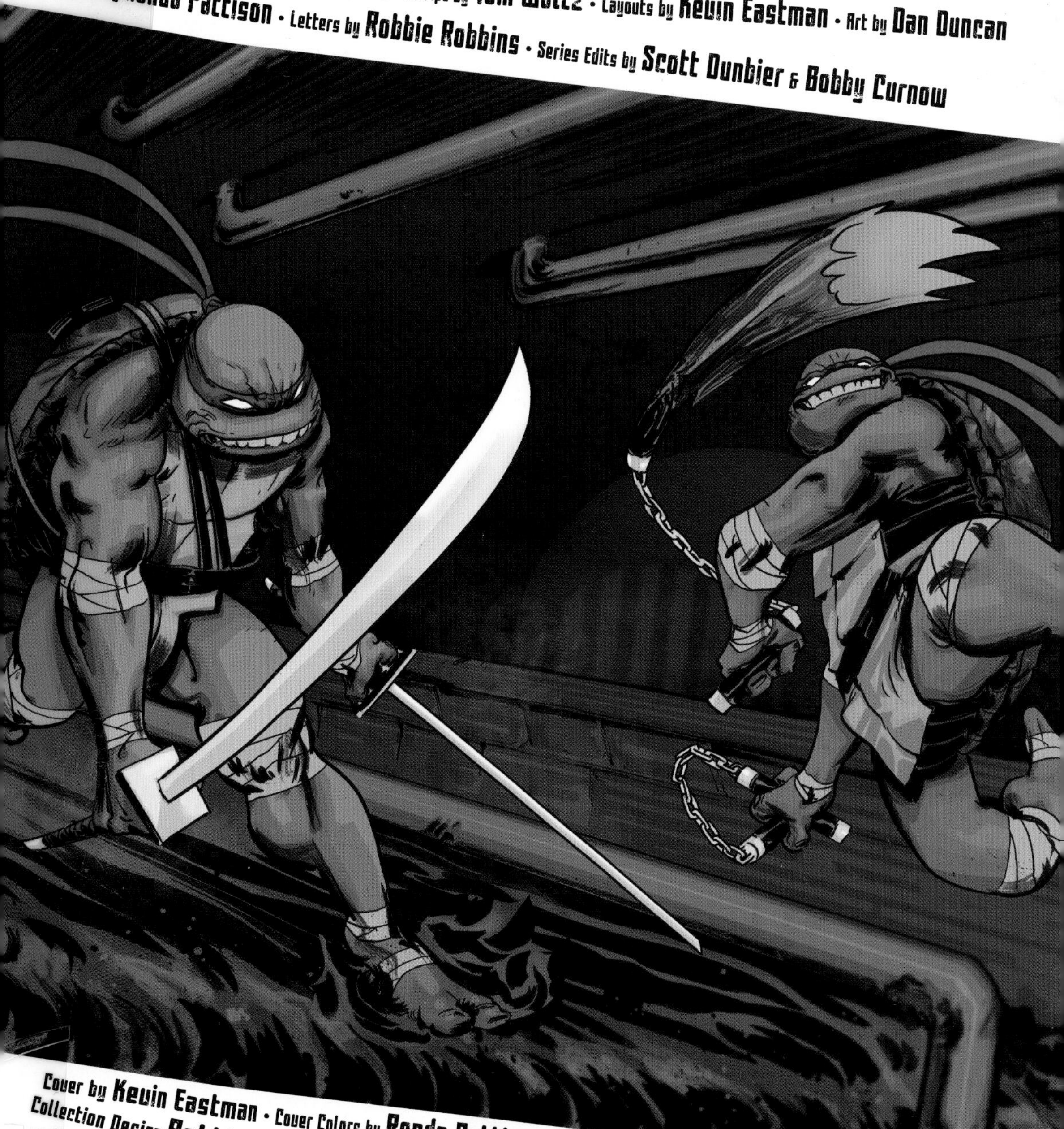

Cover by Kevin Eastman • Cover Colors by Ronda Pattison • Collection Edits Justin Eisinger & Alonzo Simon
Collection Design Robbie Robbins • Pages 1, 2, 3 art by Dan Duncan, Colors by Ronda Pattison
Page 4 art by Kevin Eastman • Colors by Ronda Pattison

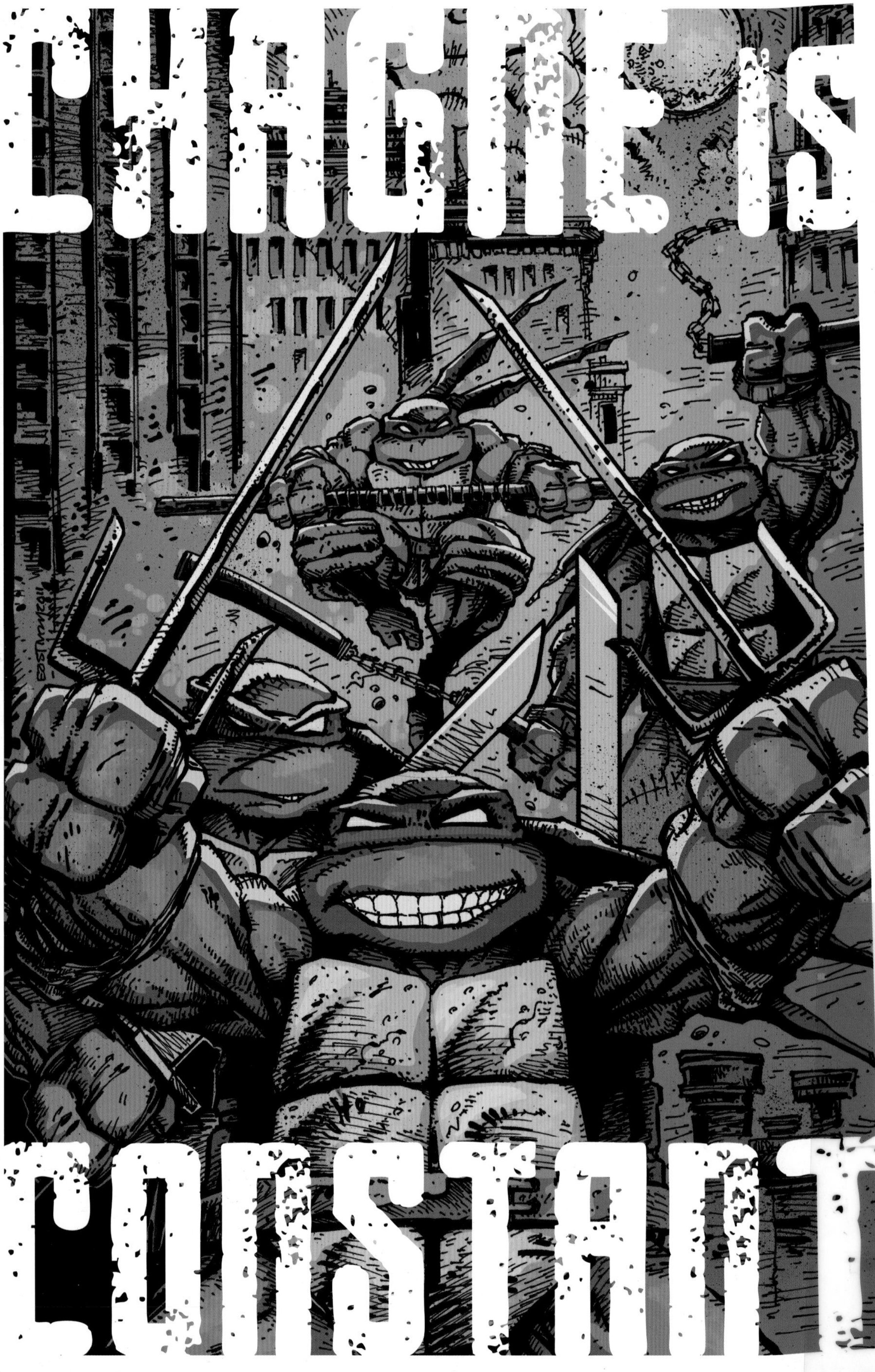
CHANGE IS
CONSTANT

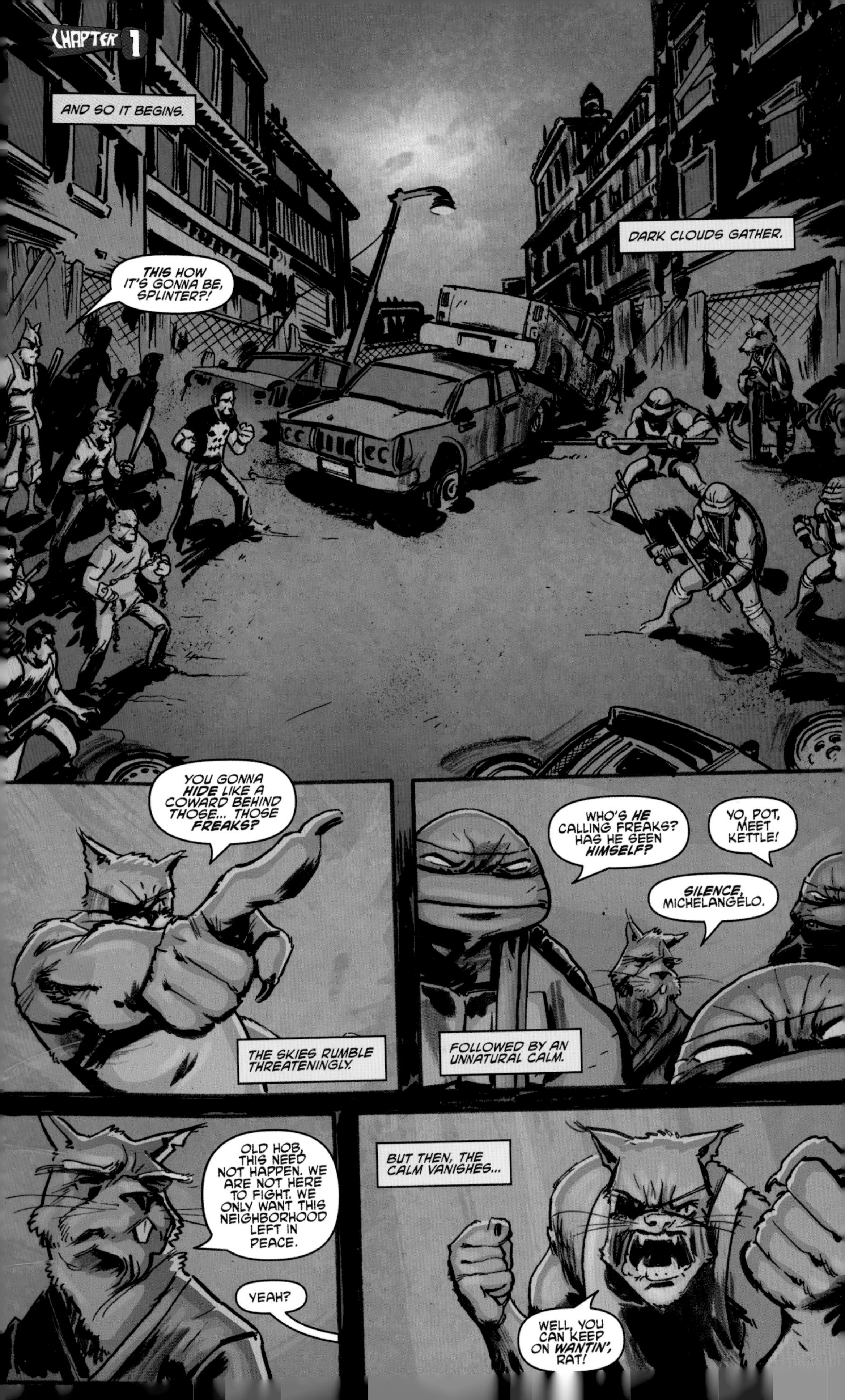
CHAPTER 1
AND SO IT BEGINS.
DARK CLOUDS GATHER.
THIS HOW IT'S GONNA BE, SPLINTER?!
YOU GONNA HIDE LIKE A COWARD BEHIND THOSE... THOSE FREAKS?
THE SKIES RUMBLE THREATENINGLY.
WHO'S HE CALLING FREAKS? HAS HE SEEN HIMSELF?
YO, POT, MEET KETTLE!
SILENCE, MICHELANGELO.
FOLLOWED BY AN UNNATURAL CALM.
OLD HOB, THIS NEED NOT HAPPEN. WE ARE NOT HERE TO FIGHT. WE ONLY WANT THIS NEIGHBORHOOD LEFT IN PEACE.
YEAH?
BUT THEN, THE CALM VANISHES...
WELL, YOU CAN KEEP ON WANTIN', RAT!

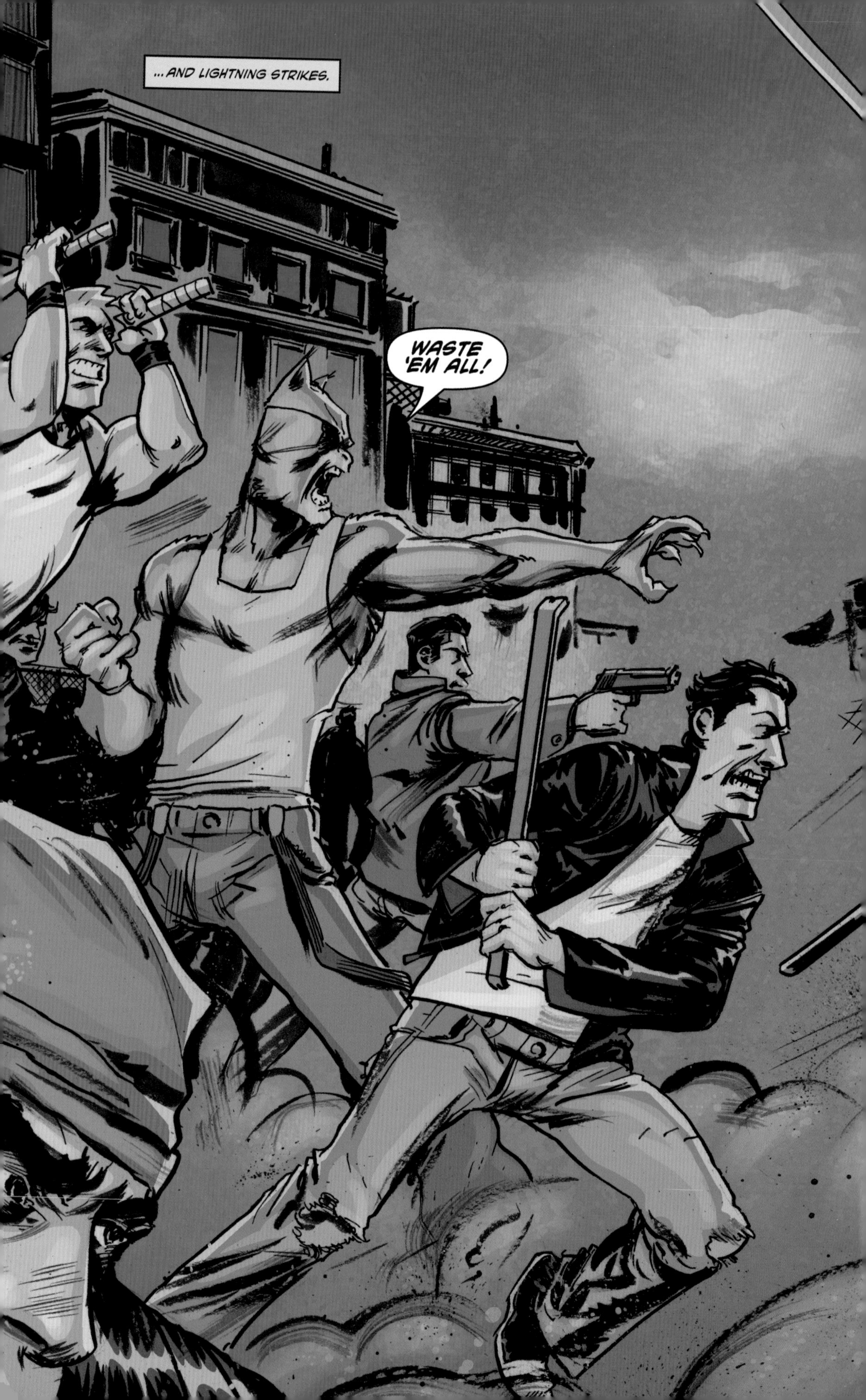
...AND LIGHTNING STRIKES.
WASTE 'EM ALL!

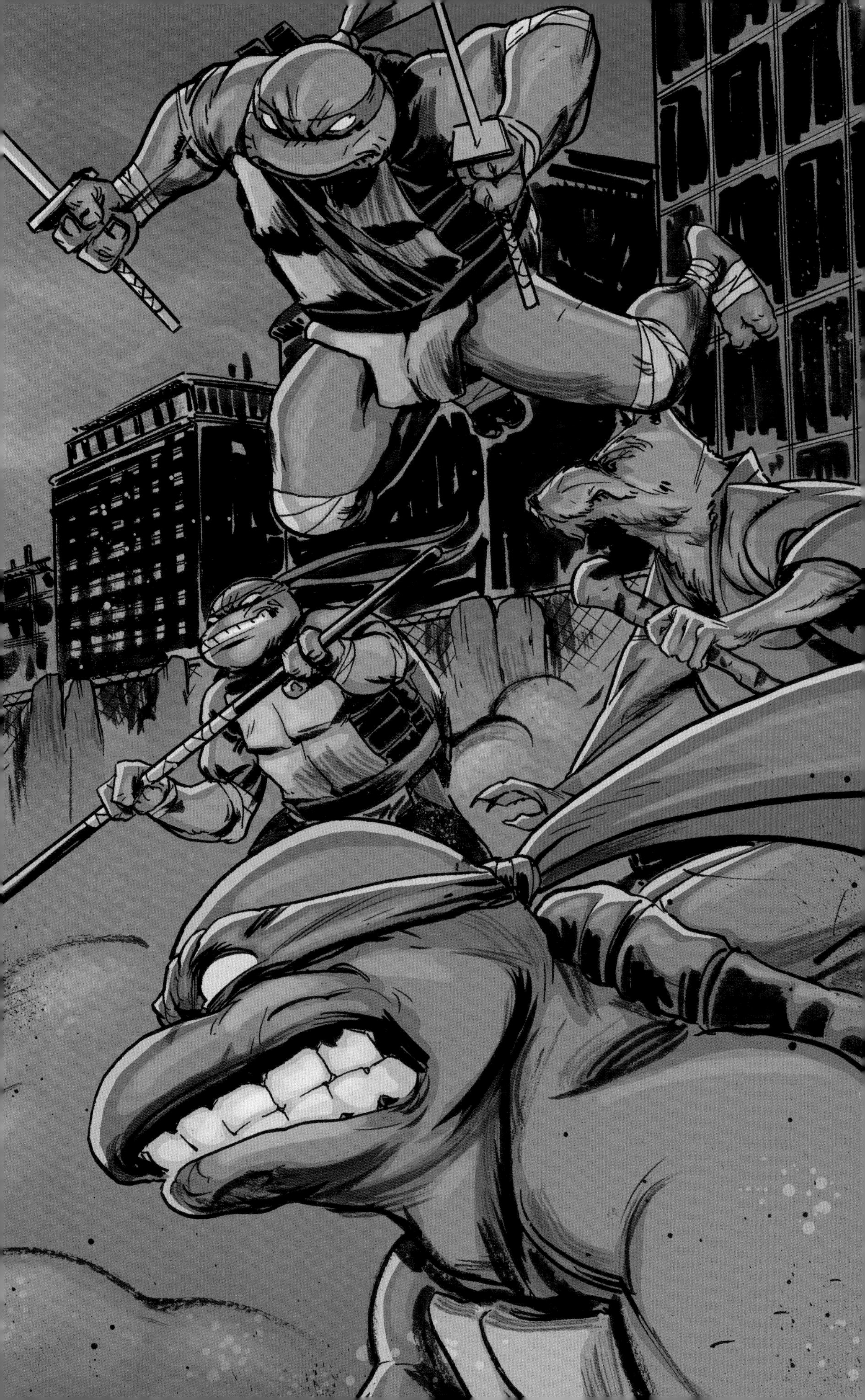

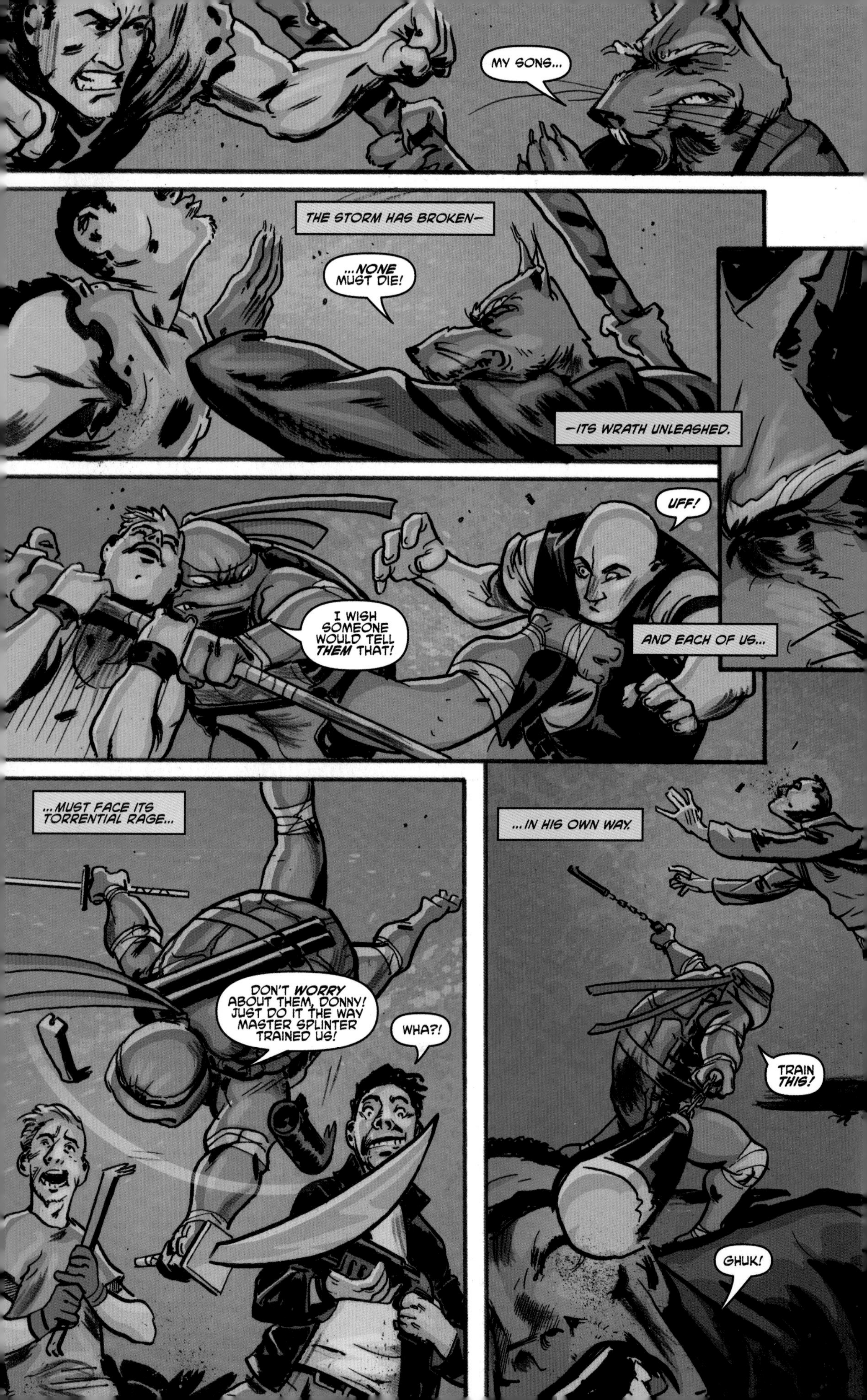
MY SONS...
THE STORM HAS BROKEN—
...NONE MUST DIE!
—ITS WRATH UNLEASHED.
UFF!
I WISH SOMEONE WOULD TELL THEM THAT!
AND EACH OF US...
...MUST FACE ITS TORRENTIAL RAGE...
DON'T WORRY ABOUT THEM, DONNY! JUST DO IT THE WAY MASTER SPLINTER TRAINED US!
WHA?!
...IN HIS OWN WAY.
TRAIN THIS!
GHUK!

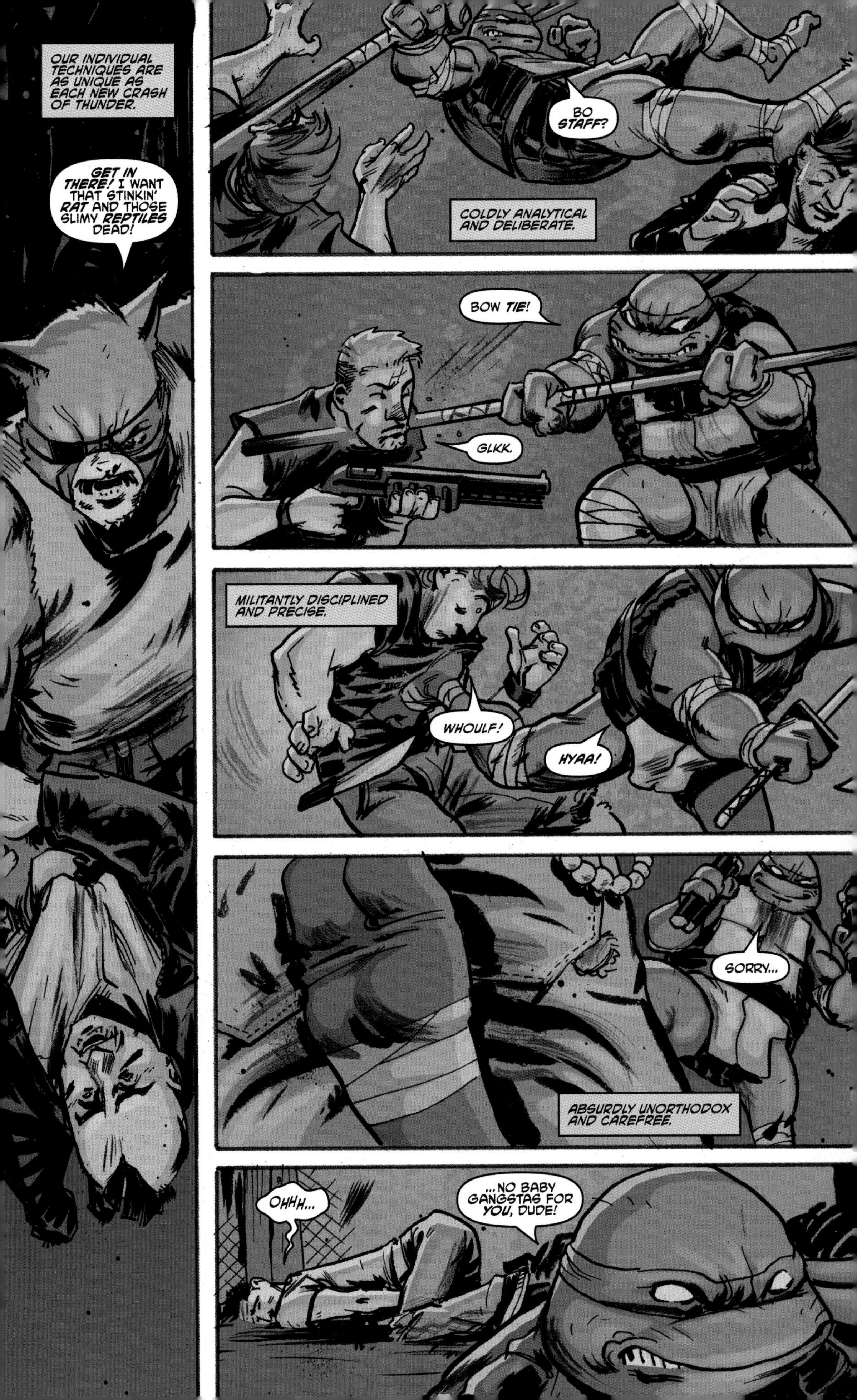
OUR INDIVIDUAL TECHNIQUES ARE AS UNIQUE AS EACH NEW CRASH OF THUNDER.
GET IN THERE! I WANT THAT STINKIN' RAT AND THOSE SLIMY REPTILES DEAD!
BO STAFF?
COLDLY ANALYTICAL AND DELIBERATE.
BOW TIE!
GLKK.
MILITANTLY DISCIPLINED AND PRECISE.
WHOULF!
HYAA!
SORRY...
ABSURDLY UNORTHODOX AND CAREFREE.
OHHH...
...NO BABY GANGSTAS FOR YOU, DUDE!

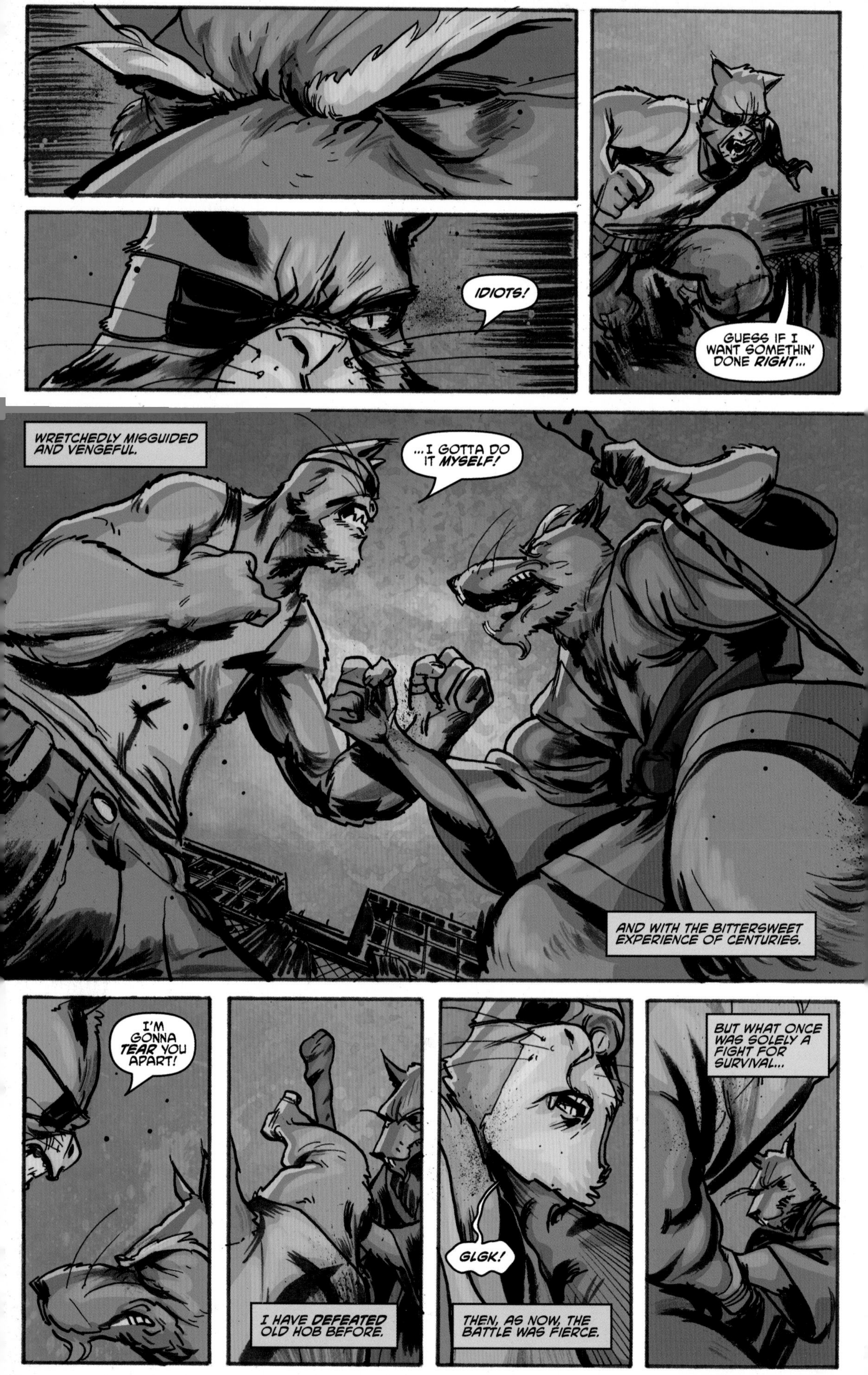
IDIOTS!
GUESS IF I WANT SOMETHIN' DONE RIGHT...
WRETCHEDLY MISGUIDED AND VENGEFUL.
...I GOTTA DO IT MYSELF!
AND WITH THE BITTERSWEET EXPERIENCE OF CENTURIES.
I'M GONNA TEAR YOU APART!
I HAVE DEFEATED OLD HOB BEFORE.
GLGK!
THEN, AS NOW, THE BATTLE WAS FIERCE.
BUT WHAT ONCE WAS SOLELY A FIGHT FOR SURVIVAL...

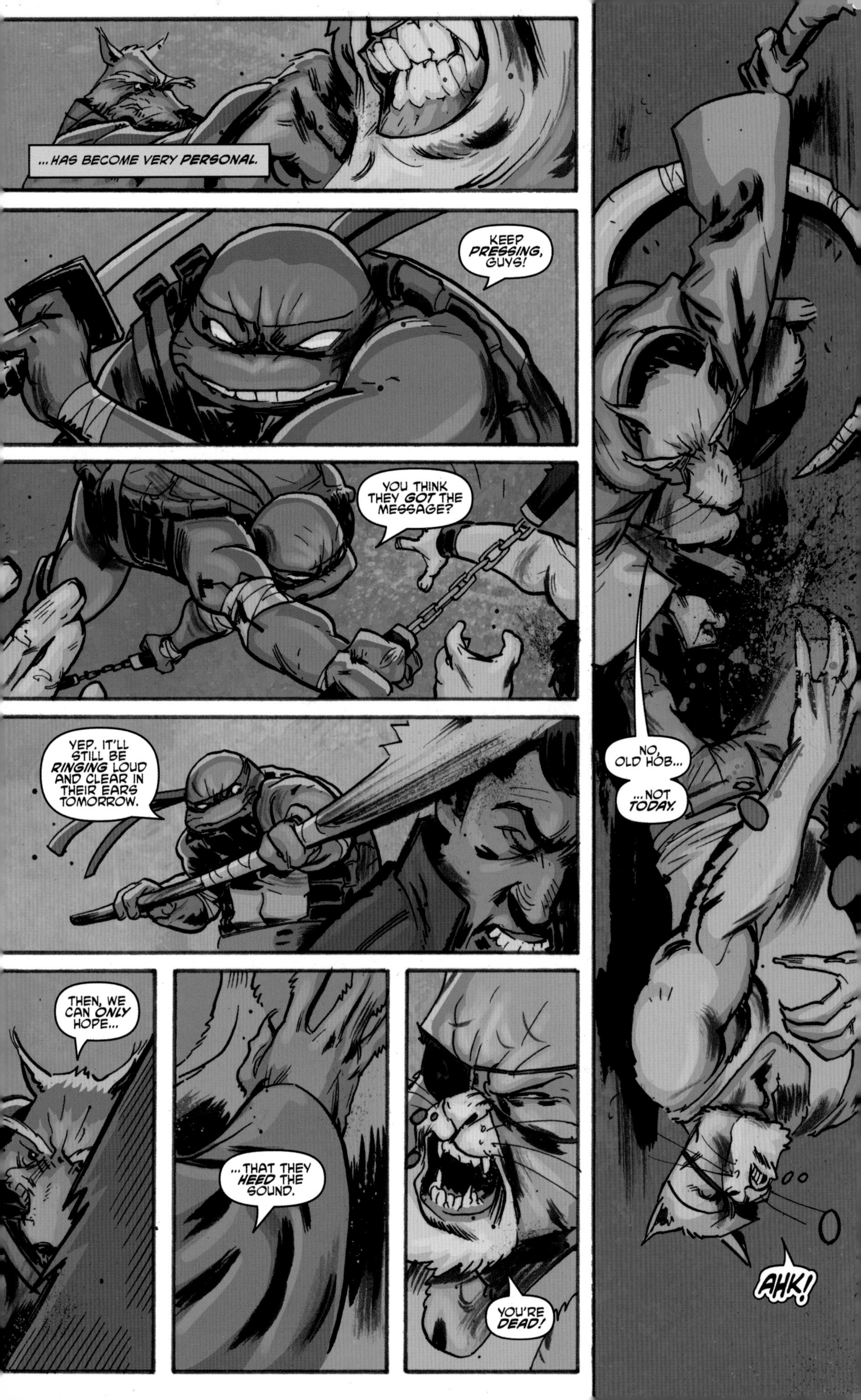
...HAS BECOME VERY PERSONAL.
KEEP PRESSING, GUYS!
YOU THINK THEY GOT THE MESSAGE?
YEP. IT'LL STILL BE RINGING LOUD AND CLEAR IN THEIR EARS TOMORROW.
THEN, WE CAN ONLY HOPE...
...THAT THEY HEED THE SOUND.
YOU'RE DEAD!
NO, OLD HOB...
...NOT TODAY.
AHK!

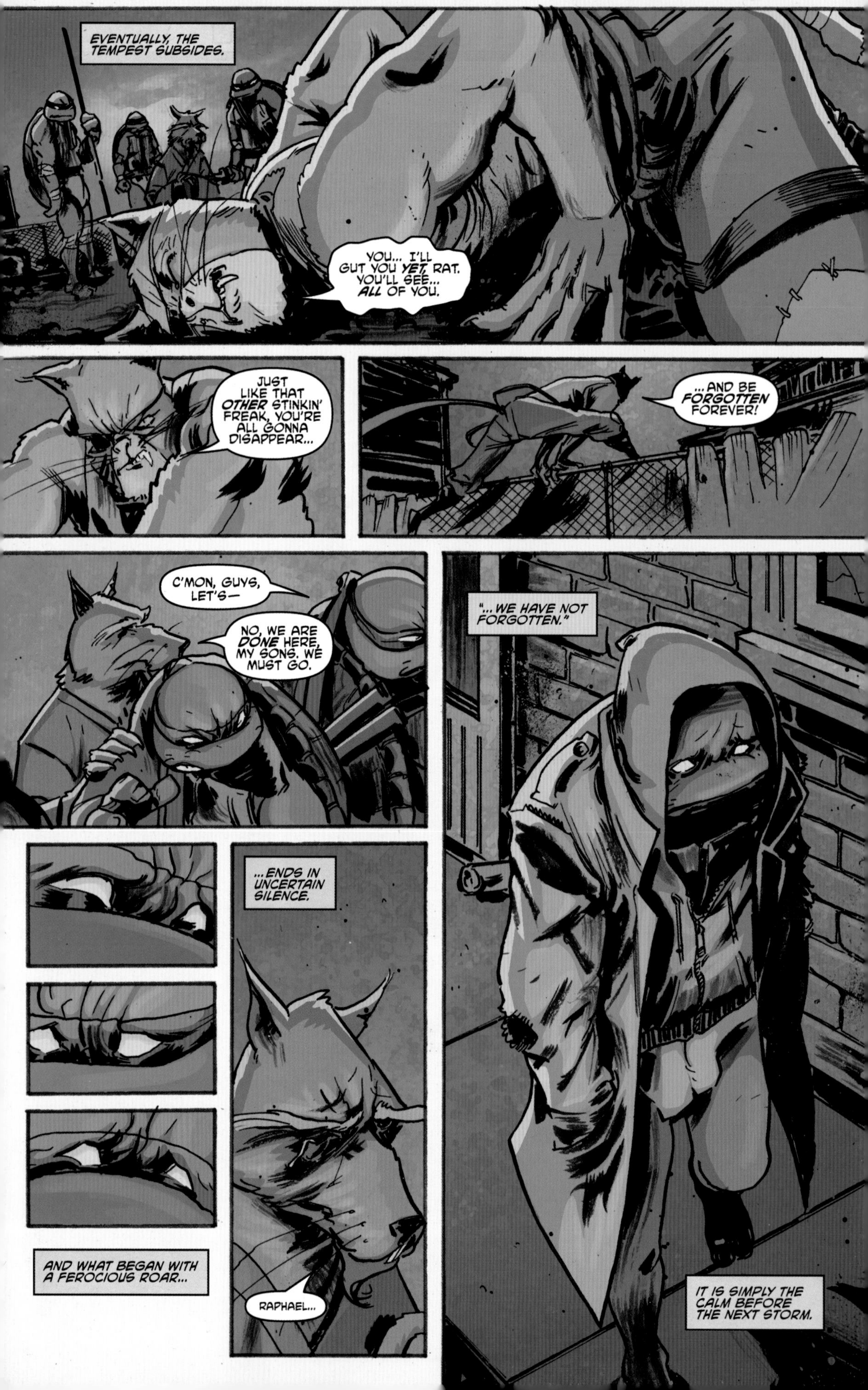
EVENTUALLY, THE TEMPEST SUBSIDES.
YOU... I'LL GUT YOU YET, RAT. YOU'LL SEE... ALL OF YOU.
JUST LIKE THAT OTHER STINKIN' FREAK, YOU'RE ALL GONNA DISAPPEAR...
...AND BE FORGOTTEN FOREVER!
C'MON, GUYS, LET'S—
NO, WE ARE DONE HERE, MY SONS. WE MUST GO.
"...WE HAVE NOT FORGOTTEN."
AND WHAT BEGAN WITH A FEROCIOUS ROAR...
...ENDS IN UNCERTAIN SILENCE.
RAPHAEL...
IT IS SIMPLY THE CALM BEFORE THE NEXT STORM.

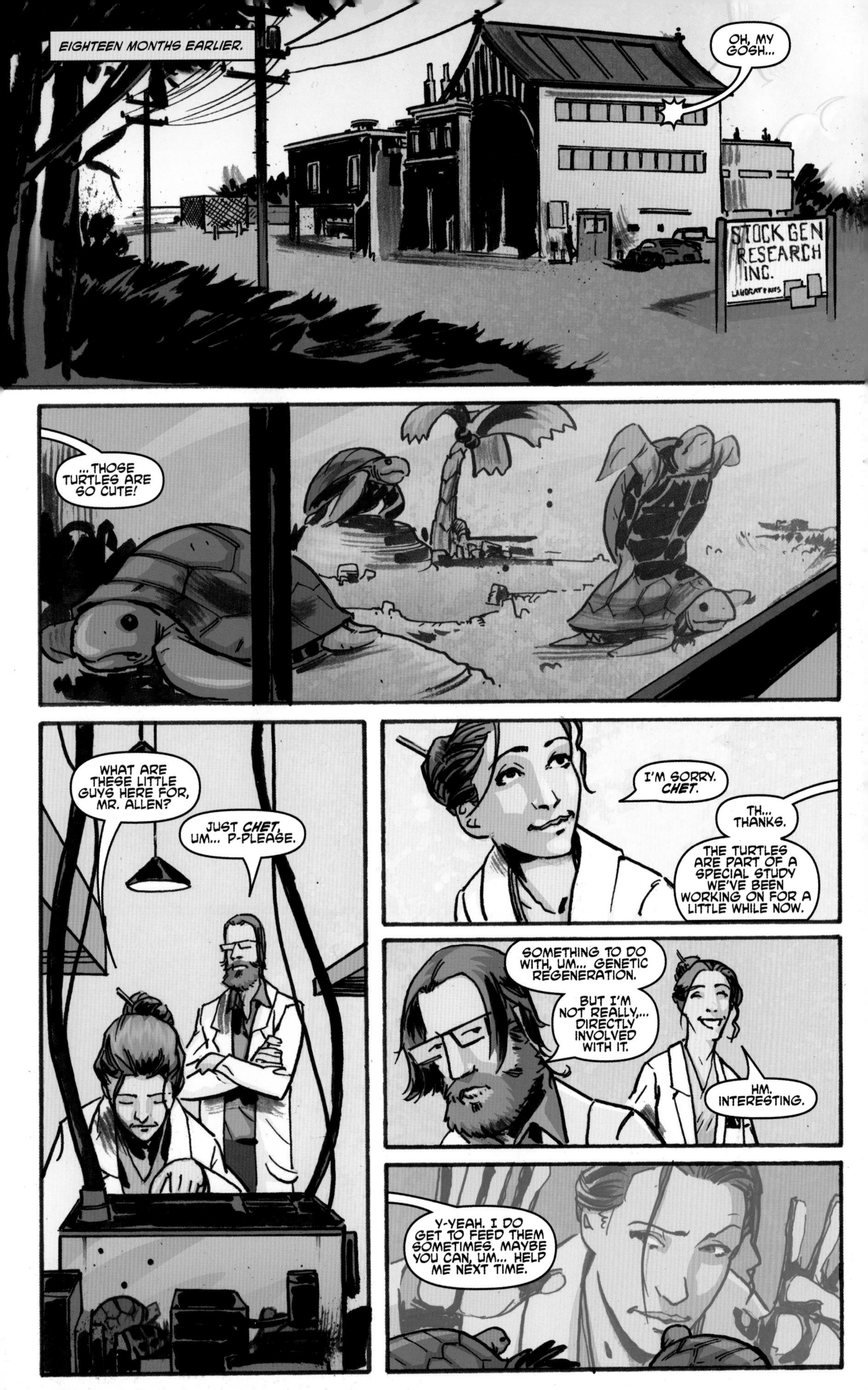
EIGHTEEN MONTHS EARLIER.
OH, MY GOSH...
STOCK GEN RESEARCH INC.
...THOSE TURTLES ARE SO CUTE!
WHAT ARE THESE LITTLE GUYS HERE FOR, MR. ALLEN?
JUST CHET, UM... P-PLEASE.
I'M SORRY. CHET.
TH... THANKS.
THE TURTLES ARE PART OF A SPECIAL STUDY WE'VE BEEN WORKING ON FOR A LITTLE WHILE NOW.
SOMETHING TO DO WITH, UM... GENETIC REGENERATION.
BUT I'M NOT REALLY,... DIRECTLY INVOLVED WITH IT.
HM. INTERESTING.
Y-YEAH. I DO GET TO FEED THEM SOMETIMES. MAYBE YOU CAN, UM... HELP ME NEXT TIME.

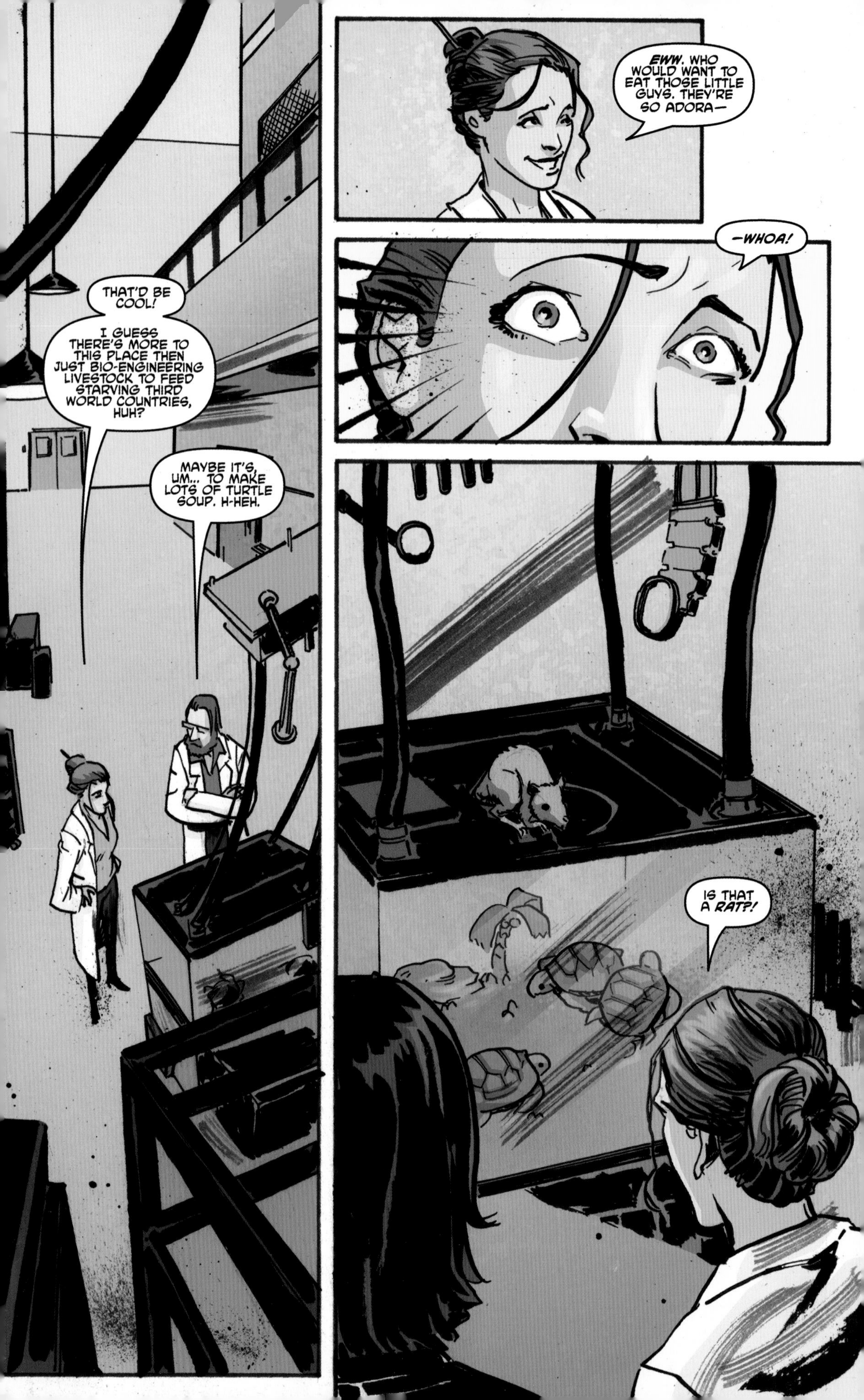
THAT'D BE COOL!
I GUESS THERE'S MORE TO THIS PLACE THEN JUST BIO-ENGINEERING LIVESTOCK TO FEED STARVING THIRD WORLD COUNTRIES, HUH?
MAYBE IT'S, UM... TO MAKE LOTS OF TURTLE SOUP. H-HEH.
EWW. WHO WOULD WANT TO EAT THOSE LITTLE GUYS. THEY'RE SO ADORA—
—WHOA!
IS THAT A RAT?!

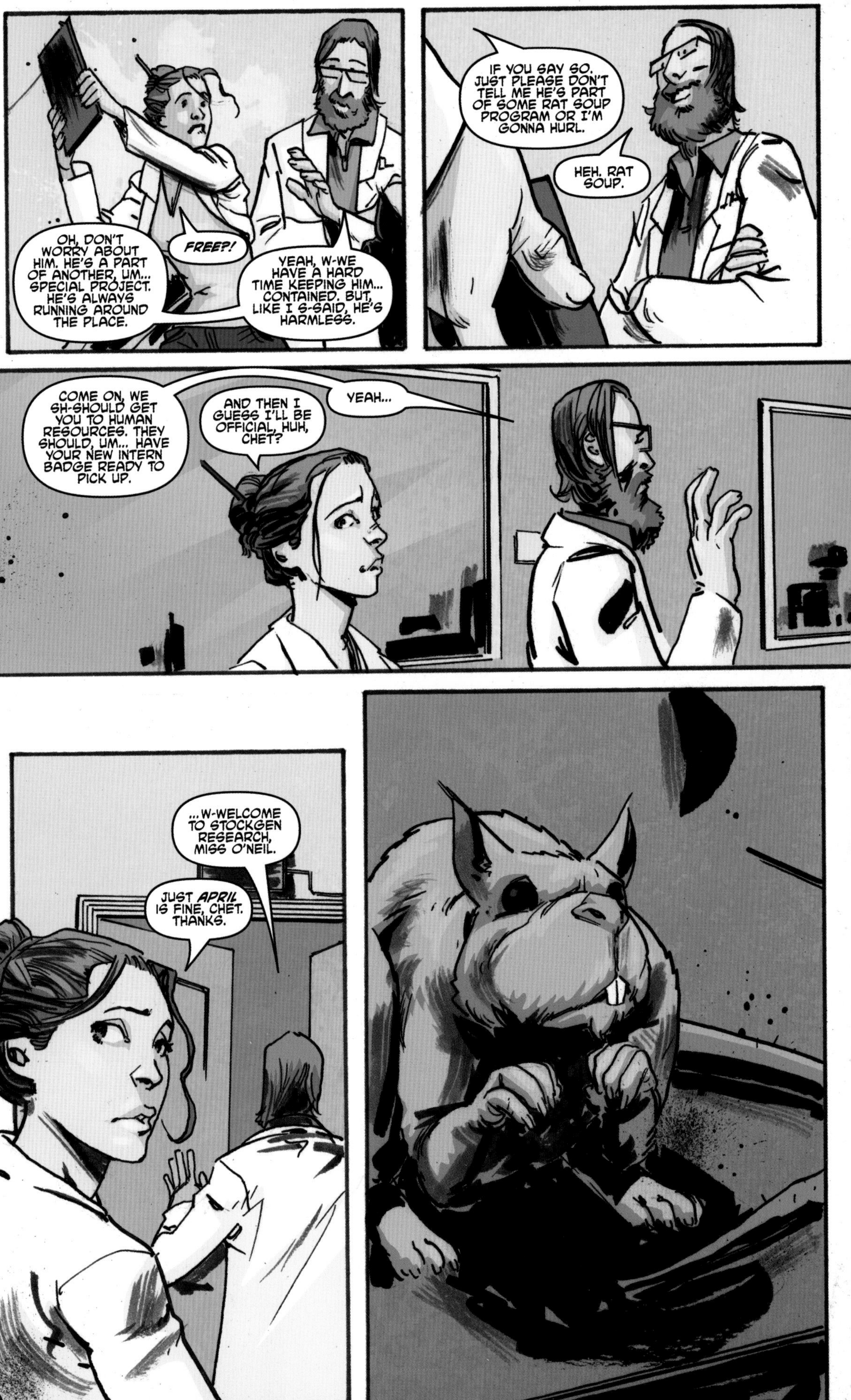

FREE?!
OH, DON'T WORRY ABOUT HIM. HE'S A PART OF ANOTHER, UM... SPECIAL PROJECT. HE'S ALWAYS RUNNING AROUND THE PLACE.
YEAH, W-WE HAVE A HARD TIME KEEPING HIM... CONTAINED. BUT, LIKE I S-SAID, HE'S HARMLESS.
IF YOU SAY SO. JUST PLEASE DON'T TELL ME HE'S PART OF SOME RAT SOUP PROGRAM OR I'M GONNA HURL.
HEH. RAT SOUP.
COME ON, WE SH-SHOULD GET YOU TO HUMAN RESOURCES. THEY SHOULD, UM... HAVE YOUR NEW INTERN BADGE READY TO PICK UP.
AND THEN I GUESS I'LL BE OFFICIAL, HUH, CHET?
YEAH...
...W-WELCOME TO STOCKGEN RESEARCH, MISS O'NEIL.
JUST APRIL IS FINE, CHET. THANKS.

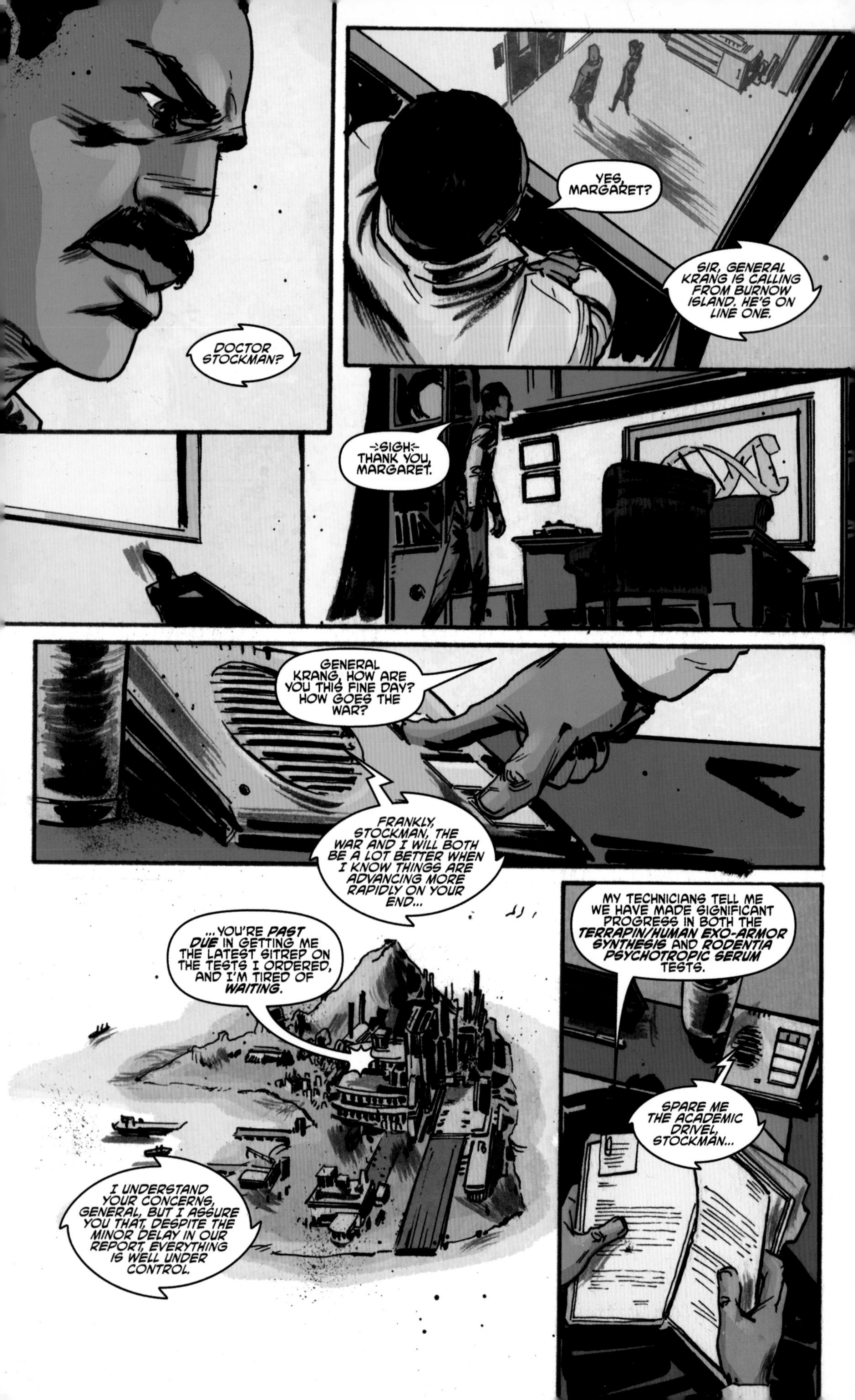
DOCTOR STOCKMAN?
YES, MARGARET?
SIR, GENERAL KRANG IS CALLING FROM BURNOW ISLAND. HE'S ON LINE ONE.
-SIGH- THANK YOU, MARGARET.
GENERAL KRANG, HOW ARE YOU THIS FINE DAY? HOW GOES THE WAR?
FRANKLY, STOCKMAN, THE WAR AND I WILL BOTH BE A LOT BETTER WHEN I KNOW THINGS ARE ADVANCING MORE RAPIDLY ON YOUR END...
...YOU'RE PAST DUE IN GETTING ME THE LATEST SITREP ON THE TESTS I ORDERED, AND I'M TIRED OF WAITING.
I UNDERSTAND YOUR CONCERNS, GENERAL, BUT I ASSURE YOU THAT, DESPITE THE MINOR DELAY IN OUR REPORT, EVERYTHING IS WELL UNDER CONTROL.
MY TECHNICIANS TELL ME WE HAVE MADE SIGNIFICANT PROGRESS IN BOTH THE TERRAPIN/HUMAN EXO-ARMOR SYNTHESIS AND RODENTIA PSYCHOTROPIC SERUM TESTS.
SPARE ME THE ACADEMIC DRIVEL, STOCKMAN...

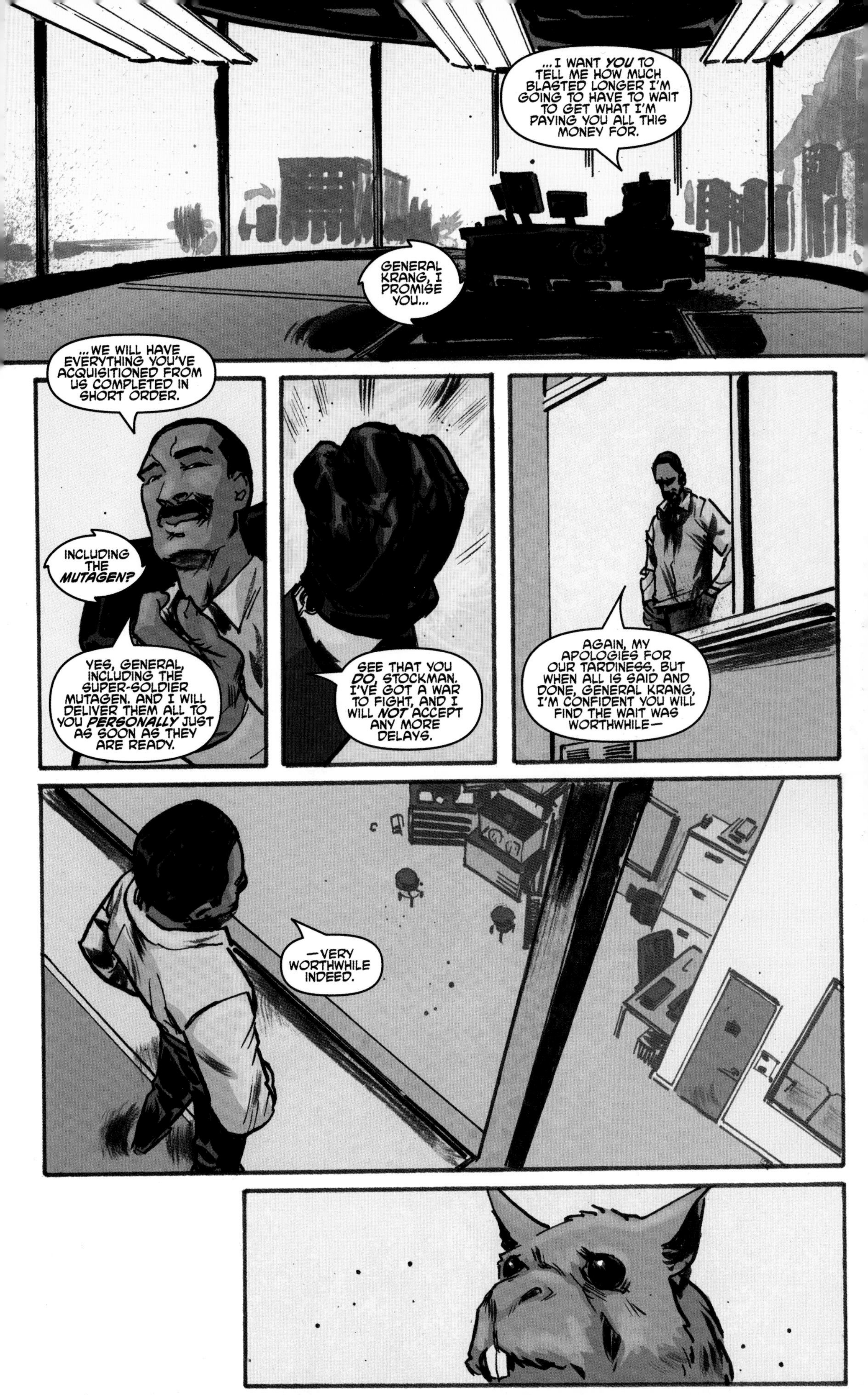
...I WANT *YOU* TO TELL ME HOW MUCH BLASTED LONGER I'M GOING TO HAVE TO WAIT TO GET WHAT I'M PAYING YOU ALL THIS MONEY FOR.
GENERAL KRANG, I PROMISE YOU...
...WE WILL HAVE EVERYTHING YOU'VE ACQUISITIONED FROM US COMPLETED IN SHORT ORDER.
INCLUDING THE *MUTAGEN?*
YES, GENERAL, INCLUDING THE SUPER-SOLDIER MUTAGEN. AND I WILL DELIVER THEM ALL TO YOU *PERSONALLY* JUST AS SOON AS THEY ARE READY.
SEE THAT YOU *DO*, STOCKMAN. I'VE GOT A WAR TO FIGHT, AND I WILL *NOT* ACCEPT ANY MORE DELAYS.
AGAIN, MY APOLOGIES FOR OUR TARDINESS. BUT WHEN ALL IS SAID AND DONE, GENERAL KRANG, I'M CONFIDENT YOU WILL FIND THE WAIT WAS WORTHWHILE—
—VERY WORTHWHILE INDEED.

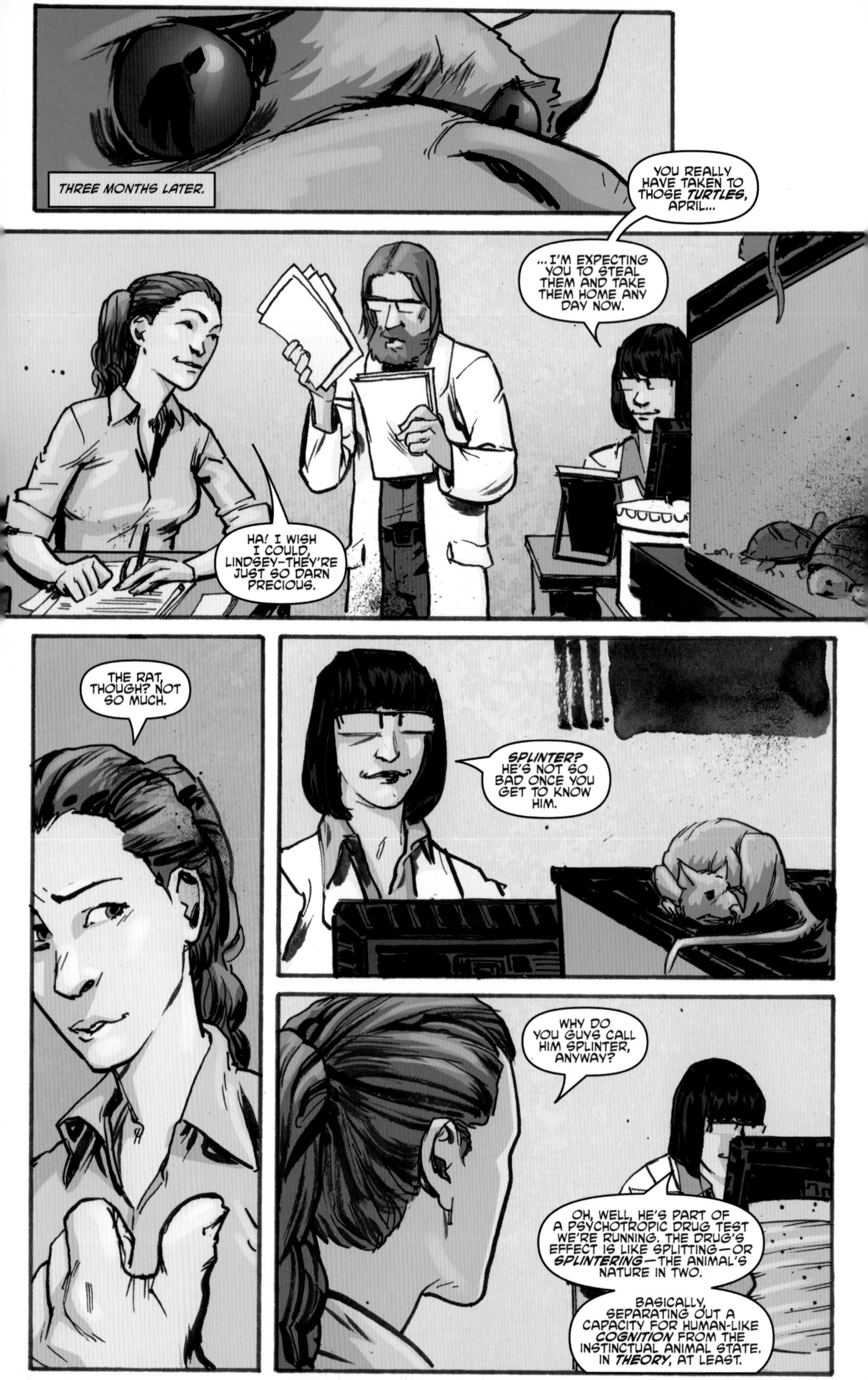
THREE MONTHS LATER.
YOU REALLY HAVE TAKEN TO THOSE *TURTLES*, APRIL...
...I'M EXPECTING YOU TO STEAL THEM AND TAKE THEM HOME ANY DAY NOW.
HA! I WISH I COULD, LINDSEY—THEY'RE JUST SO DARN PRECIOUS.
THE RAT, THOUGH? NOT SO MUCH.
SPLINTER? HE'S NOT SO BAD ONCE YOU GET TO KNOW HIM.
WHY DO YOU GUYS CALL HIM SPLINTER, ANYWAY?
OH, WELL, HE'S PART OF A PSYCHOTROPIC DRUG TEST WE'RE RUNNING. THE DRUG'S EFFECT IS LIKE SPLITTING—OR *SPLINTERING*—THE ANIMAL'S NATURE IN TWO.
BASICALLY, SEPARATING OUT A CAPACITY FOR HUMAN-LIKE *COGNITION* FROM THE INSTINCTUAL ANIMAL STATE. IN *THEORY*, AT LEAST.

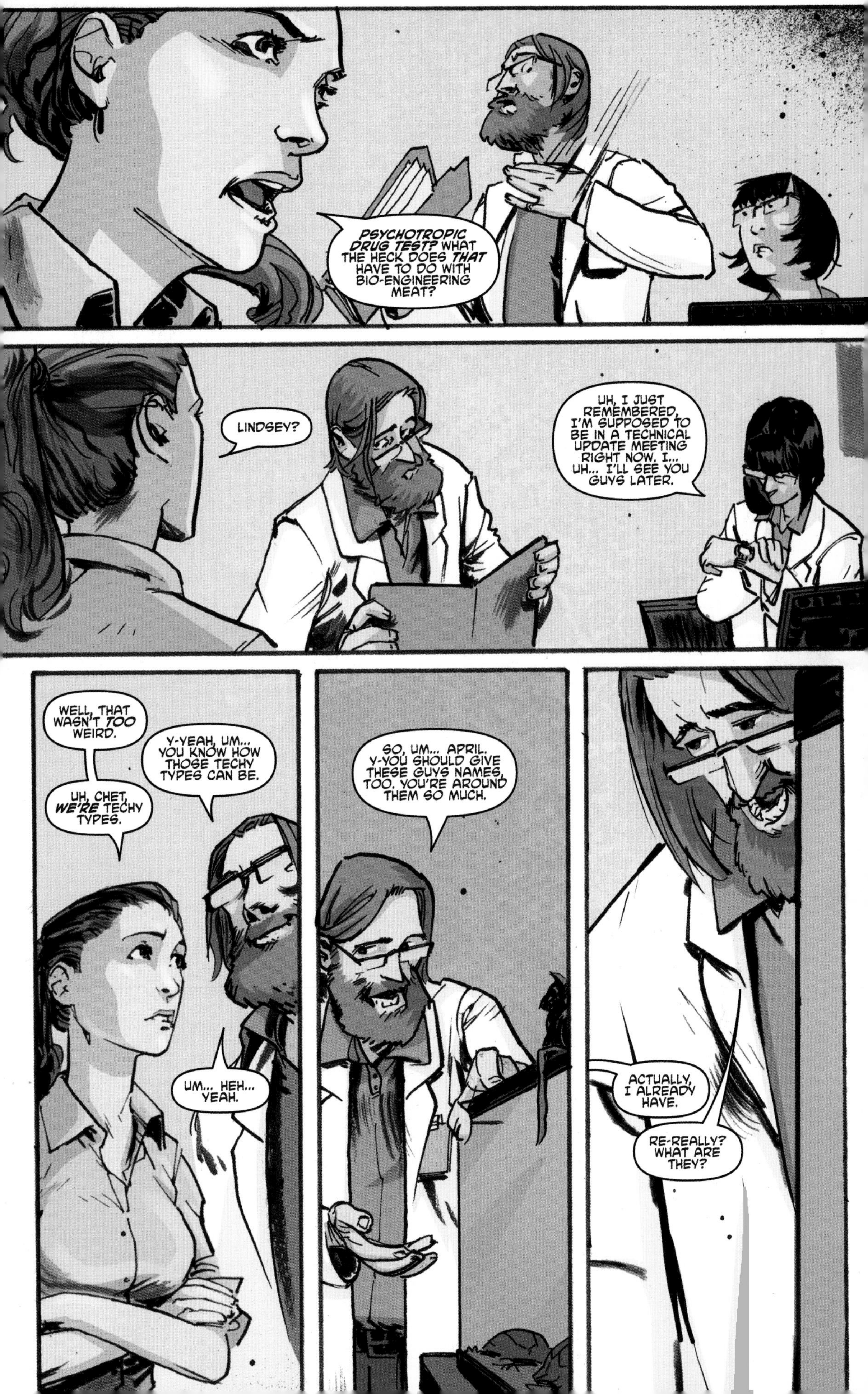
PSYCHOTROPIC DRUG TEST? WHAT THE HECK DOES *THAT* HAVE TO DO WITH BIO-ENGINEERING MEAT?
LINDSEY?
UH, I JUST REMEMBERED, I'M SUPPOSED TO BE IN A TECHNICAL UPDATE MEETING RIGHT NOW. I... UH... I'LL SEE YOU GUYS LATER.
WELL, THAT WASN'T *TOO* WEIRD.
Y-YEAH, UM... YOU KNOW HOW THOSE TECHY TYPES CAN BE.
UH, CHET, *WE'RE* TECHY TYPES.
UM... HEH... YEAH.
SO, UM... APRIL. Y-YOU SHOULD GIVE THESE GUYS NAMES, TOO. YOU'RE AROUND THEM SO MUCH.
ACTUALLY, I ALREADY HAVE.
RE-REALLY? WHAT ARE THEY?

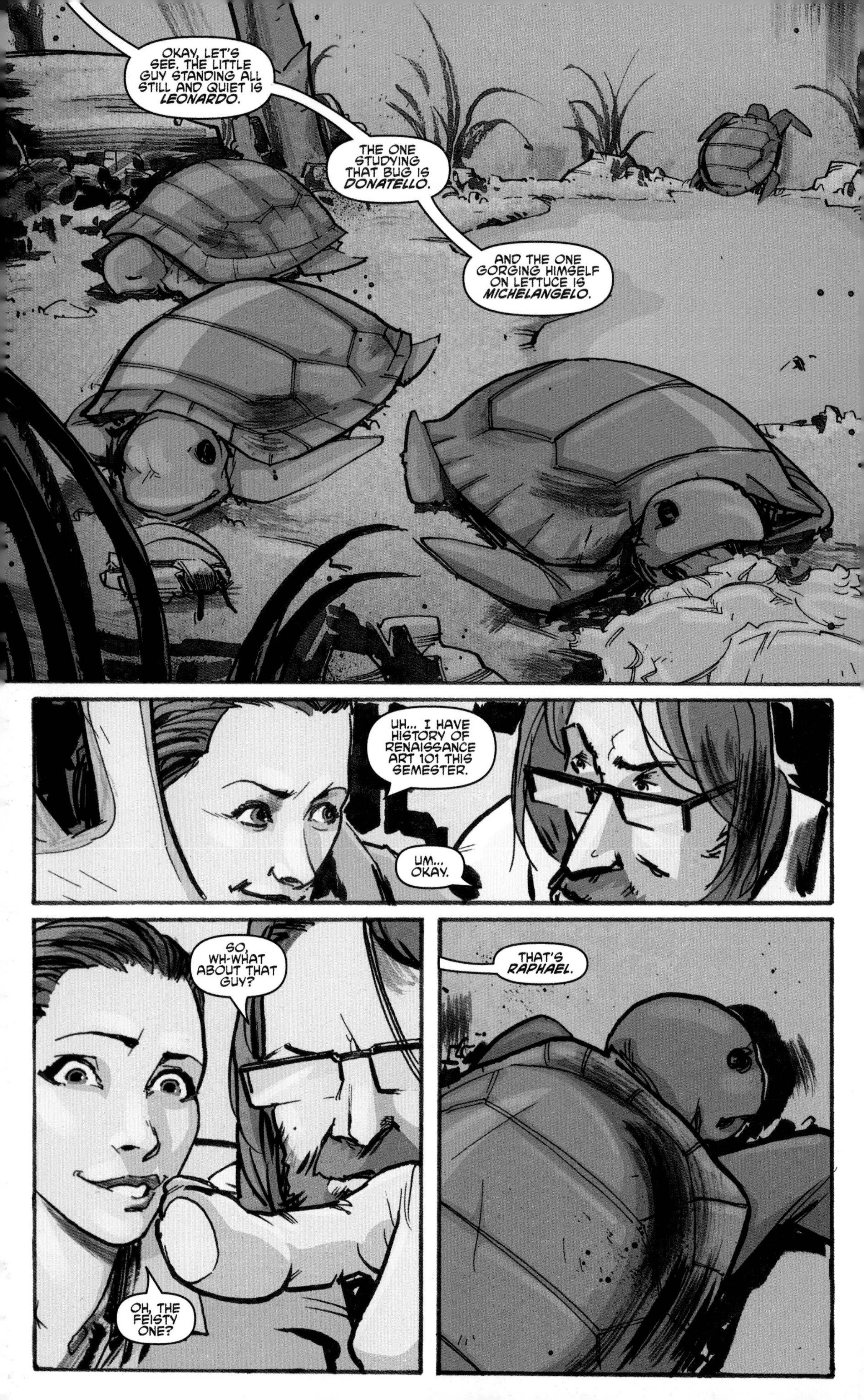
OKAY, LET'S SEE. THE LITTLE GUY STANDING ALL STILL AND QUIET IS *LEONARDO*.
THE ONE STUDYING THAT BUG IS *DONATELLO*.
AND THE ONE GORGING HIMSELF ON LETTUCE IS *MICHELANGELO*.
UH... I HAVE HISTORY OF RENAISSANCE ART 101 THIS SEMESTER.
UM... OKAY.
SO, WH-WHAT ABOUT THAT GUY?
OH, THE FEISTY ONE?
THAT'S *RAPHAEL*.

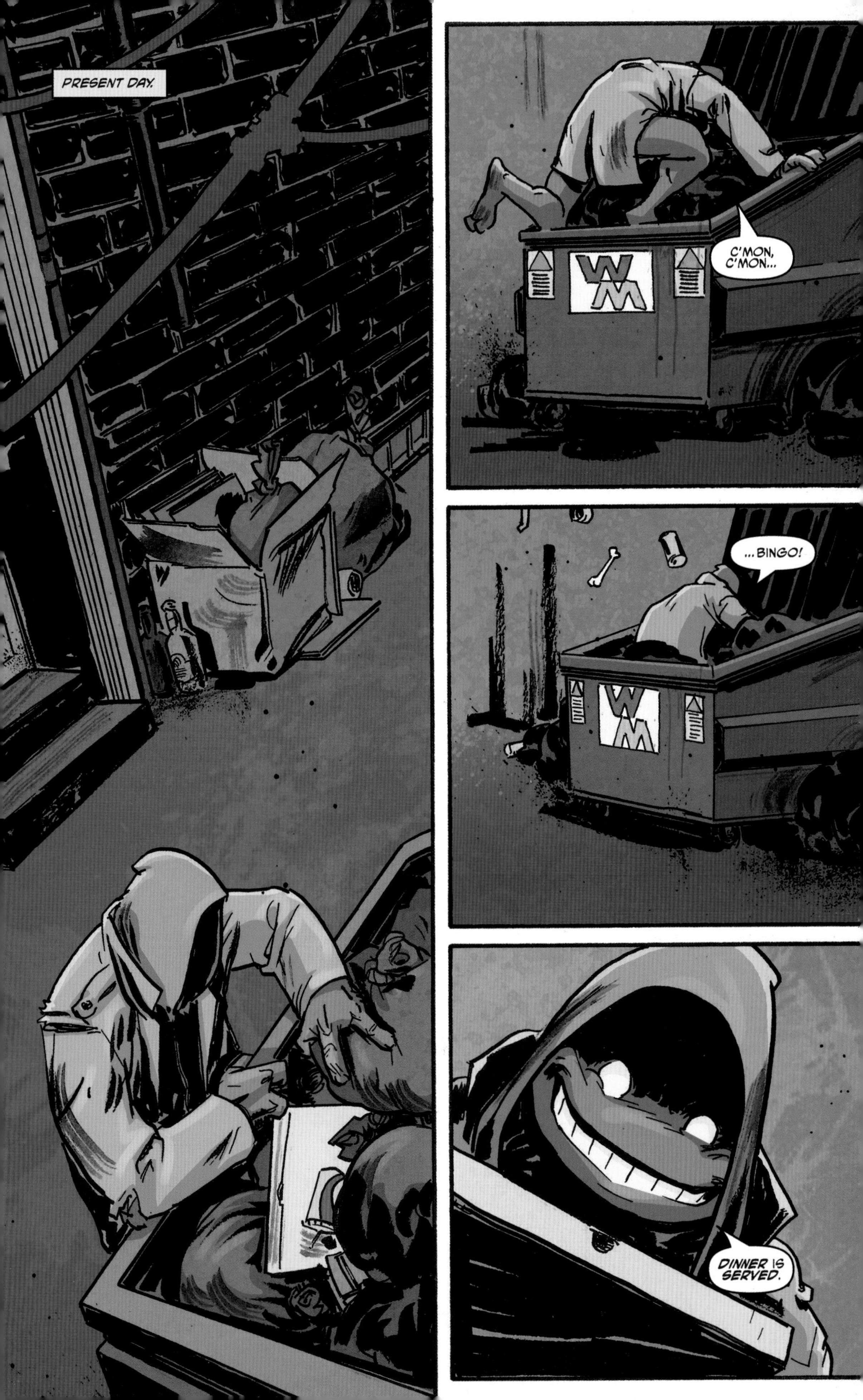
PRESENT DAY.
C'MON, C'MON...
...BINGO!
DINNER IS SERVED.

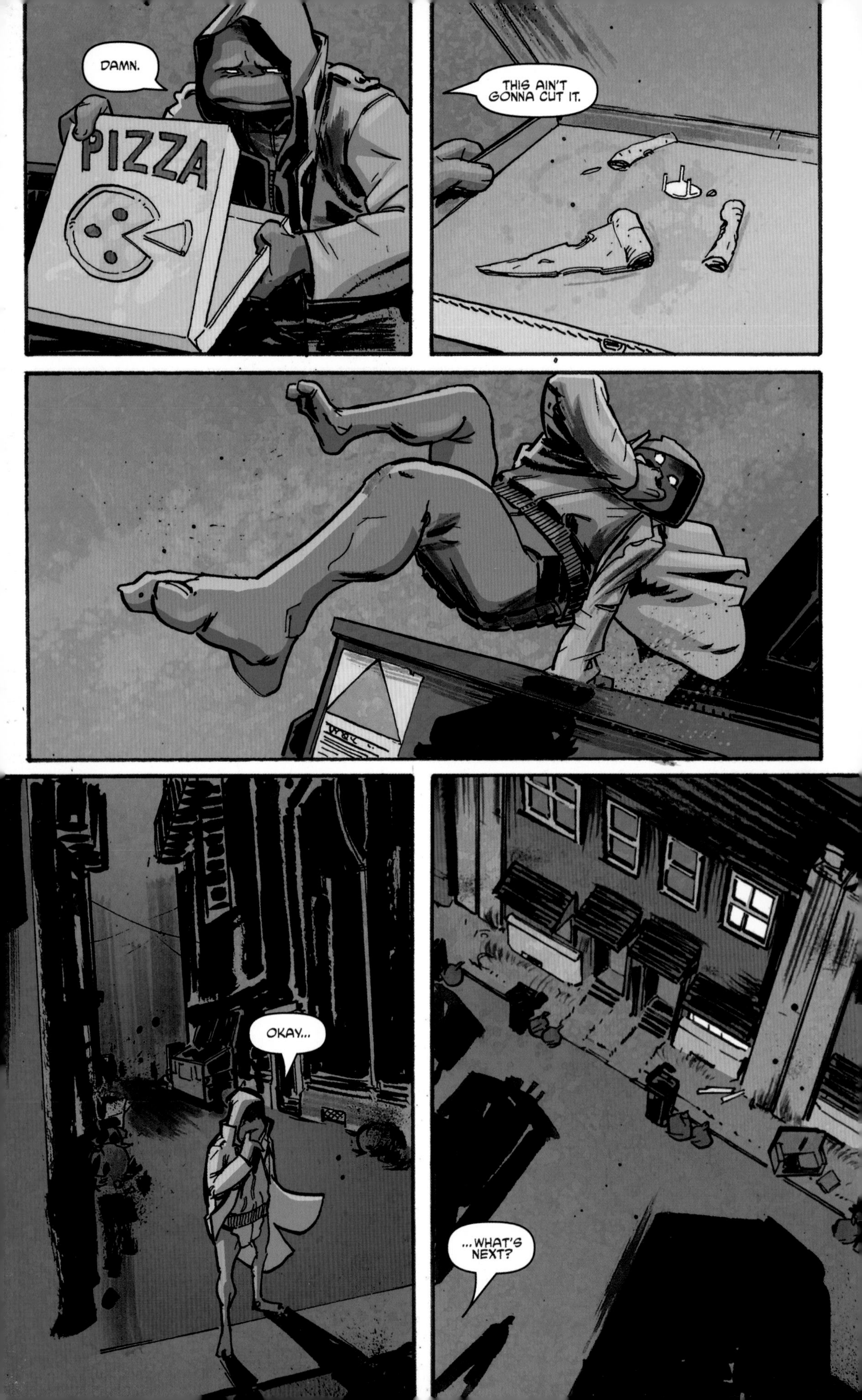
DAMN.
PIZZA
THIS AIN'T GONNA CUT IT.
OKAY...
...WHAT'S NEXT?

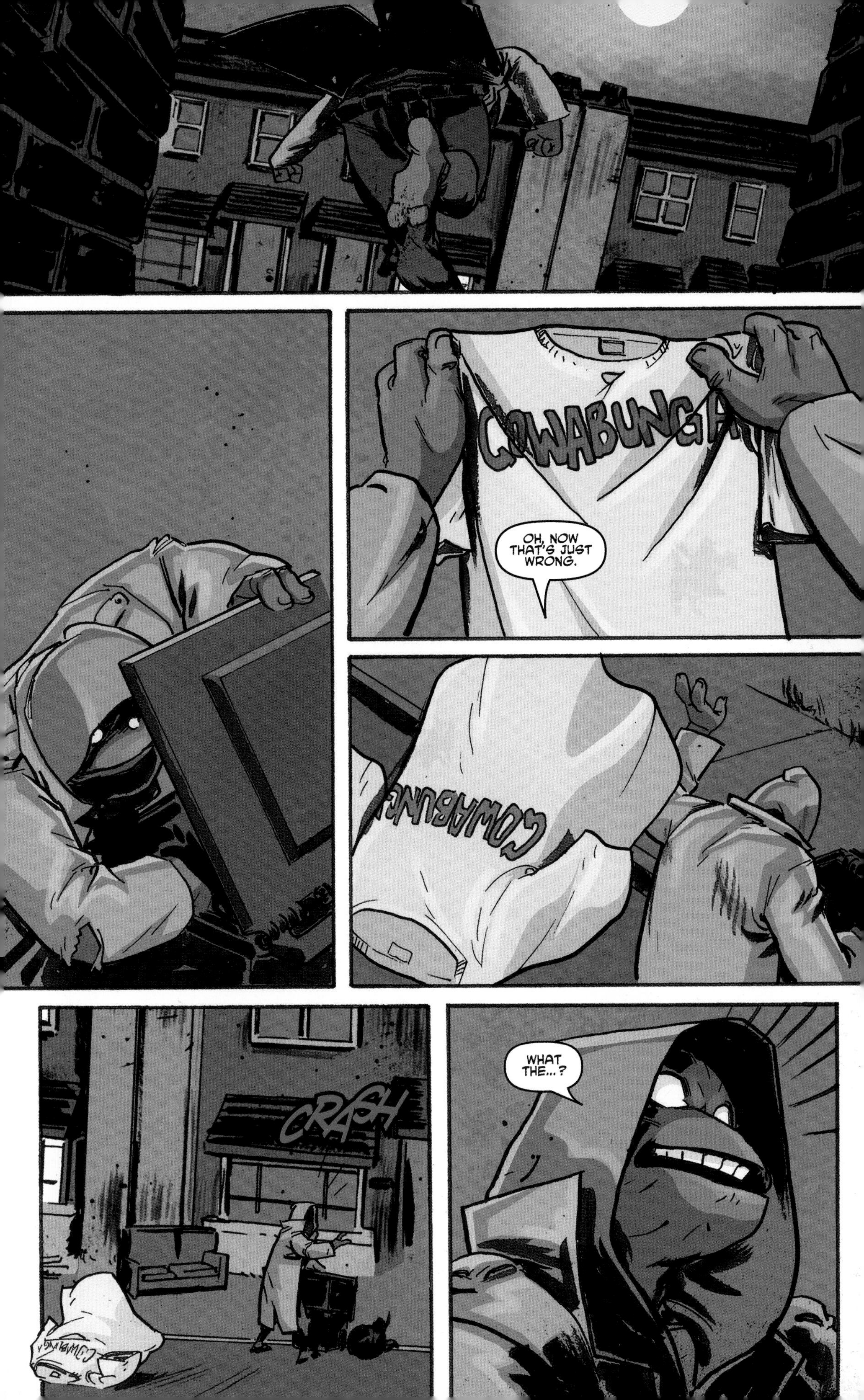
COWABUNGA
OH, NOW THAT'S JUST WRONG.
CRASH
WHAT THE...?

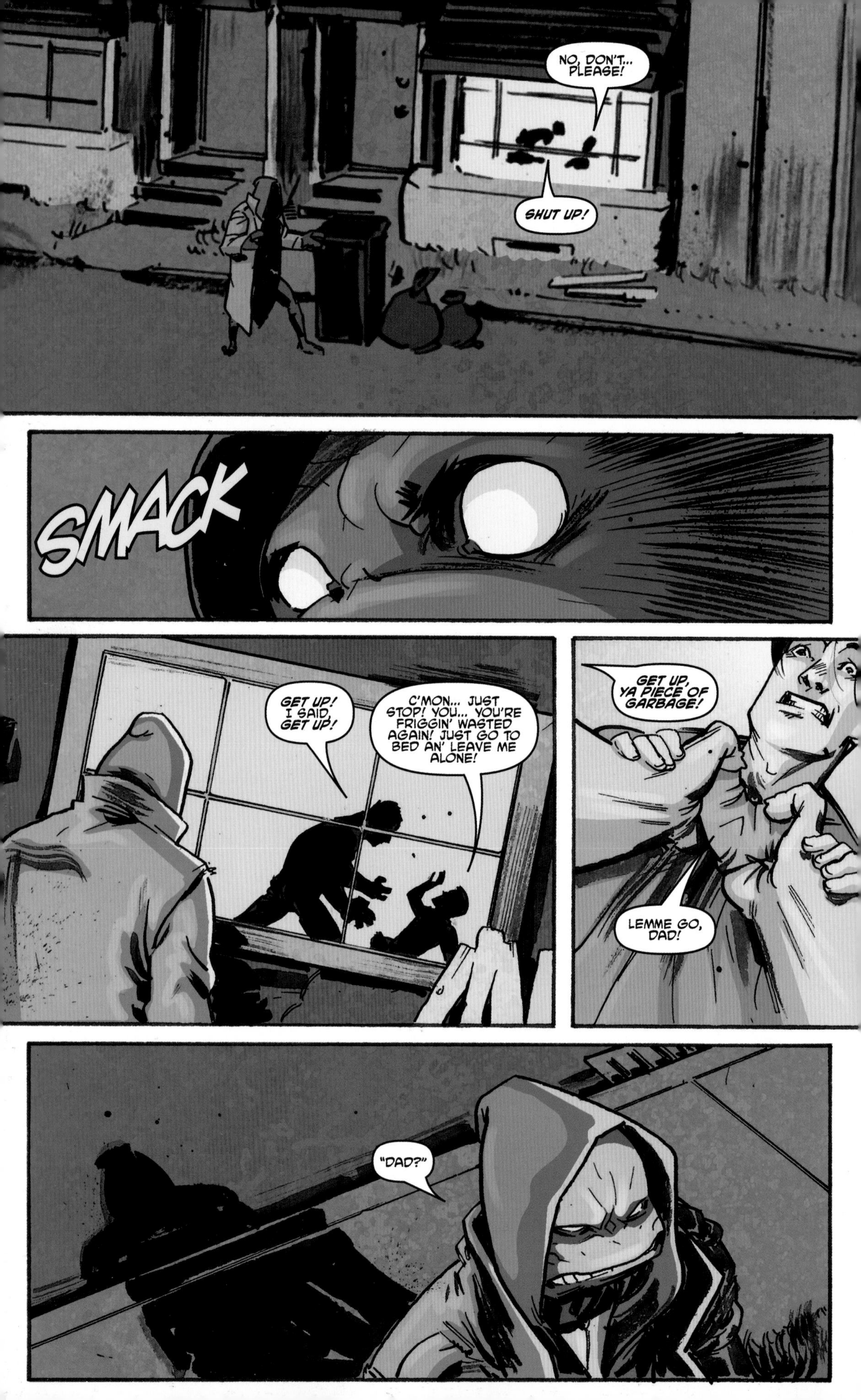

NO, DON'T... PLEASE!
SHUT UP!
SMACK
GET UP! I SAID, GET UP!
C'MON... JUST STOP! YOU... YOU'RE FRIGGIN' WASTED AGAIN! JUST GO TO BED AN' LEAVE ME ALONE!
GET UP, YA PIECE OF GARBAGE!
LEMME GO, DAD!
"DAD?"

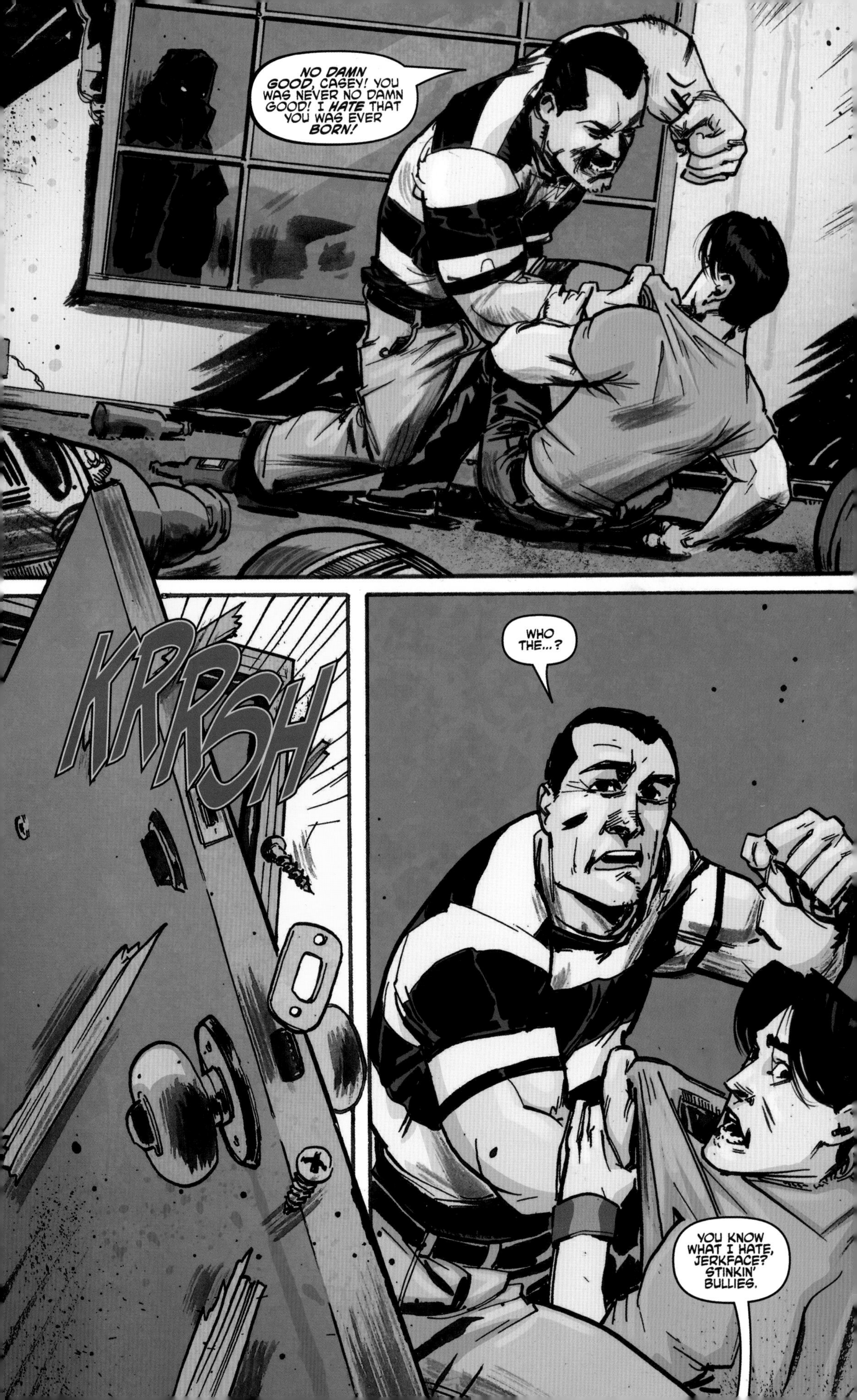
NO DAMN GOOD, CASEY! YOU WAS NEVER NO DAMN GOOD! I HATE THAT YOU WAS EVER BORN!
KRRSH
WHO THE...?
YOU KNOW WHAT I HATE, JERKFACE? STINKIN' BULLIES.

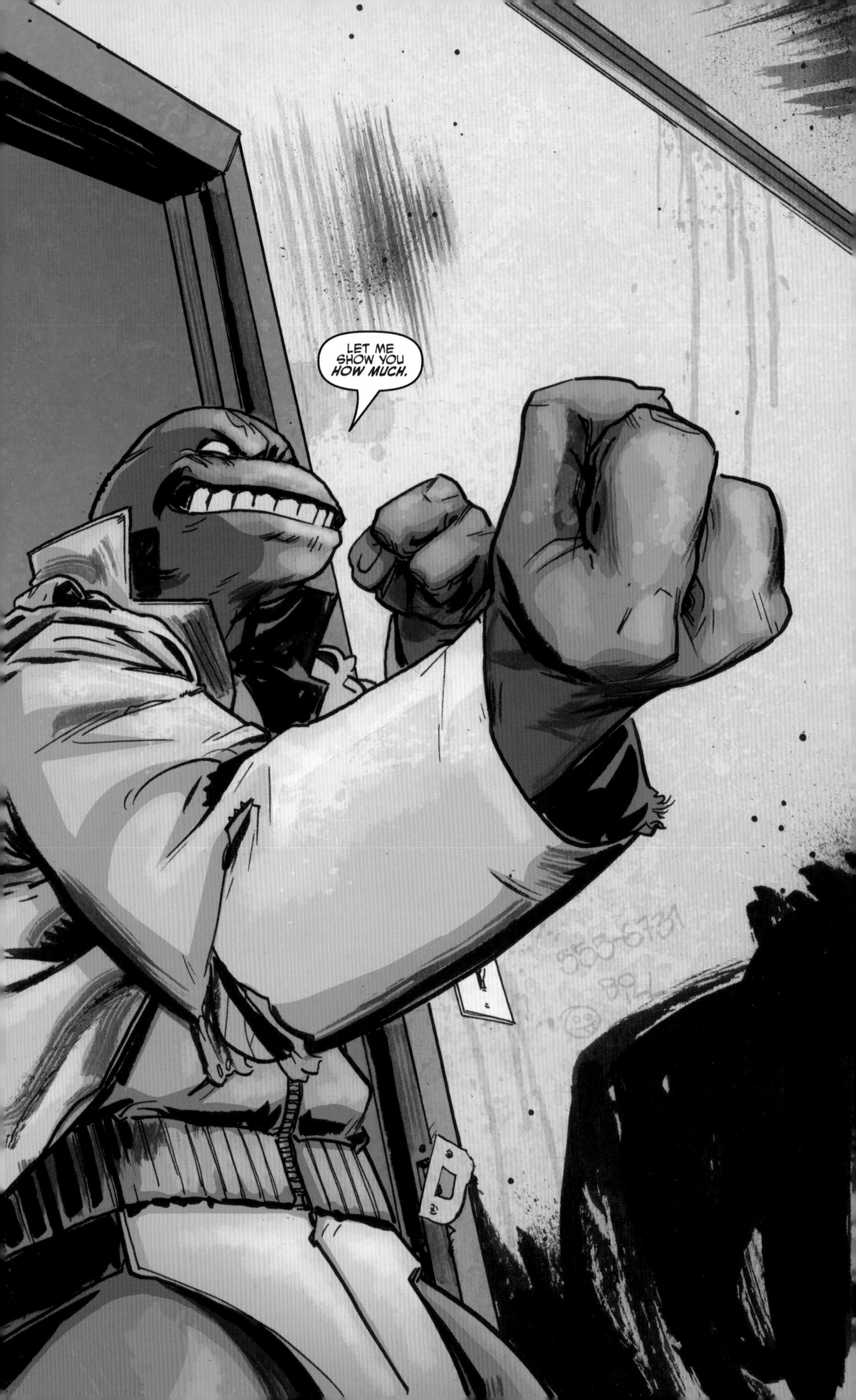
LET ME SHOW YOU *HOW MUCH.*
555-6731
BILL

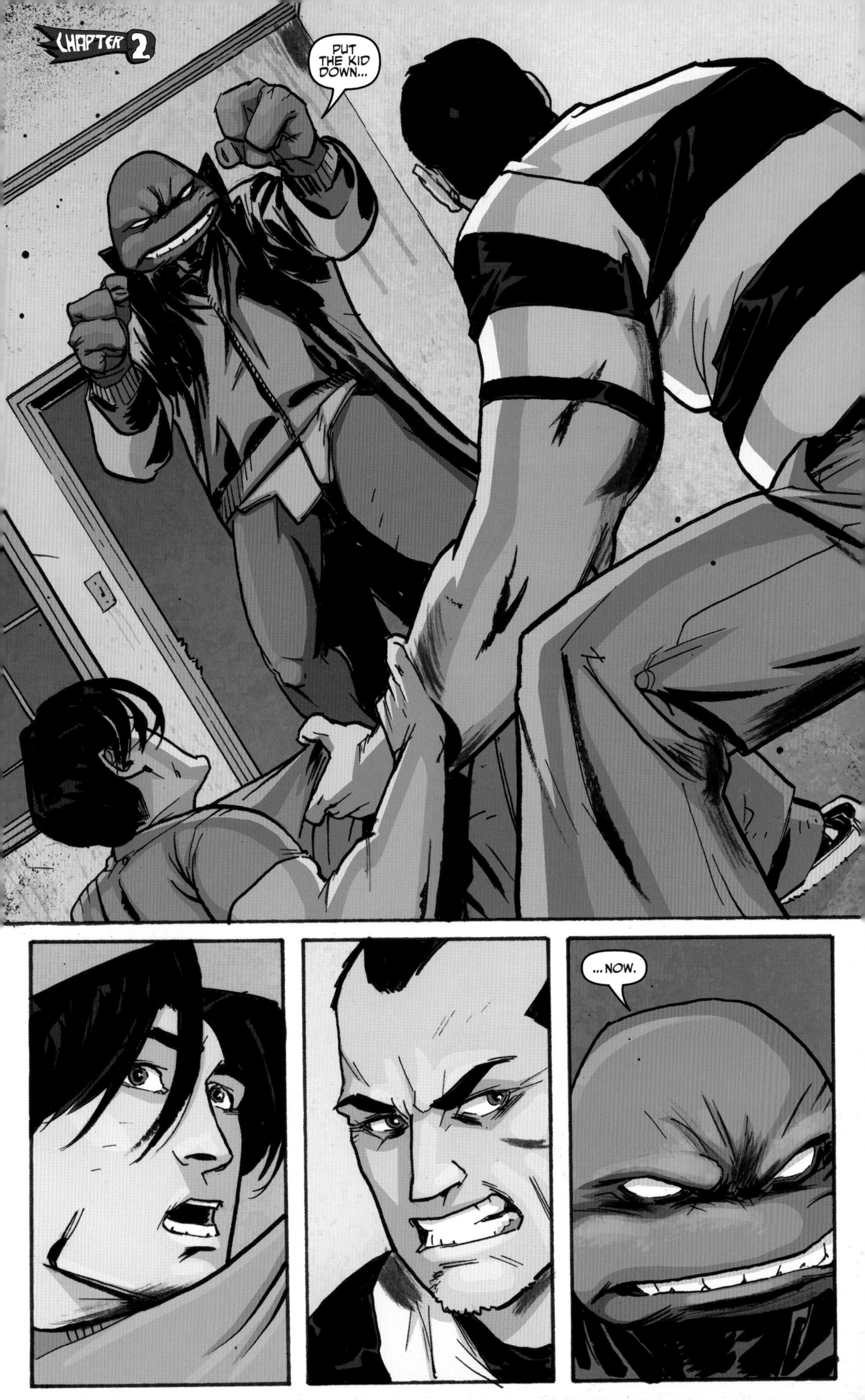
CHAPTER 2
PUT THE KID DOWN...
...NOW.

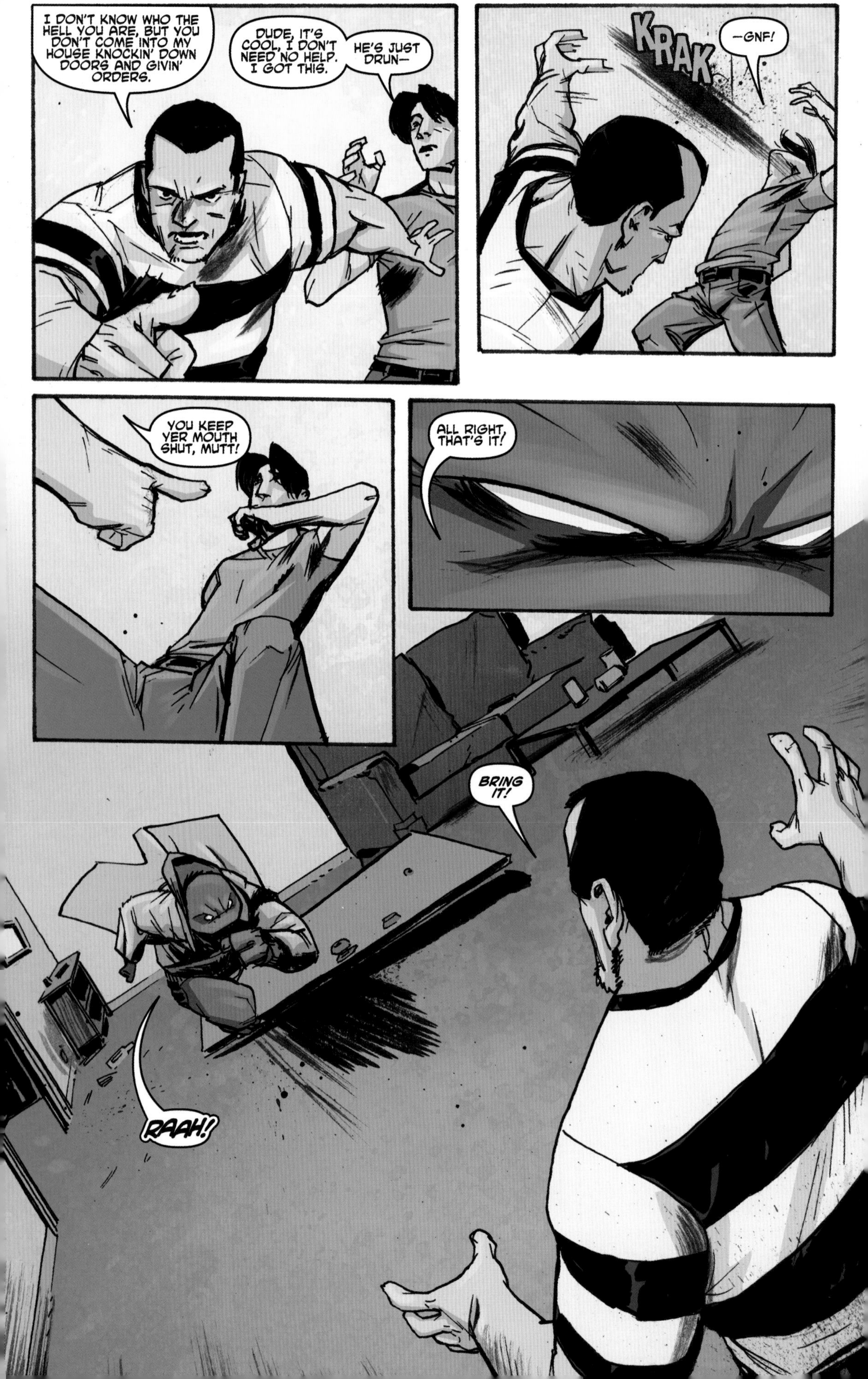
I DON'T KNOW WHO THE HELL YOU ARE, BUT YOU DON'T COME INTO MY HOUSE KNOCKIN' DOWN DOORS AND GIVIN' ORDERS.
DUDE, IT'S COOL, I DON'T NEED NO HELP. I GOT THIS.
HE'S JUST DRUN—
KRAK
—GNF!
YOU KEEP YER MOUTH SHUT, MUTT!
ALL RIGHT, THAT'S IT!
BRING IT!
RAAH!

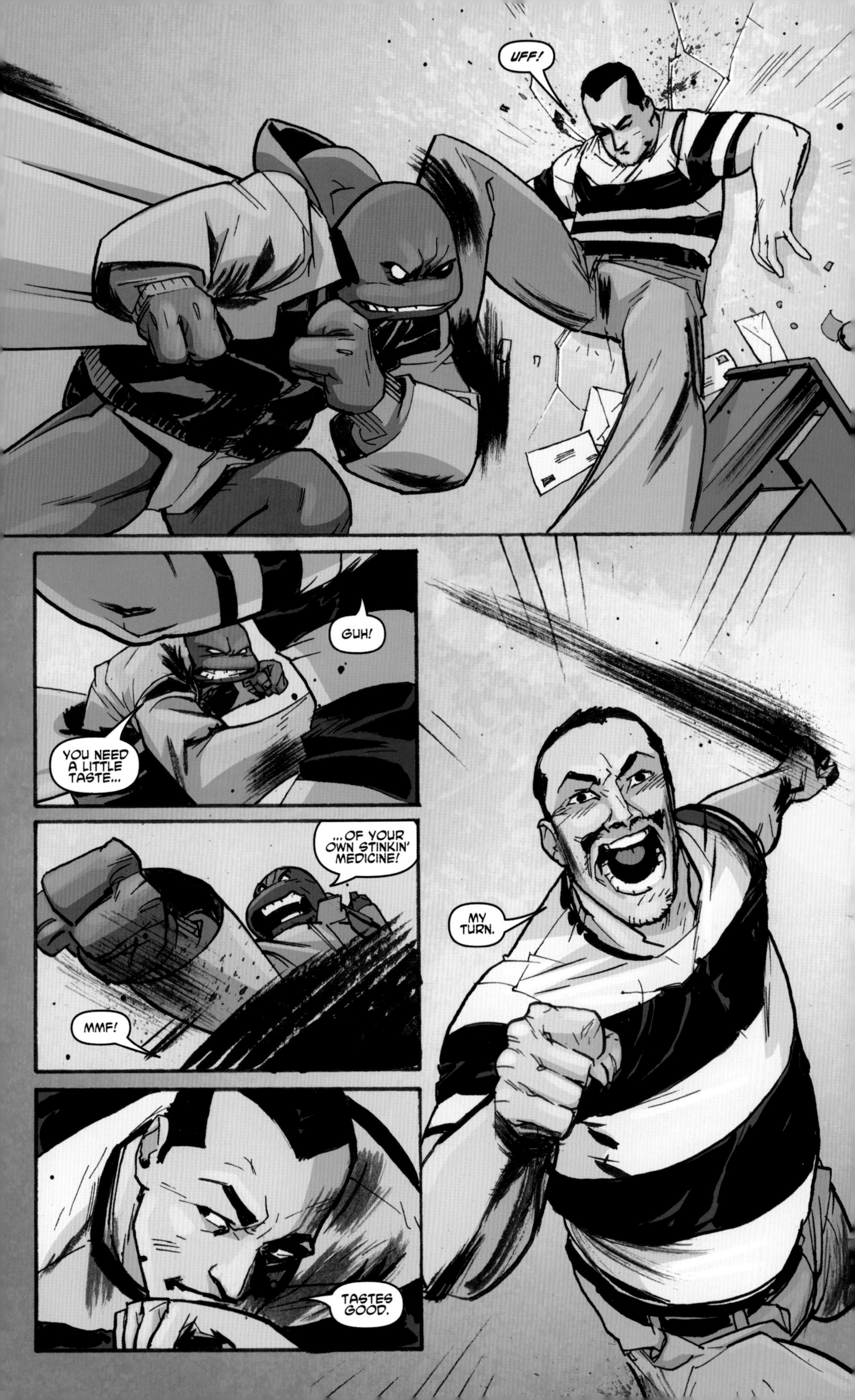
UFF!
GUH!
YOU NEED A LITTLE TASTE...
...OF YOUR OWN STINKIN' MEDICINE!
MMF!
TASTES GOOD.
MY TURN.

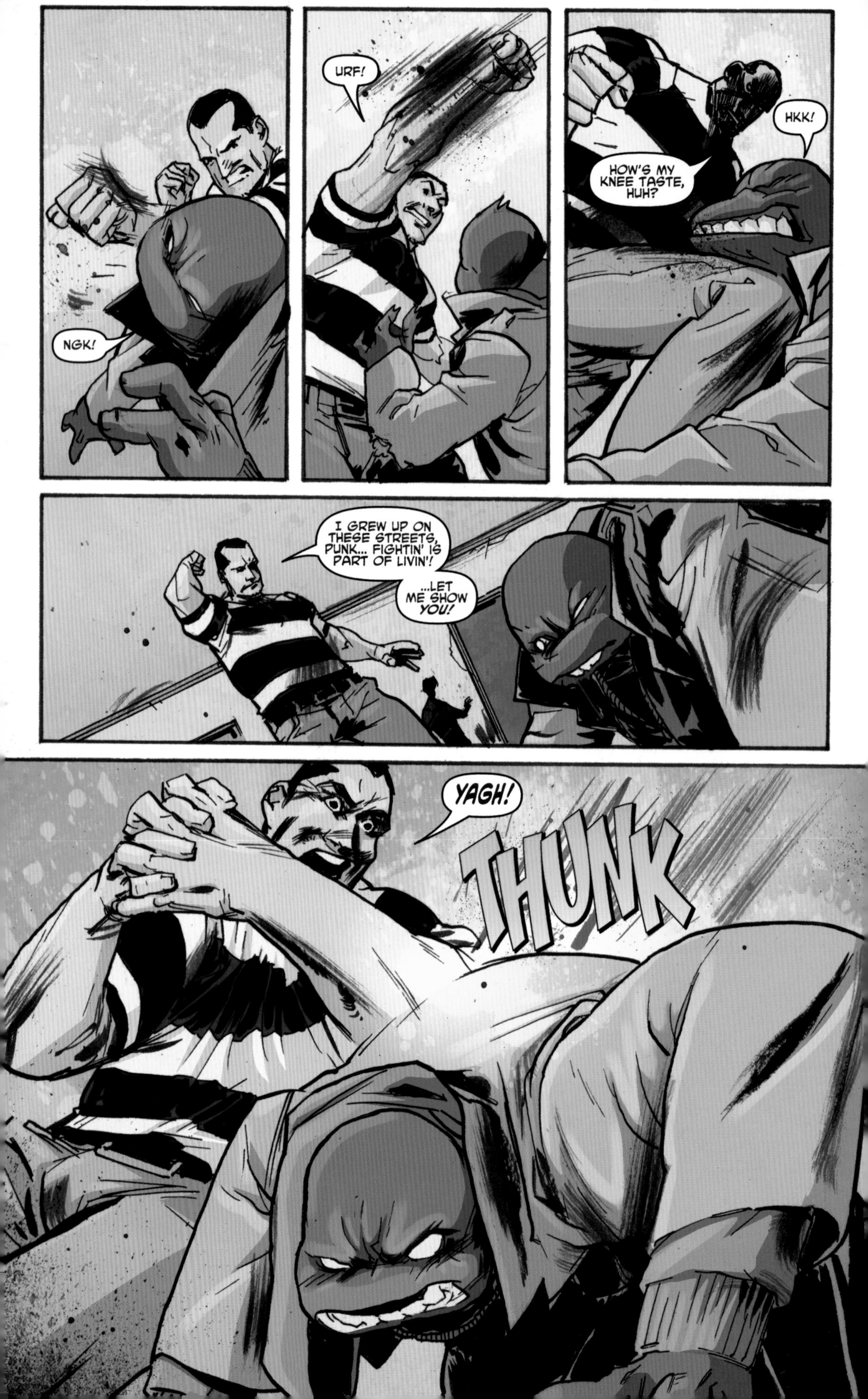
NGK!
URF!
HKK!
HOW'S MY KNEE TASTE, HUH?
I GREW UP ON THESE STREETS, PUNK... FIGHTIN' IS PART OF LIVIN'!
...LET ME SHOW YOU!
YAGH!
THUNK

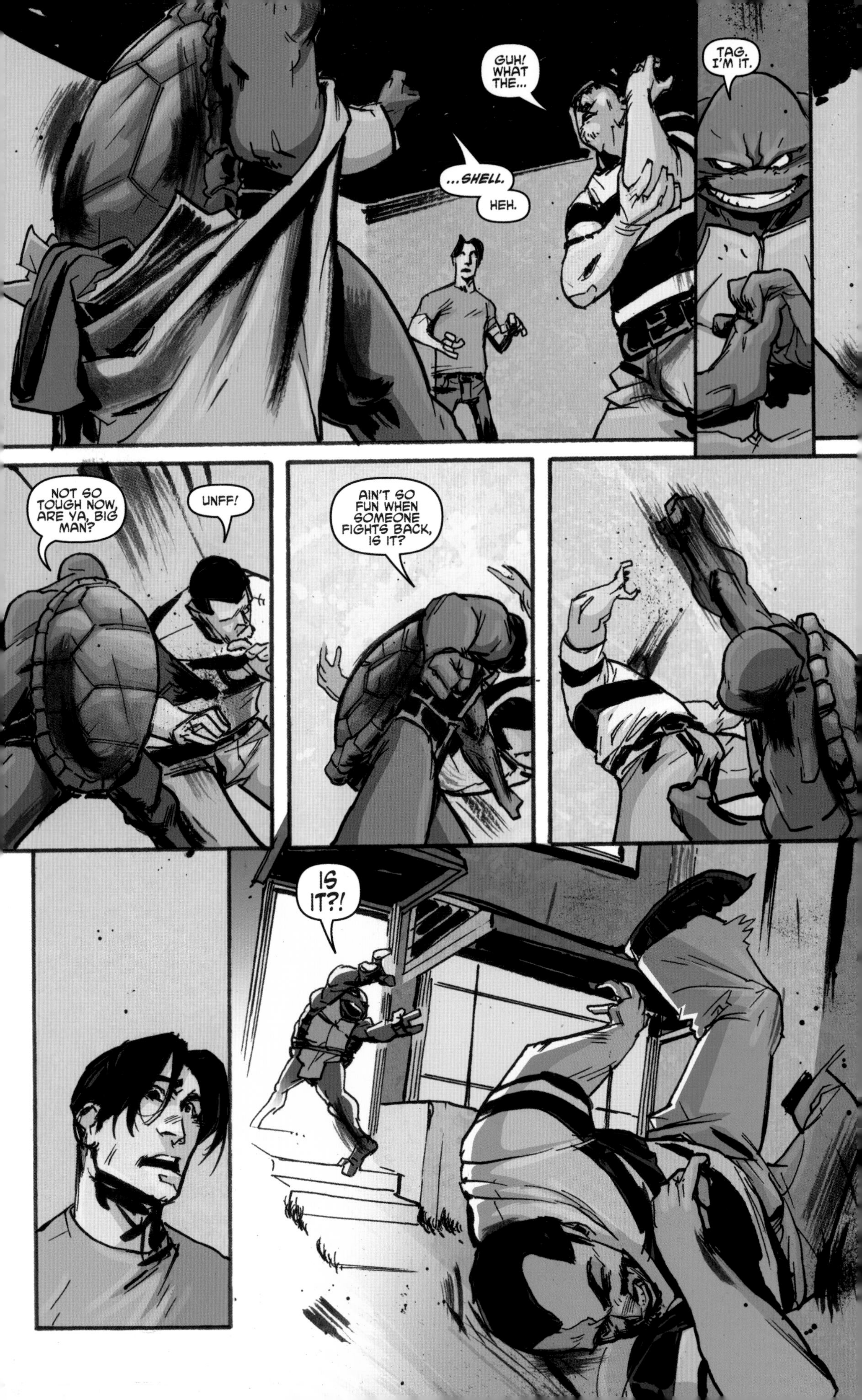
GUH! WHAT THE...
TAG. I'M IT.
...SHELL.
HEH.
NOT SO TOUGH NOW, ARE YA, BIG MAN?
UNFF!
AIN'T SO FUN WHEN SOMEONE FIGHTS BACK, IS IT?
IS IT?!

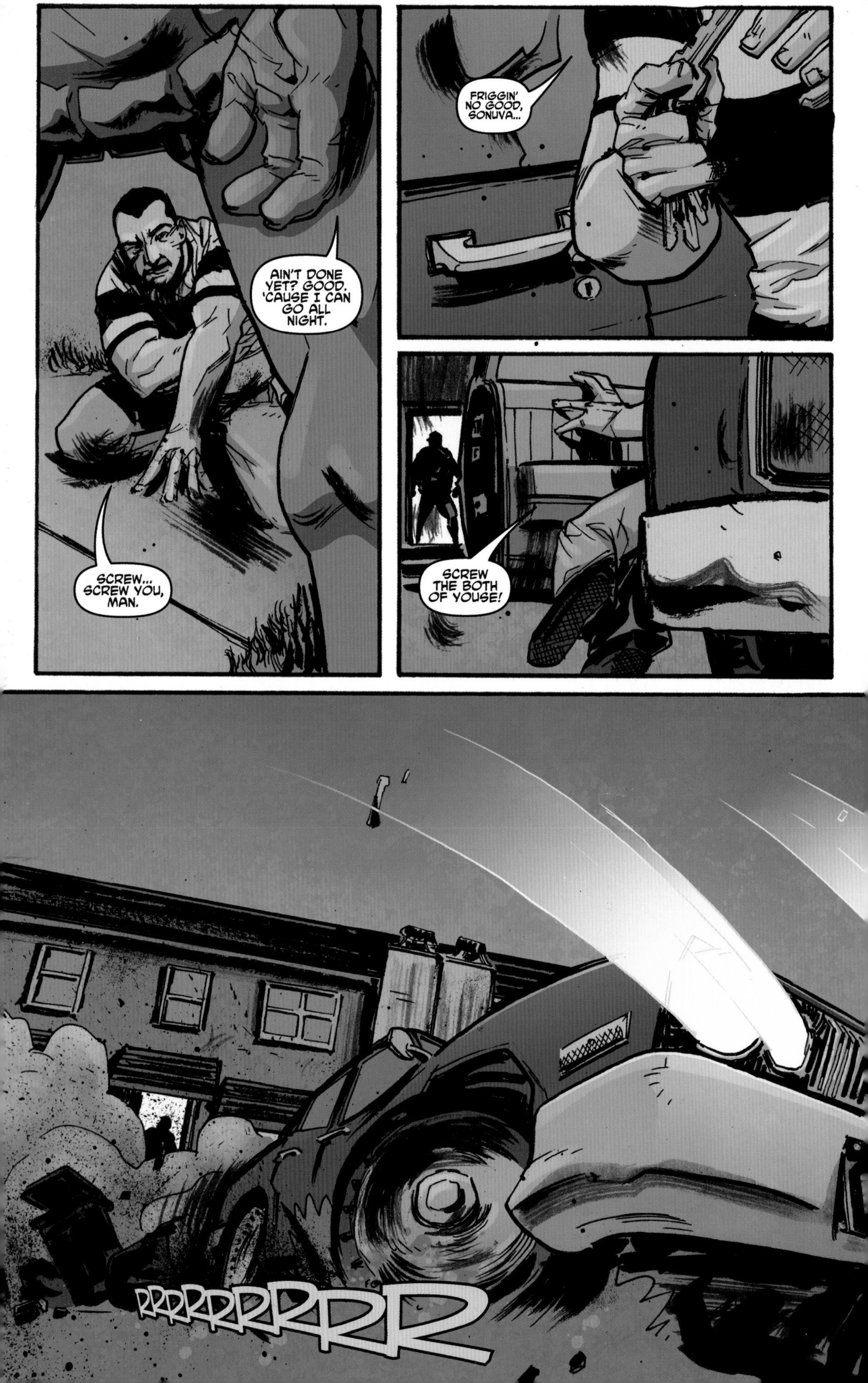
AIN'T DONE YET? GOOD. 'CAUSE I CAN GO ALL NIGHT.
SCREW... SCREW YOU, MAN.
FRIGGIN' NO GOOD, SONUVA...
SCREW THE BOTH OF YOUSE!
RRRRRRRR

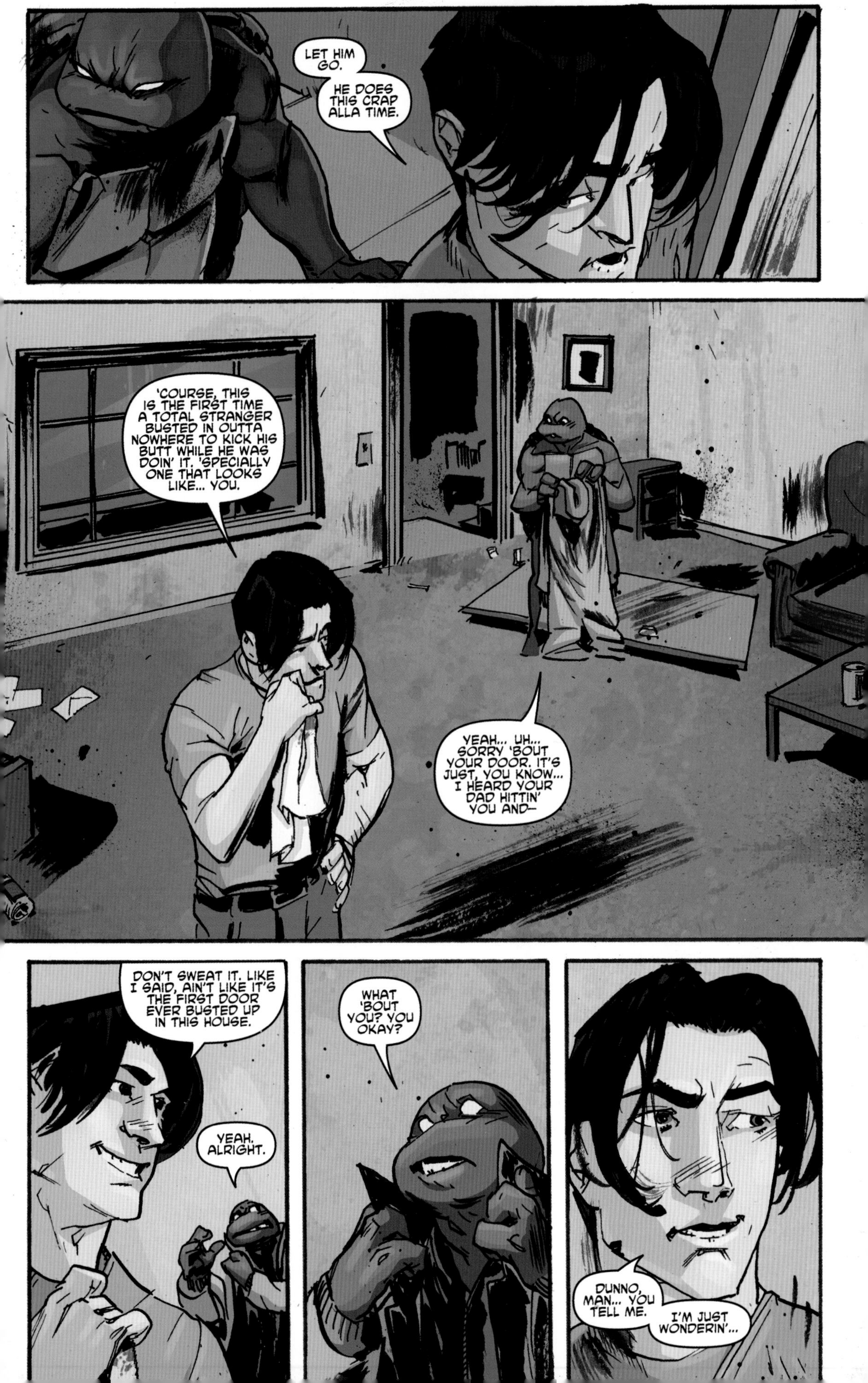

LET HIM GO.
HE DOES THIS CRAP ALLA TIME.
'COURSE, THIS IS THE FIRST TIME A TOTAL STRANGER BUSTED IN OUTTA NOWHERE TO KICK HIS BUTT WHILE HE WAS DOIN' IT. 'SPECIALLY ONE THAT LOOKS LIKE... YOU.
YEAH... UH... SORRY 'BOUT YOUR DOOR. IT'S JUST, YOU KNOW... I HEARD YOUR DAD HITTIN' YOU AND—
DON'T SWEAT IT. LIKE I SAID, AIN'T LIKE IT'S THE FIRST DOOR EVER BUSTED UP IN THIS HOUSE.
YEAH. ALRIGHT.
WHAT 'BOUT YOU? YOU OKAY?
DUNNO, MAN... YOU TELL ME.
I'M JUST WONDERIN'...

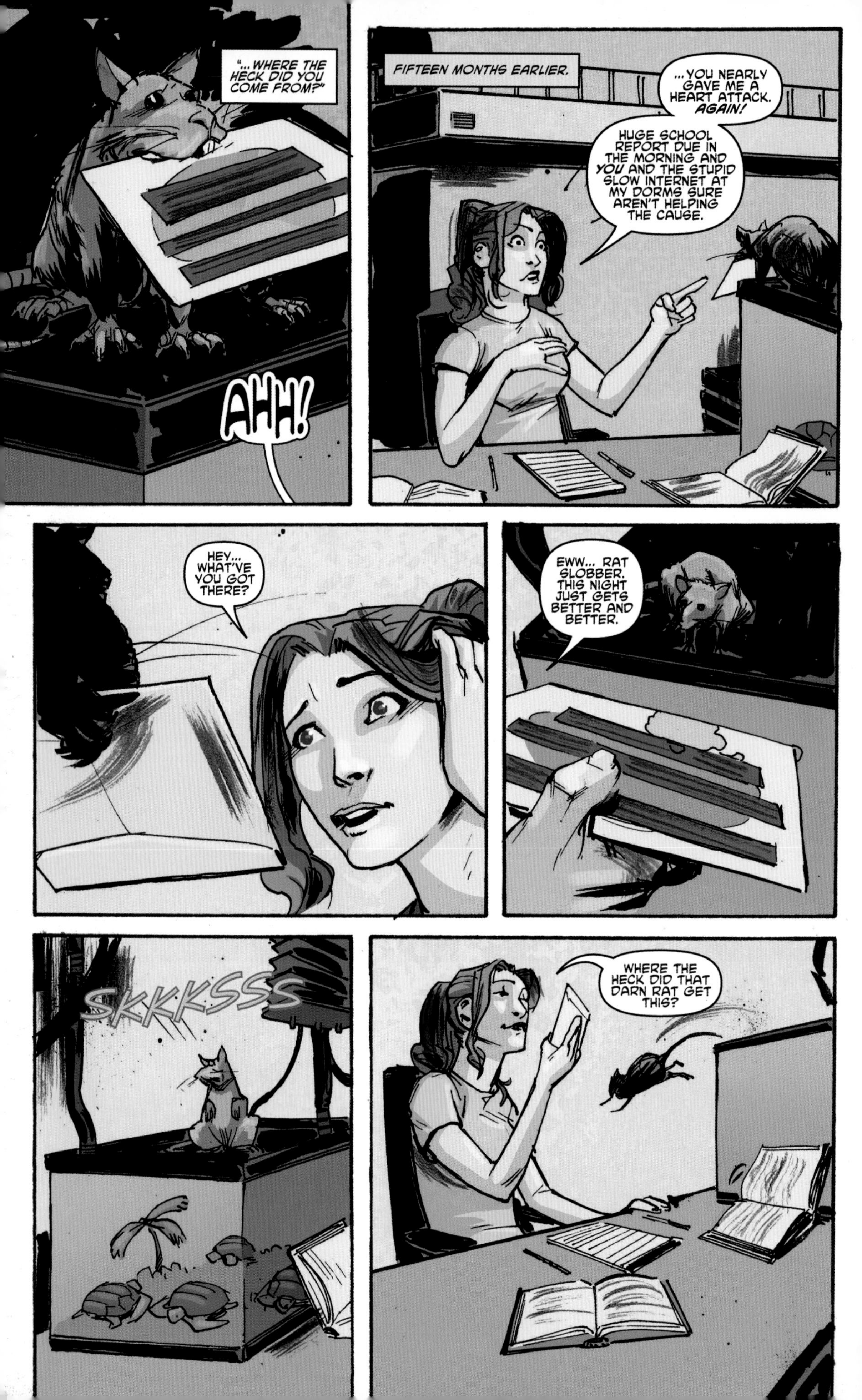
"...WHERE THE HECK DID YOU COME FROM?"
AHH!
FIFTEEN MONTHS EARLIER.
...YOU NEARLY GAVE ME A HEART ATTACK. AGAIN!
HUGE SCHOOL REPORT DUE IN THE MORNING AND YOU AND THE STUPID SLOW INTERNET AT MY DORMS SURE AREN'T HELPING THE CAUSE.
HEY... WHAT'VE YOU GOT THERE?
EWW... RAT SLOBBER. THIS NIGHT JUST GETS BETTER AND BETTER.
SKKKSSS
WHERE THE HECK DID THAT DARN RAT GET THIS?

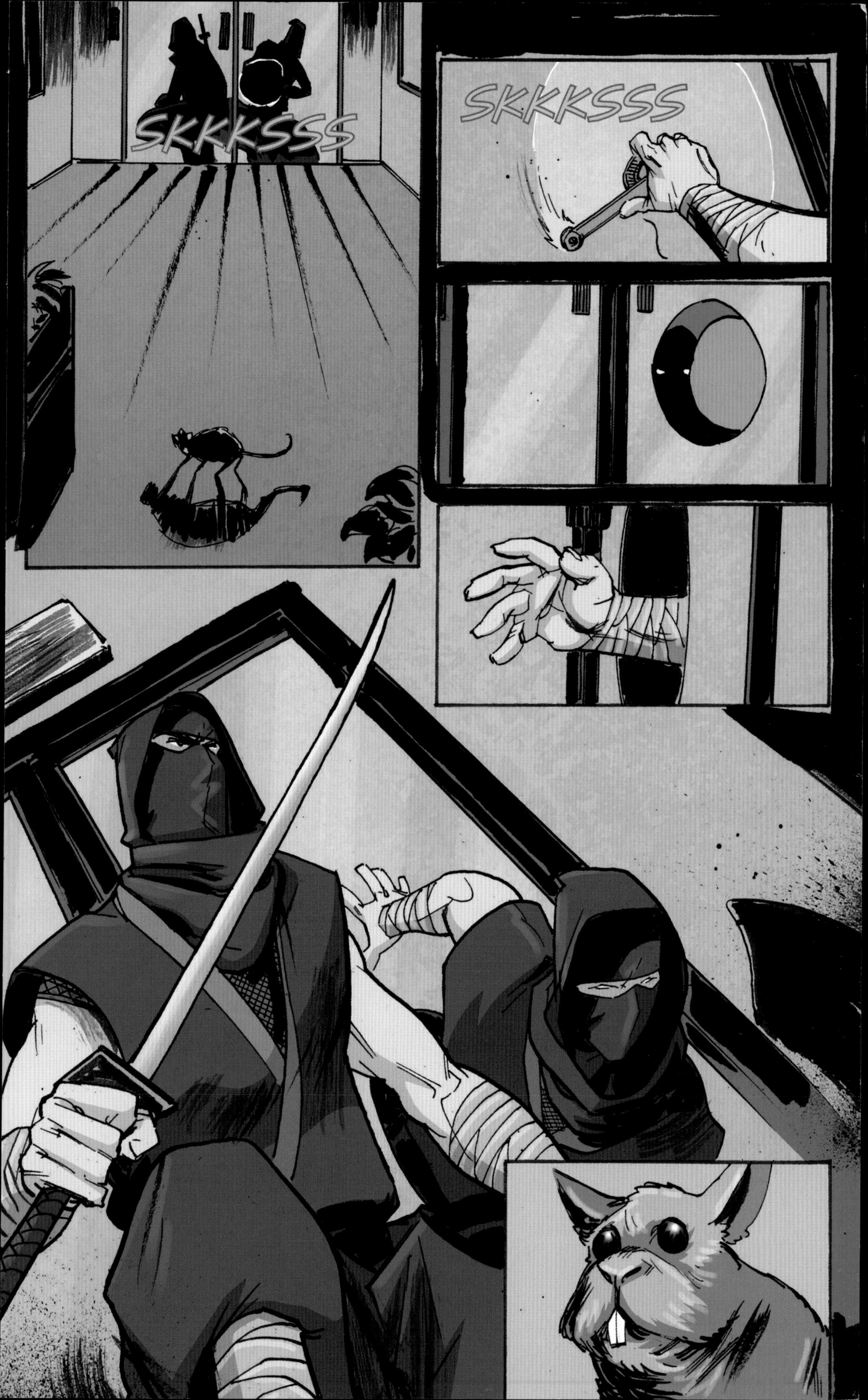
SKKKSSS
SKKKSSS

WHAT IN THE WORLD...?

CONFIDENTIAL — PROPRIETARY

TERRAPIN/HUMAN EXO-ARMOR SYNTHESIS

MILITARY APPLICA
& BATTLEFIELD A

HUH?

GEEZ, APRIL... RATS, MYSTERY DISKS, AND NOW YOU'RE SEEING THINGS. WHAT'S...

...NEXT?

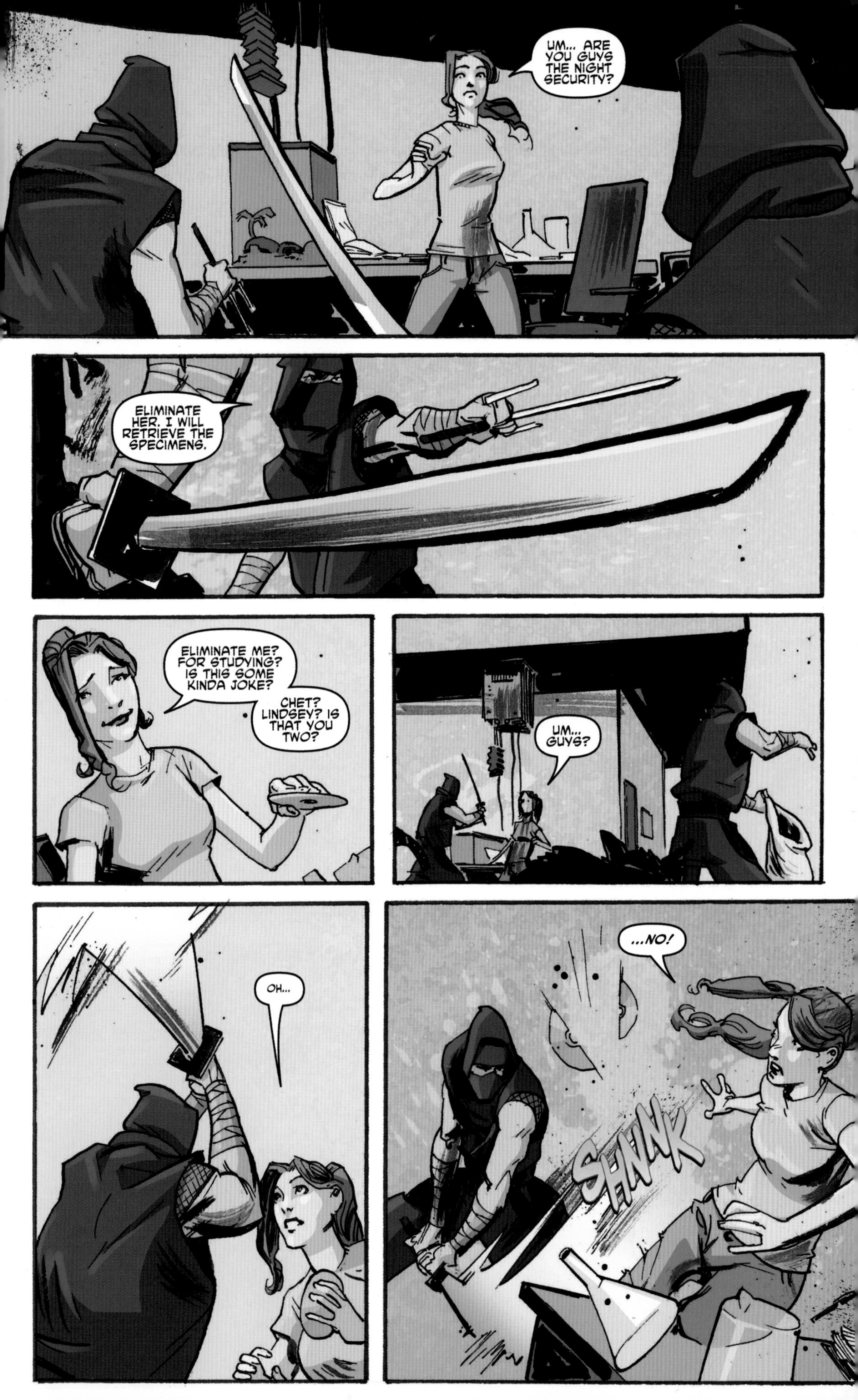
UM... ARE YOU GUYS THE NIGHT SECURITY?
ELIMINATE HER. I WILL RETRIEVE THE SPECIMENS.
ELIMINATE ME? FOR STUDYING? IS THIS SOME KINDA JOKE?
CHET? LINDSEY? IS THAT YOU TWO?
UM... GUYS?
OH...
...NO!
SHNK

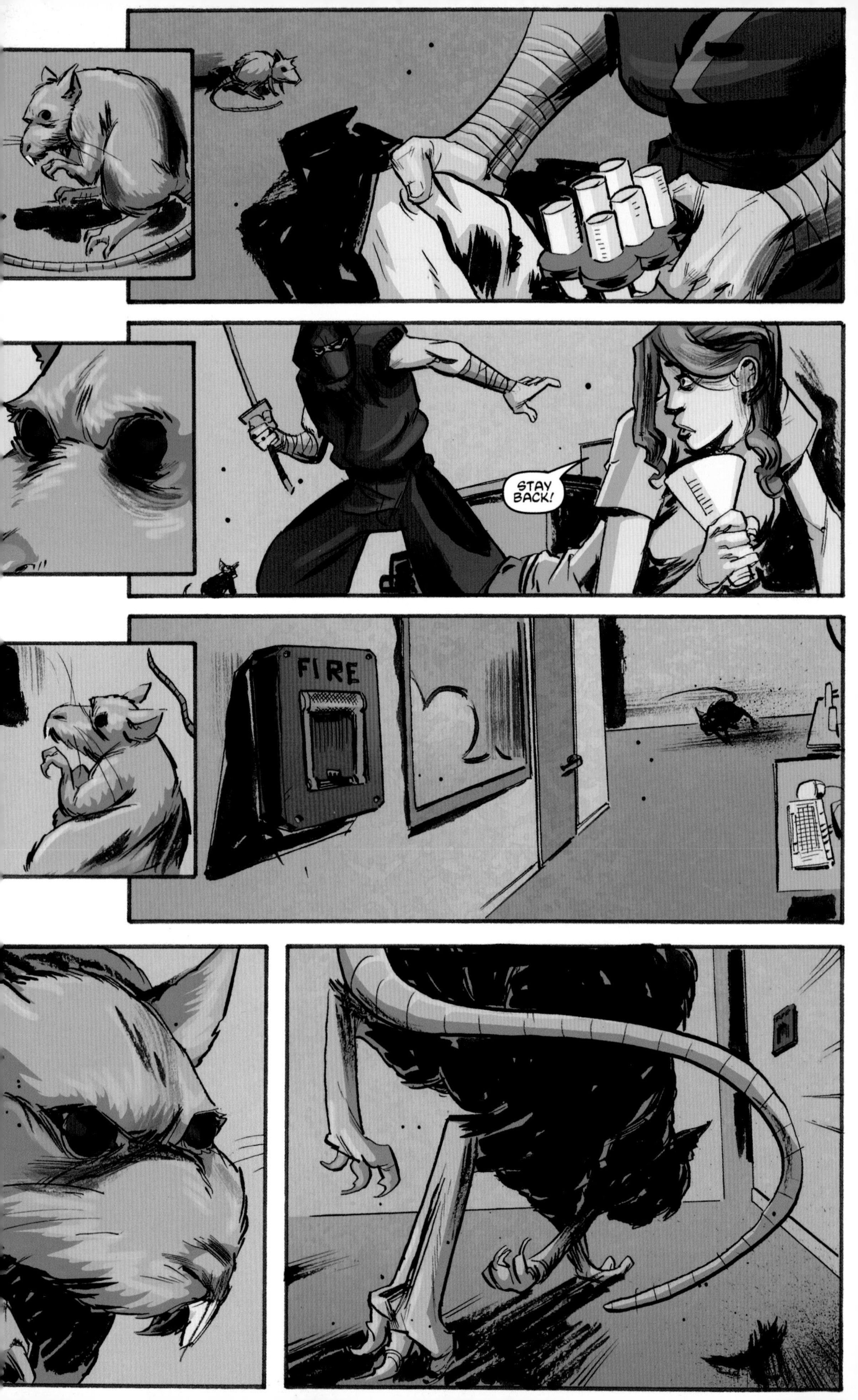
STAY BACK!
FIRE

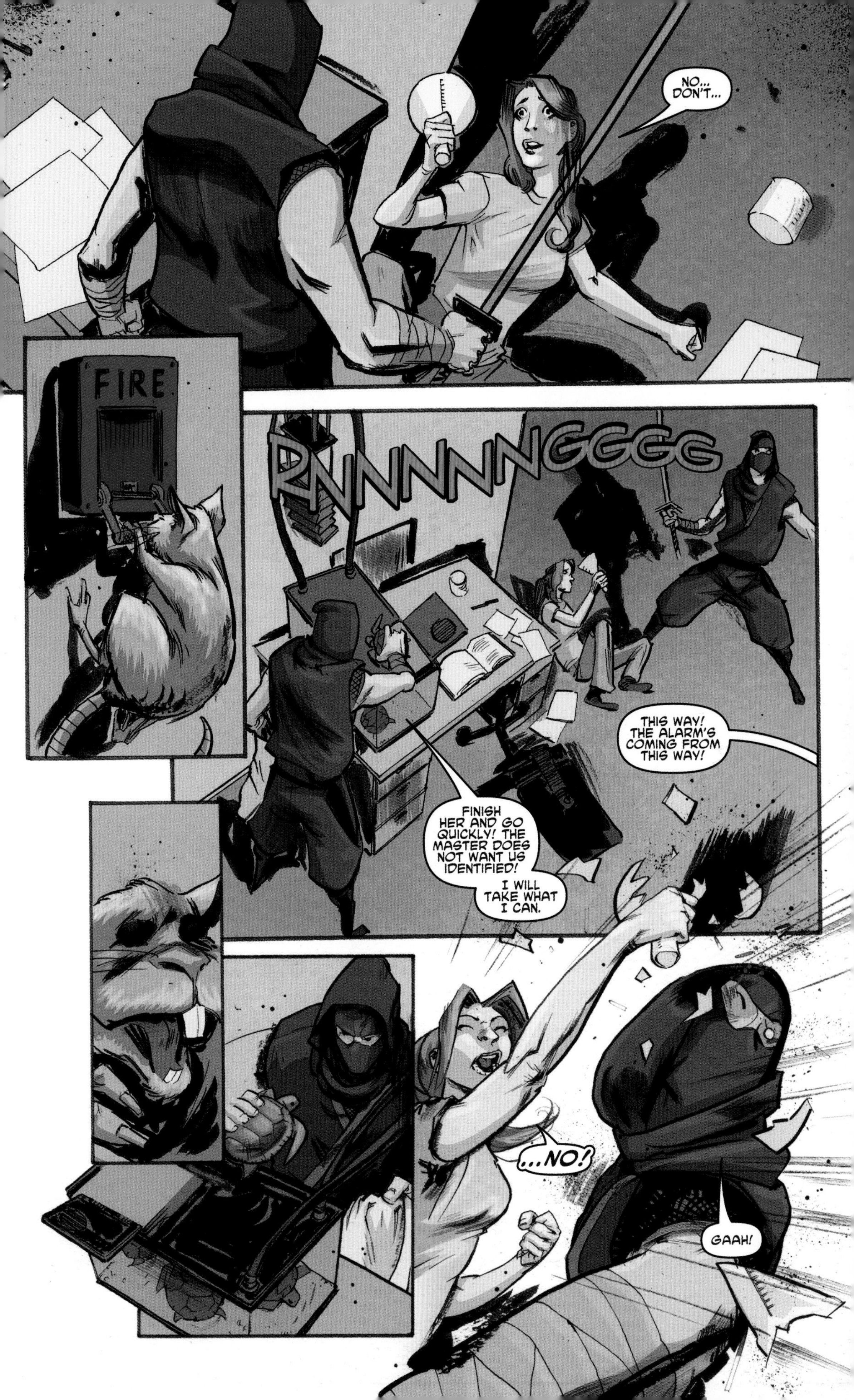
NO... DON'T...
FIRE
RNNNNNGGGG
THIS WAY! THE ALARM'S COMING FROM THIS WAY!
FINISH HER AND GO QUICKLY! THE MASTER DOES NOT WANT US IDENTIFIED!
I WILL TAKE WHAT I CAN.
...NO!
GAAH!

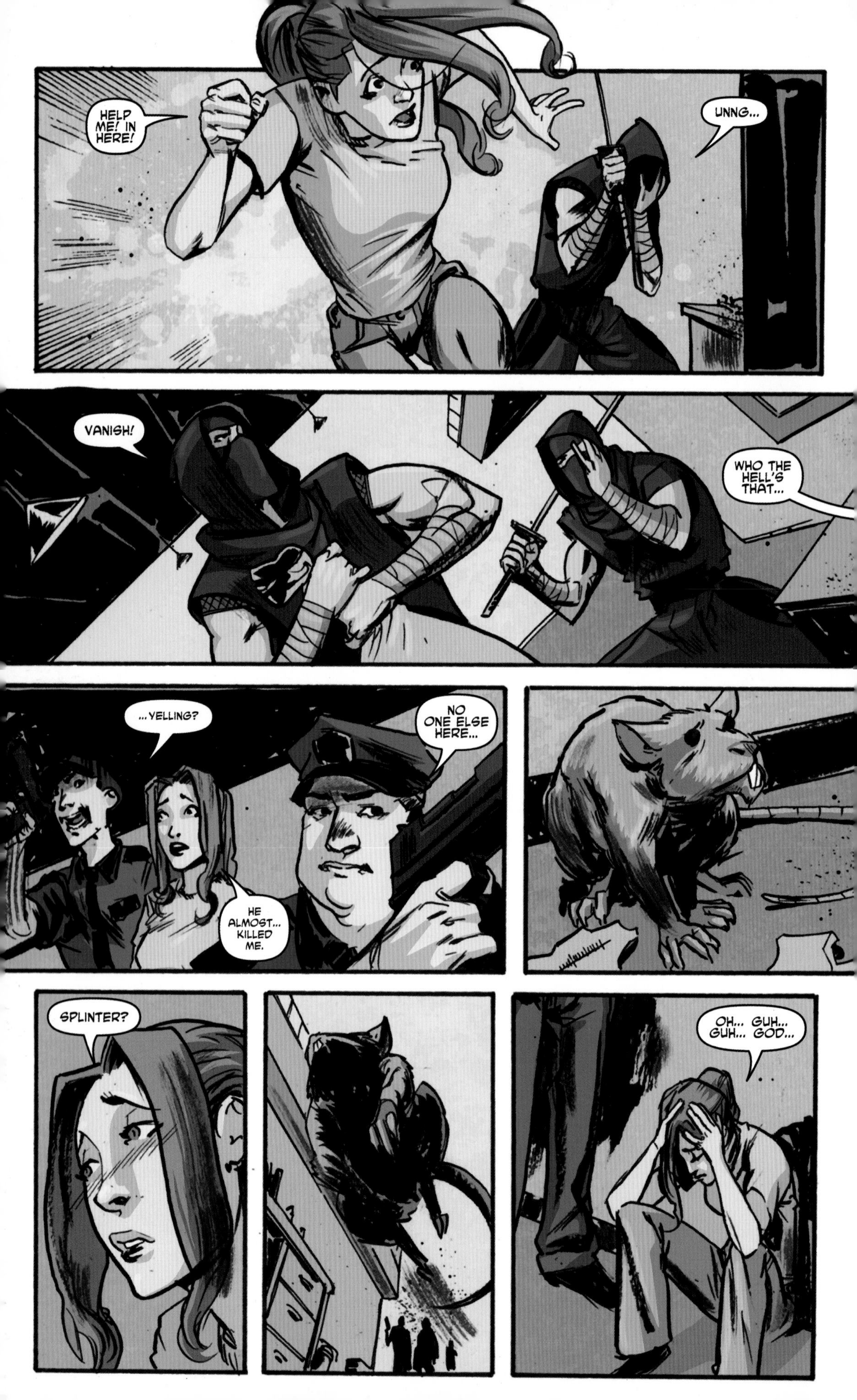
HELP ME! IN HERE!
UNNG...
VANISH!
WHO THE HELL'S THAT...
...YELLING?
NO ONE ELSE HERE...
HE ALMOST... KILLED ME.
SPLINTER?
OH... GUH... GUH... GOD...

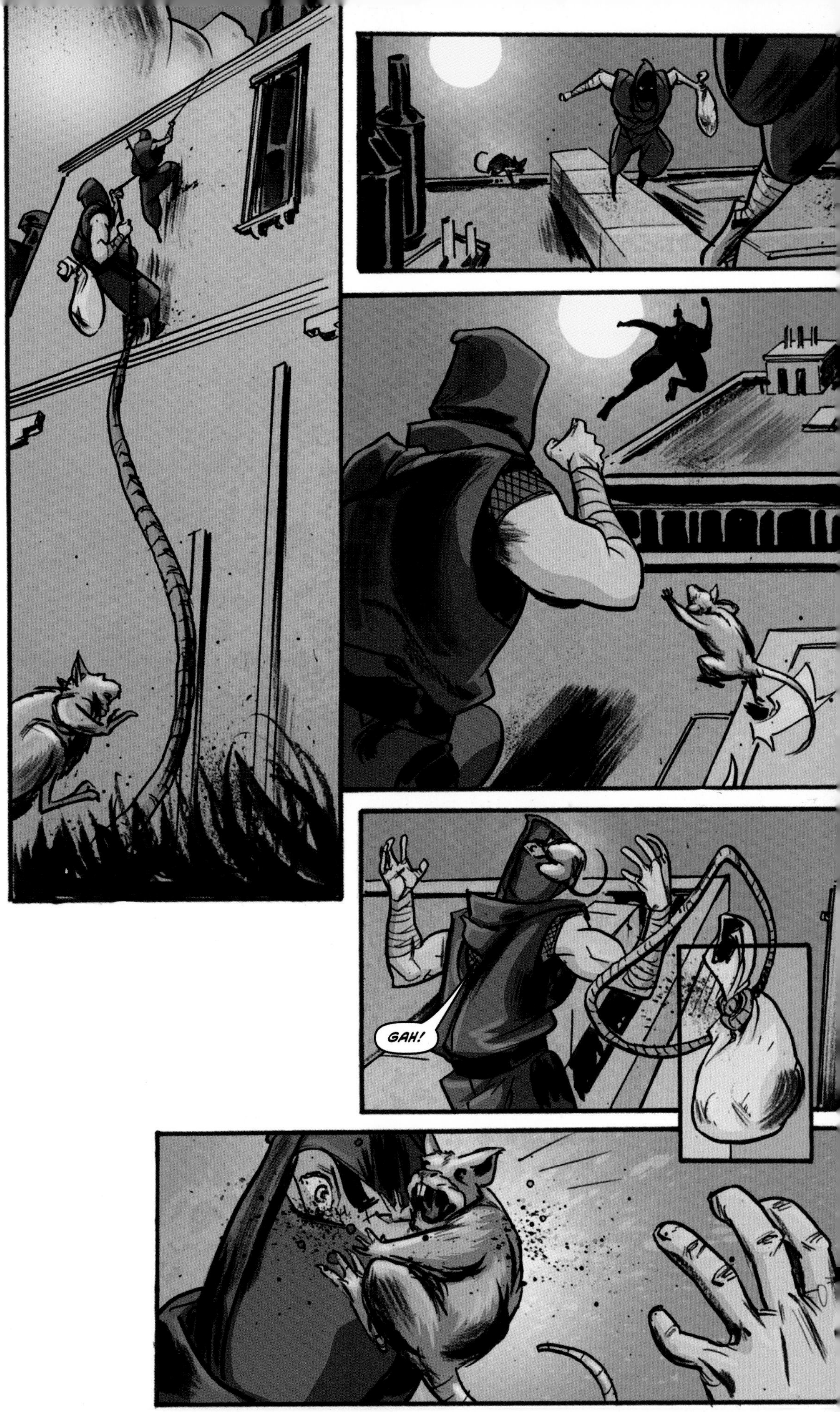
GAH!

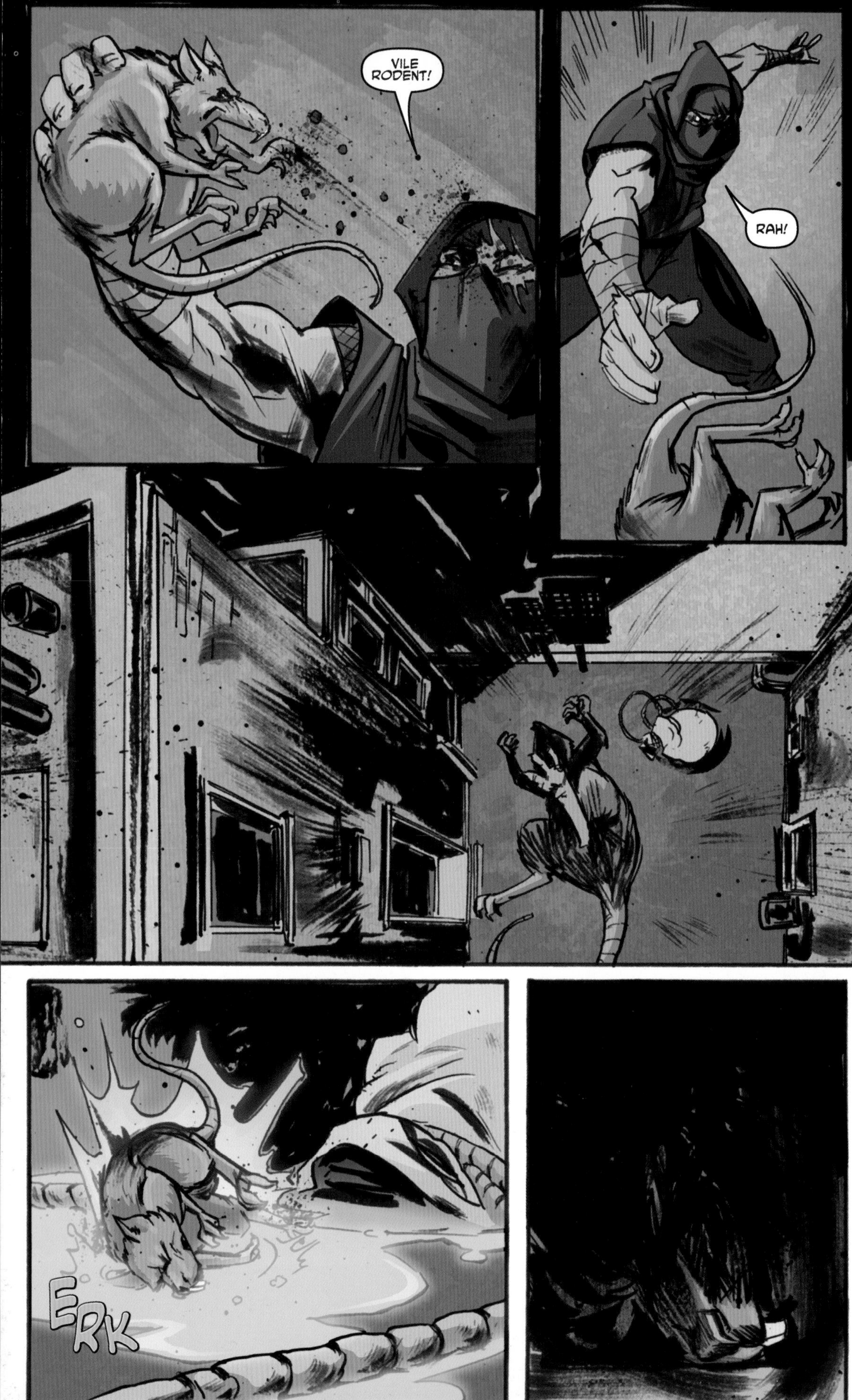
VILE RODENT!
RAH!
ERK

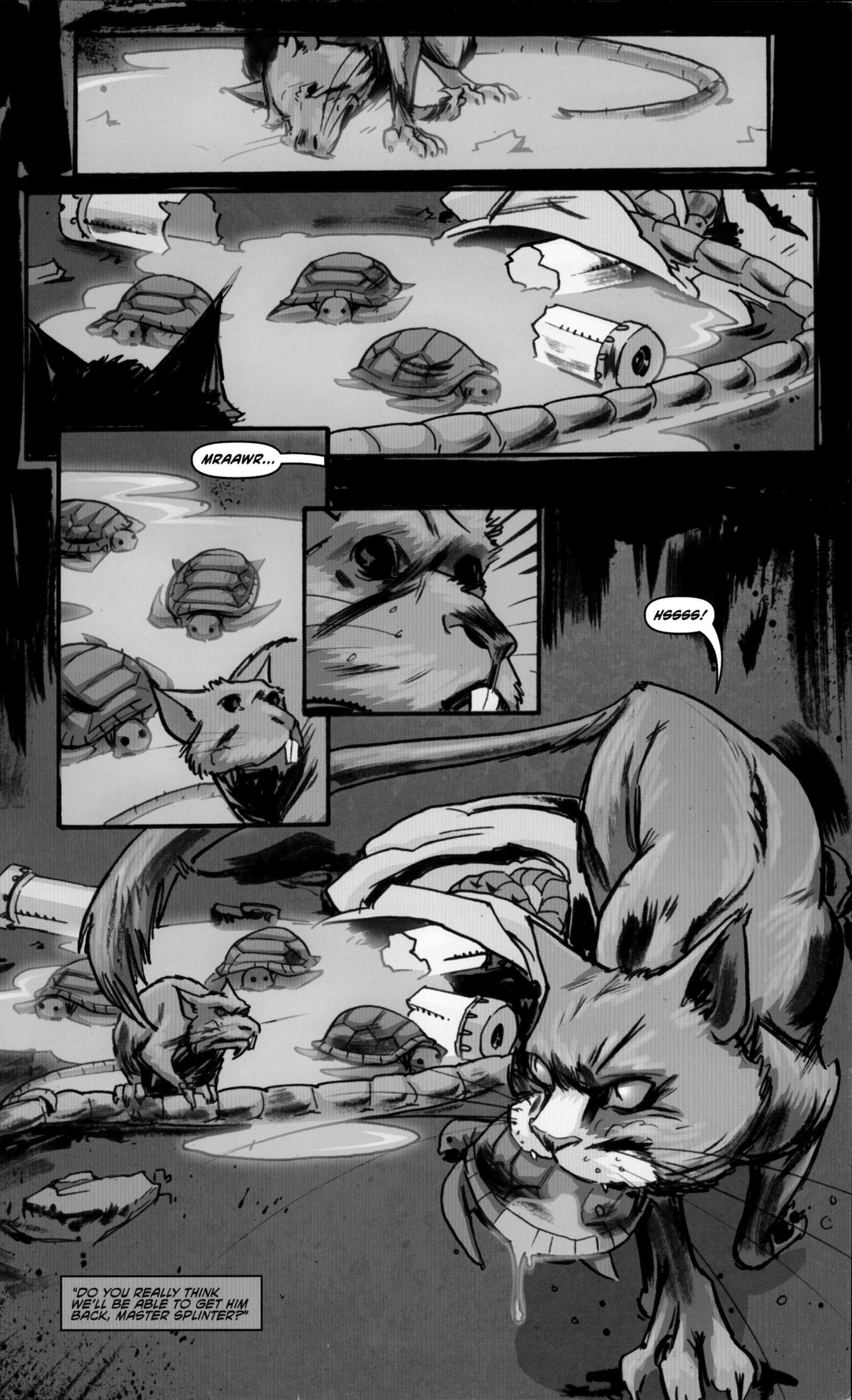
MRAAWR...
HSSSS!
"DO YOU REALLY THINK WE'LL BE ABLE TO GET HIM BACK, MASTER SPLINTER?"

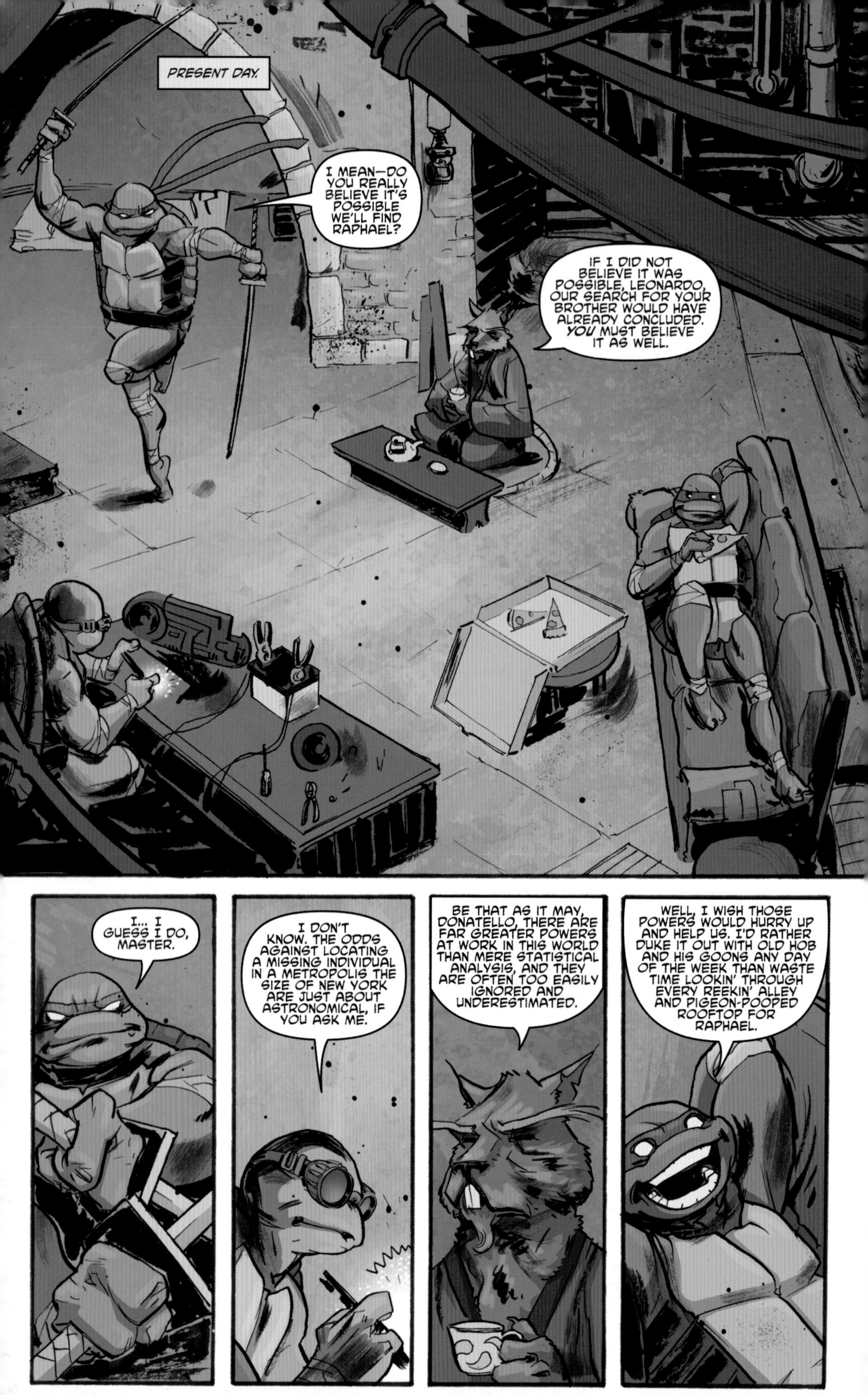
PRESENT DAY.
I MEAN—DO YOU REALLY BELIEVE IT'S POSSIBLE WE'LL FIND RAPHAEL?
IF I DID NOT BELIEVE IT WAS POSSIBLE, LEONARDO, OUR SEARCH FOR YOUR BROTHER WOULD HAVE ALREADY CONCLUDED. *YOU* MUST BELIEVE IT AS WELL.
I... I GUESS I DO, MASTER.
I DON'T KNOW. THE ODDS AGAINST LOCATING A MISSING INDIVIDUAL IN A METROPOLIS THE SIZE OF NEW YORK ARE JUST ABOUT ASTRONOMICAL, IF YOU ASK ME.
BE THAT AS IT MAY, DONATELLO, THERE ARE FAR GREATER POWERS AT WORK IN THIS WORLD THAN MERE STATISTICAL ANALYSIS, AND THEY ARE OFTEN TOO EASILY IGNORED AND UNDERESTIMATED.
WELL, I WISH THOSE POWERS WOULD HURRY UP AND HELP US. I'D RATHER DUKE IT OUT WITH OLD HOB AND HIS GOONS ANY DAY OF THE WEEK THAN WASTE TIME LOOKIN' THROUGH EVERY REEKIN' ALLEY AND PIGEON-POOPED ROOFTOP FOR RAPHAEL.

SO, THEN, MICHELANGELO, YOU CLAIM THE SEARCH FOR YOUR LOST BROTHER TO BE A POOR USE OF YOUR TIME?

NO, MASTER, IT'S NOT THAT. I MEAN, I REALLY DO WANNA FIND RAPHAEL—WE ALL DO. IT'S JUST, WELL...

...IT'S JUST THAT WE'VE BEEN LOOKIN' EVERYWHERE FOR HIM FOR LIKE A YEAR NOW. AND WE'VE GOT ZILCH TO SHOW FOR IT. MAYBE DONNIE'S RIGHT—MAYBE IT IS IMPOSSIBLE.

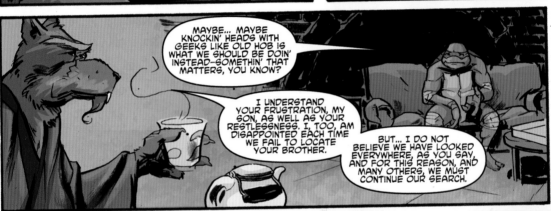

MAYBE... MAYBE KNOCKIN' HEADS WITH GEEKS LIKE OLD HOB IS WHAT WE SHOULD BE DOIN' INSTEAD—SOMETHIN' THAT MATTERS, YOU KNOW?

I UNDERSTAND YOUR FRUSTRATION, MY SON, AS WELL AS YOUR RESTLESSNESS. I, TOO, AM DISAPPOINTED EACH TIME WE FAIL TO LOCATE YOUR BROTHER.

BUT... I DO NOT BELIEVE WE HAVE LOOKED EVERYWHERE, AS YOU SAY, AND FOR THIS REASON, AND MANY OTHERS, WE MUST CONTINUE OUR SEARCH.

OUR BATTLE AGAINST OLD HOB'S GANG TONIGHT WAS—AS ARE ALL BATTLES WE WILL FIGHT—AN UNFORTUNATE NECESSITY. ANY VALUE DERIVED FROM IT IS HOLLOW AT BEST. OUR WAR HAS ONLY JUST BEGUN, AND HOB IS ONLY THE FIRST OF MANY ENEMIES I FEAR WE WILL BE FORCED TO CONFRONT.

THE ONLY VICTORY WE MUST ACTIVELY PURSUE IS THE RETURN OF RAPHAEL TO OUR CLAN—TO OUR FAMILY. ONLY THEN CAN WE ALLOW OURSELVES A MOMENT OF TRIUMPH, FOR THEN OUR CIRCLE WILL AT LAST BE COMPLETE AND WE WILL BE TRULY READY TO FACE THE HARDSHIPS THAT LIE AHEAD.

UNTIL THEN, HOWEVER, WE MUST CONTINUE TO SEARCH FOR YOUR BROTHER, FOR WITHOUT HIM...

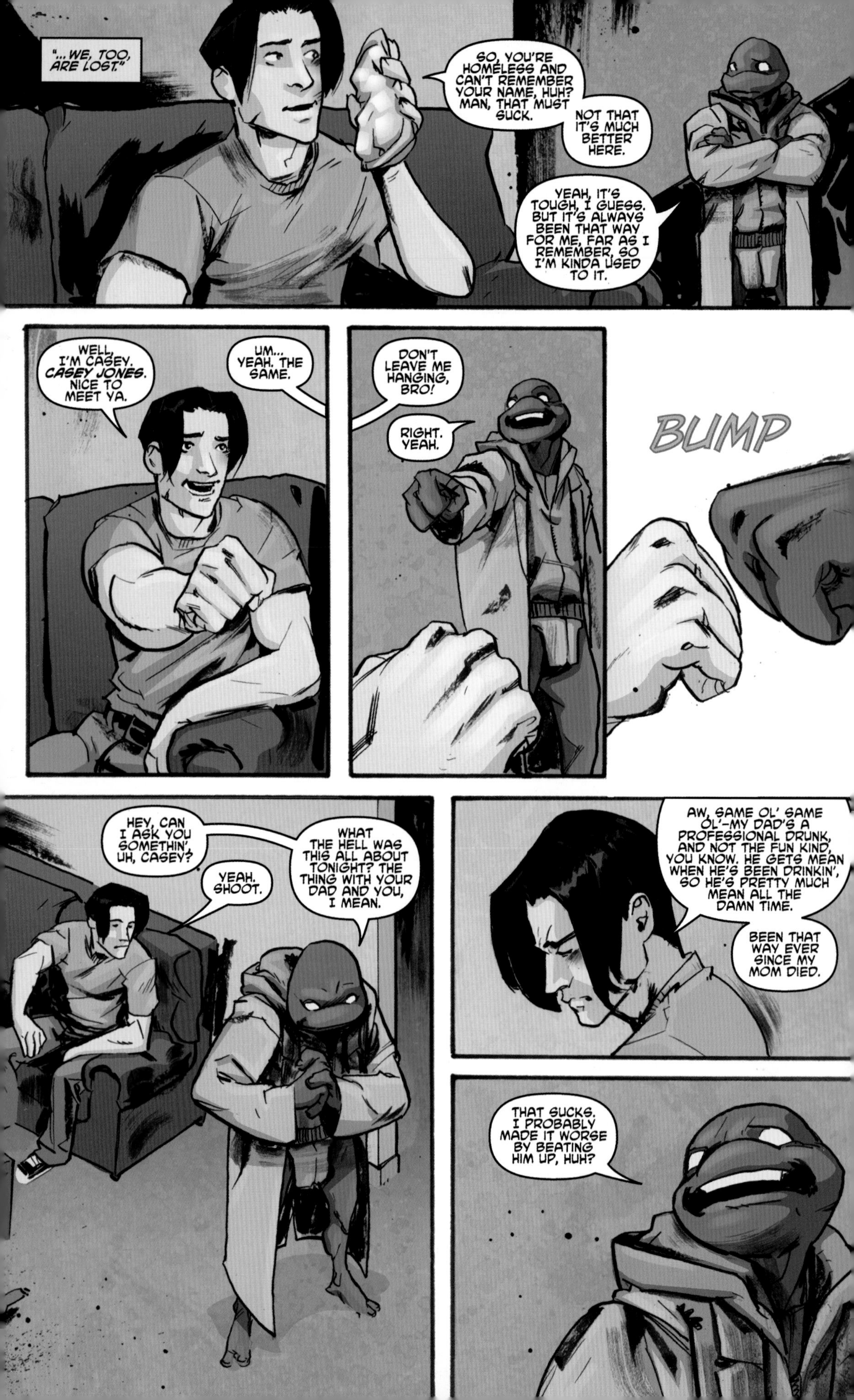
"...WE, TOO, ARE LOST."
SO, YOU'RE HOMELESS AND CAN'T REMEMBER YOUR NAME, HUH? MAN, THAT MUST SUCK.
NOT THAT IT'S MUCH BETTER HERE.
YEAH, IT'S TOUGH, I GUESS. BUT IT'S ALWAYS BEEN THAT WAY FOR ME, FAR AS I REMEMBER, SO I'M KINDA USED TO IT.
WELL, I'M CASEY. *CASEY JONES*. NICE TO MEET YA.
UM... YEAH. THE SAME.
DON'T LEAVE ME HANGING, BRO!
RIGHT. YEAH.
BUMP
HEY, CAN I ASK YOU SOMETHIN', UH, CASEY?
YEAH. SHOOT.
WHAT THE HELL WAS THIS ALL ABOUT TONIGHT? THE THING WITH YOUR DAD AND YOU, I MEAN.
AW, SAME OL' SAME OL'–MY DAD'S A PROFESSIONAL DRUNK, AND NOT THE FUN KIND, YOU KNOW. HE GETS MEAN WHEN HE'S BEEN DRINKIN', SO HE'S PRETTY MUCH MEAN ALL THE DAMN TIME.
BEEN THAT WAY EVER SINCE MY MOM DIED.
THAT SUCKS. I PROBABLY MADE IT WORSE BY BEATING HIM UP, HUH?

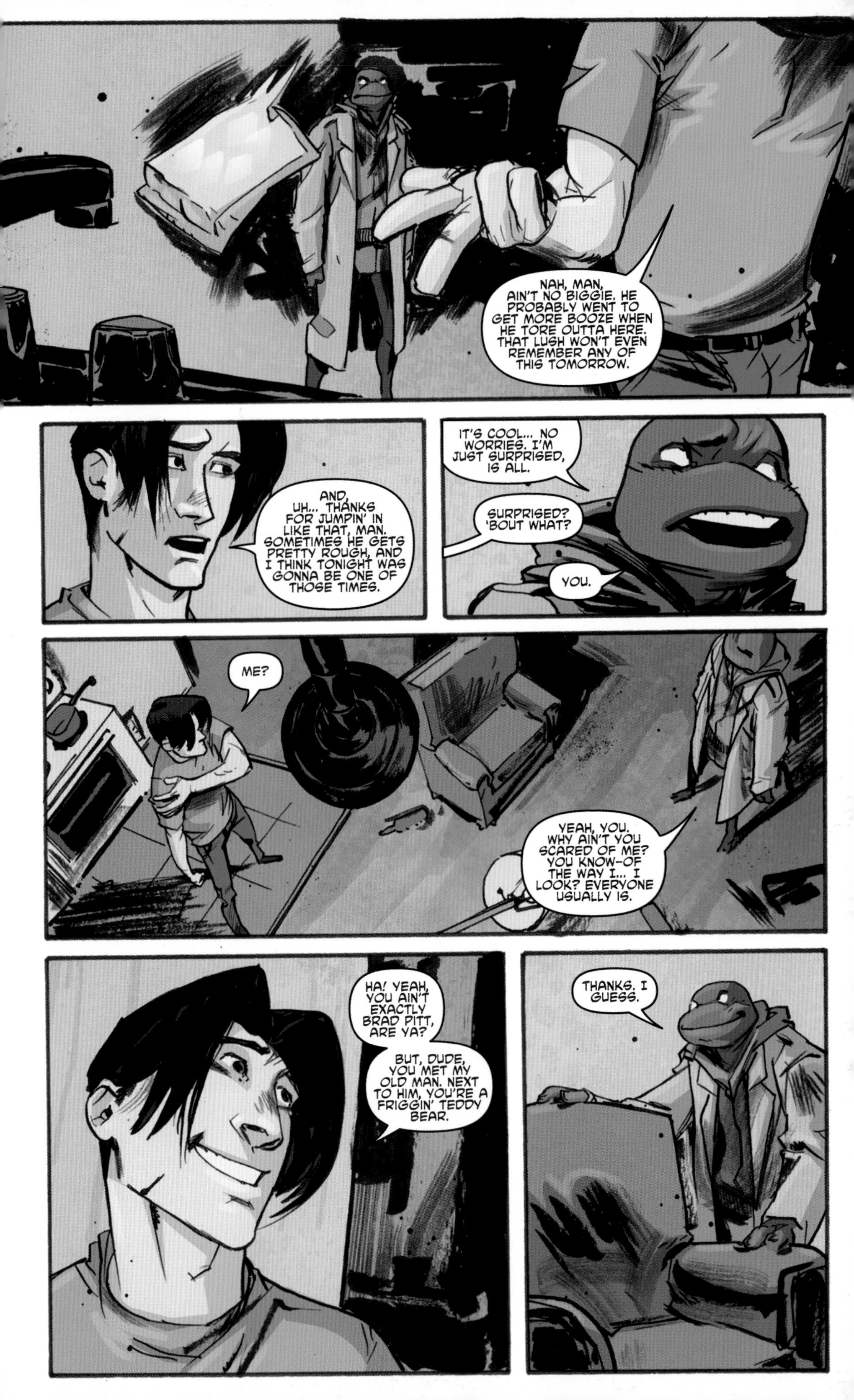
NAH, MAN, AIN'T NO BIGGIE. HE PROBABLY WENT TO GET MORE BOOZE WHEN HE TORE OUTTA HERE. THAT LUSH WON'T EVEN REMEMBER ANY OF THIS TOMORROW.
AND, UH... THANKS FOR JUMPIN' IN LIKE THAT, MAN. SOMETIMES HE GETS PRETTY ROUGH, AND I THINK TONIGHT WAS GONNA BE ONE OF THOSE TIMES.
IT'S COOL... NO WORRIES. I'M JUST SURPRISED, IS ALL.
SURPRISED? 'BOUT WHAT?
YOU.
ME?
YEAH, YOU. WHY AIN'T YOU SCARED OF ME? YOU KNOW--OF THE WAY I... I LOOK? EVERYONE USUALLY IS.
HA! YEAH, YOU AIN'T EXACTLY BRAD PITT, ARE YA?
BUT, DUDE, YOU MET MY OLD MAN. NEXT TO HIM, YOU'RE A FRIGGIN' TEDDY BEAR.
THANKS. I GUESS.

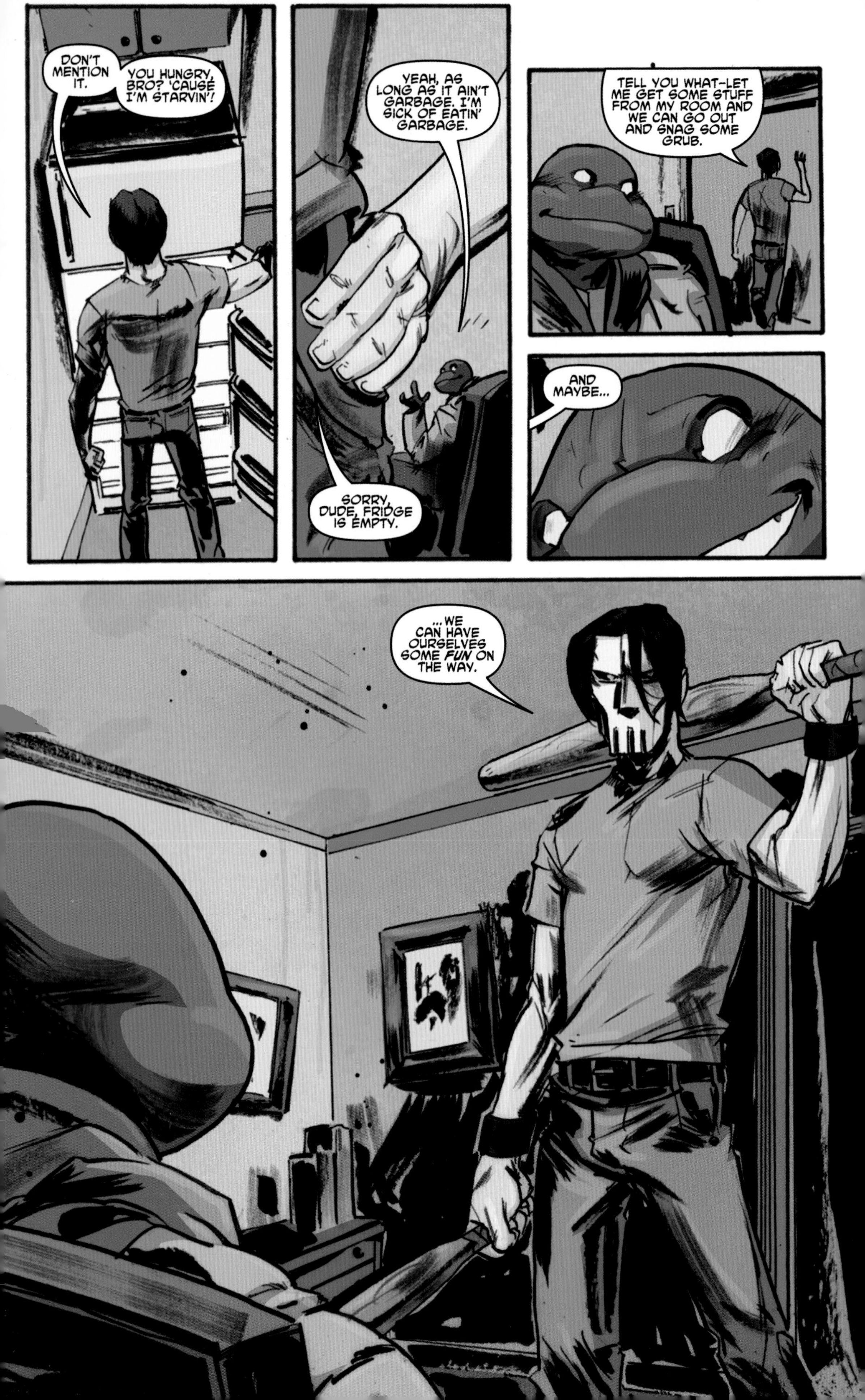
DON'T MENTION IT.
YOU HUNGRY, BRO? 'CAUSE I'M STARVIN'!
YEAH, AS LONG AS IT AIN'T GARBAGE. I'M SICK OF EATIN' GARBAGE.
SORRY, DUDE, FRIDGE IS EMPTY.
TELL YOU WHAT–LET ME GET SOME STUFF FROM MY ROOM AND WE CAN GO OUT AND SNAG SOME GRUB.
AND MAYBE...
...WE CAN HAVE OURSELVES SOME FUN ON THE WAY.

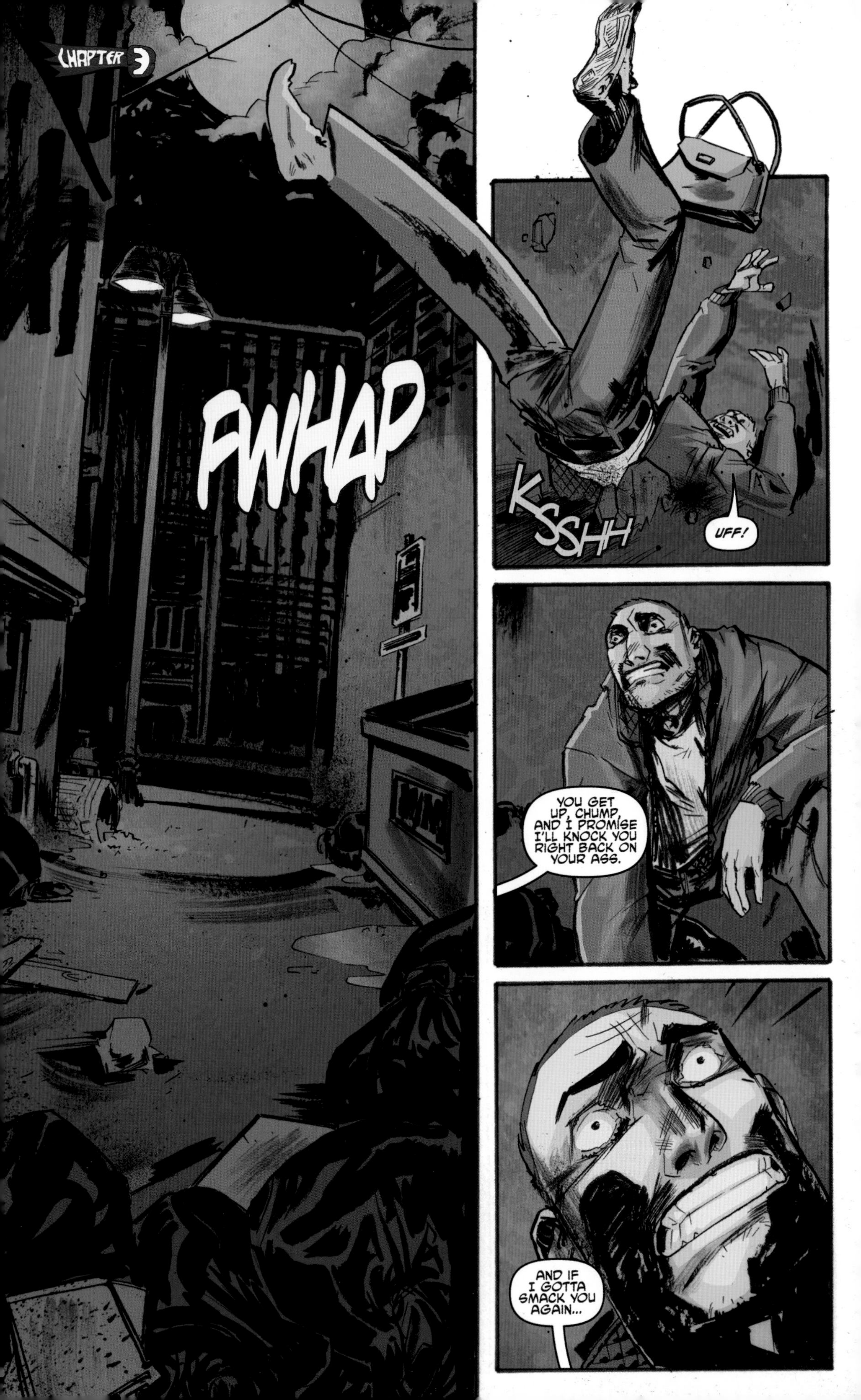
CHAPTER 3
FWHAP
KSSHH
UFF!
YOU GET UP, CHUMP, AND I PROMISE I'LL KNOCK YOU RIGHT BACK ON YOUR ASS.
AND IF I GOTTA SMACK YOU AGAIN...

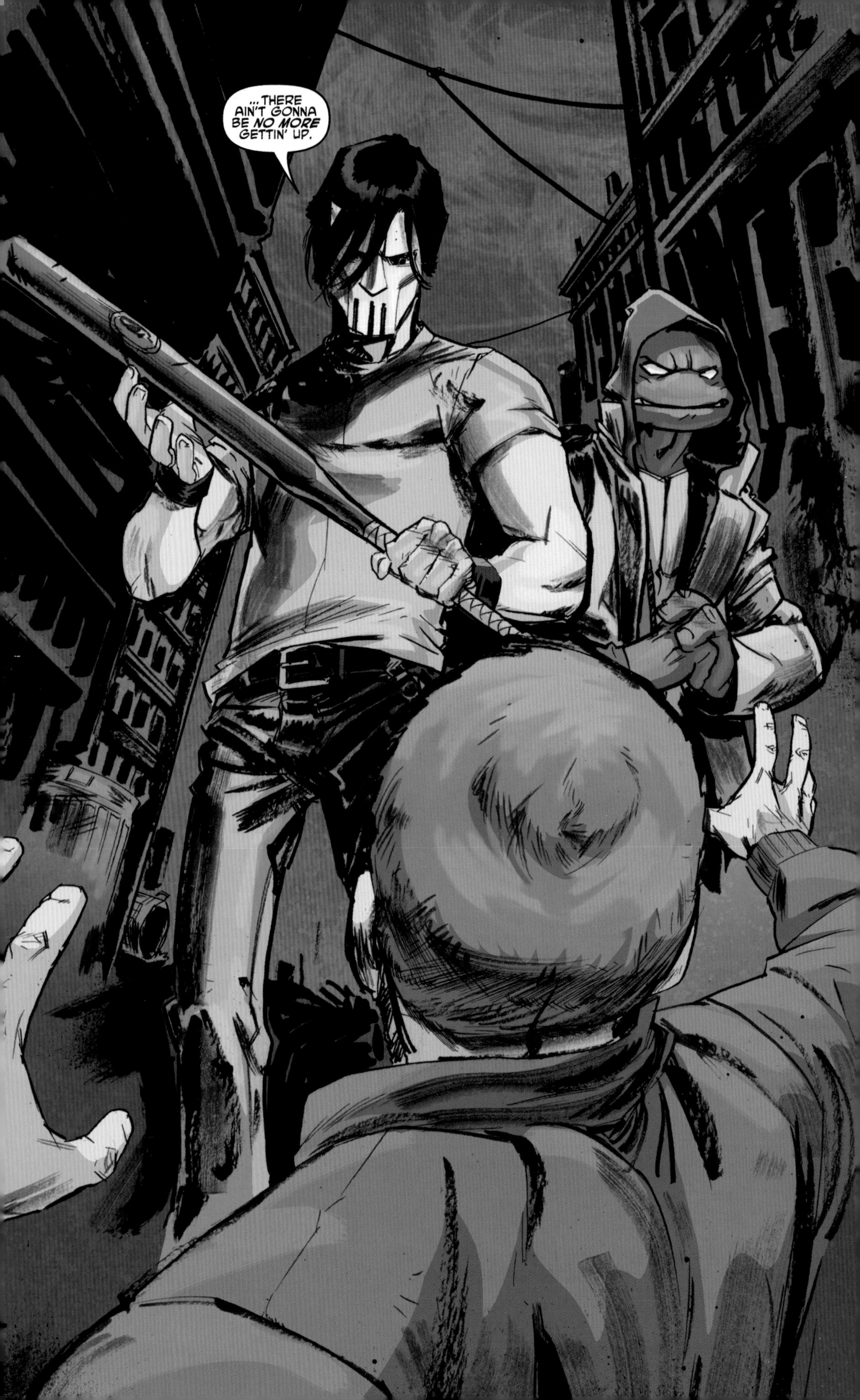
...THERE AIN'T GONNA BE NO MORE GETTIN' UP.

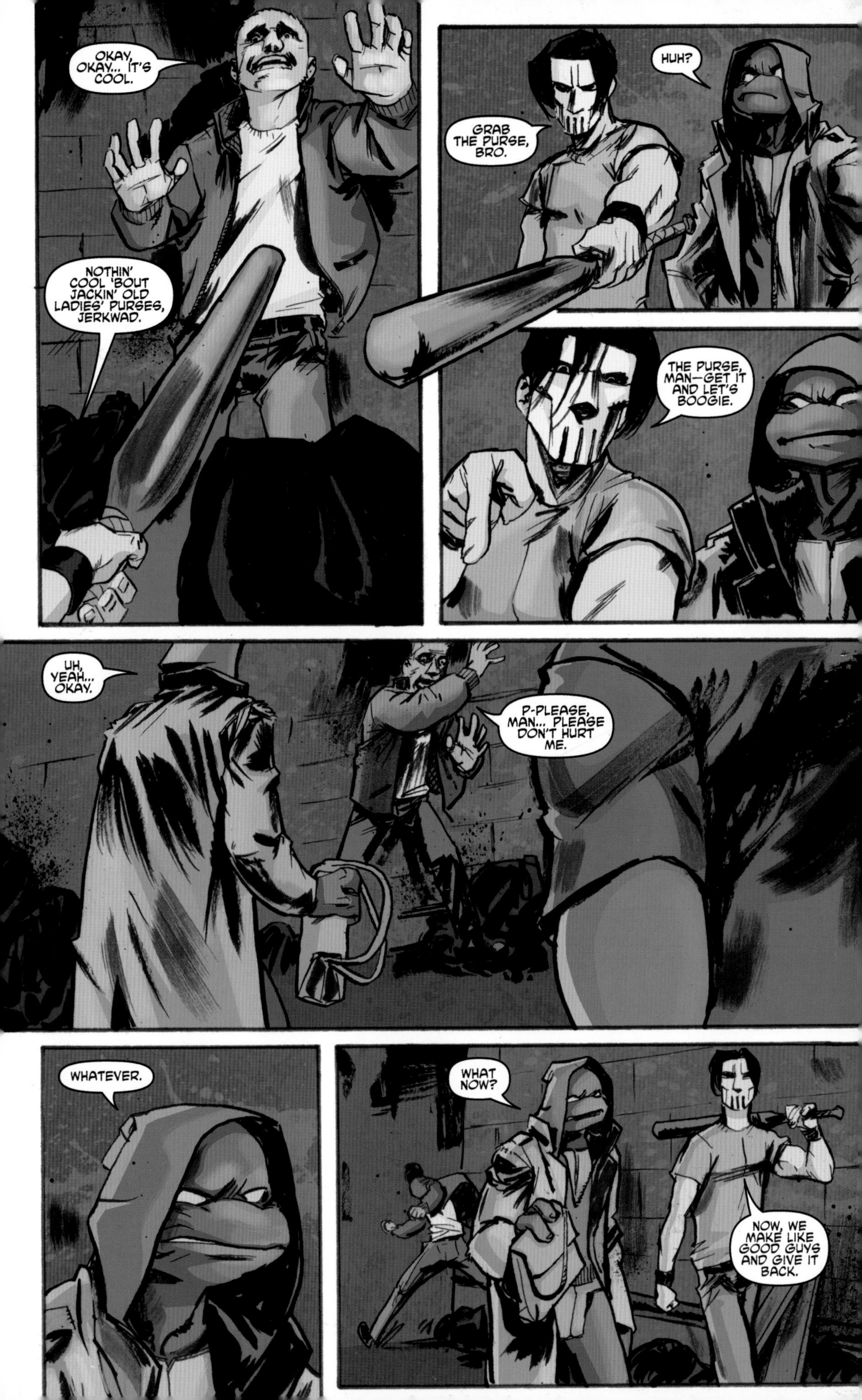
OKAY, OKAY... IT'S COOL.
NOTHIN' COOL 'BOUT JACKIN' OLD LADIES' PURSES, JERKWAD.
HUH?
GRAB THE PURSE, BRO.
THE PURSE, MAN—GET IT AND LET'S BOOGIE.
UH, YEAH... OKAY.
P-PLEASE, MAN... PLEASE DON'T HURT ME.
WHATEVER.
WHAT NOW?
NOW, WE MAKE LIKE GOOD GUYS AND GIVE IT BACK.

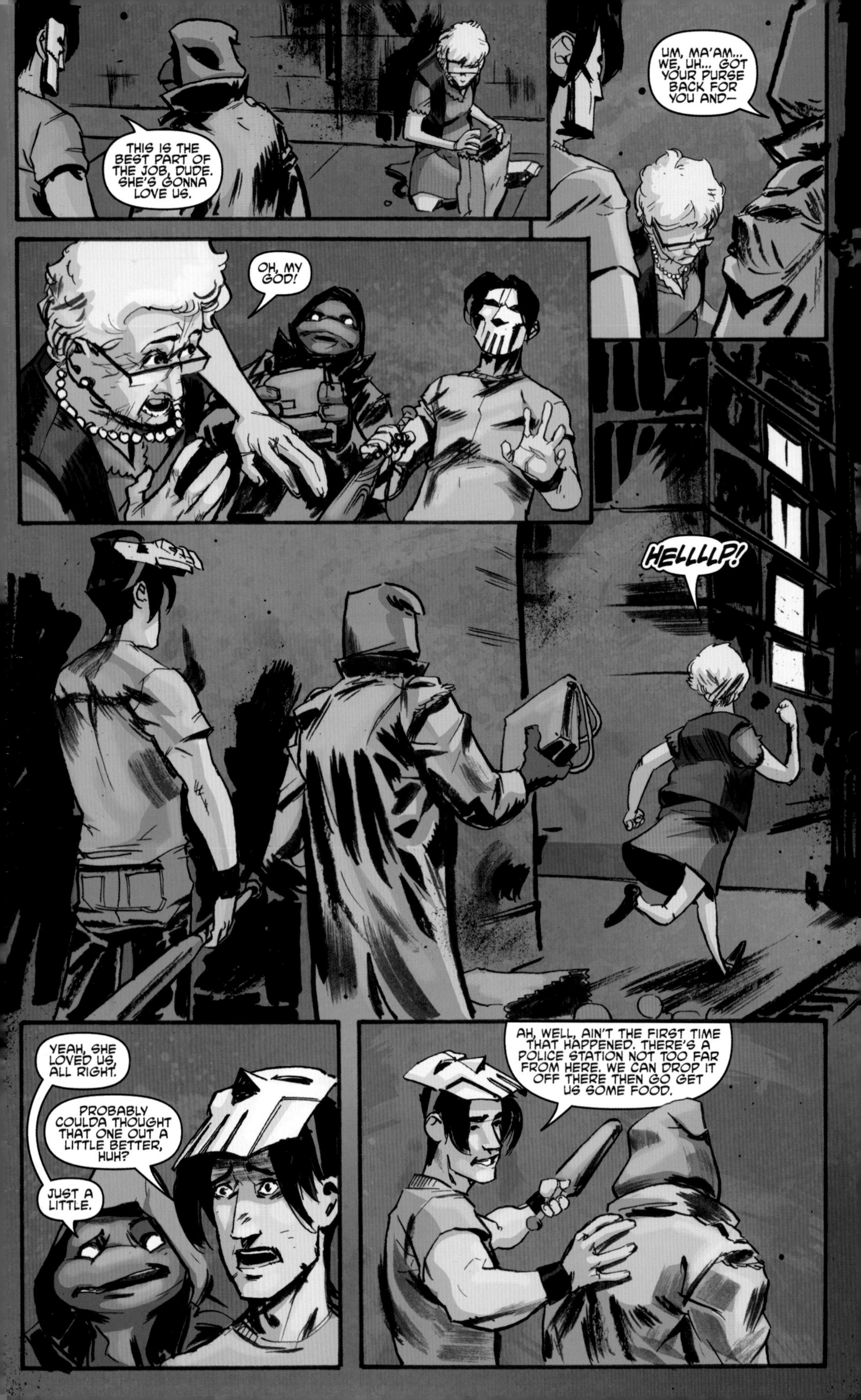
THIS IS THE BEST PART OF THE JOB, DUDE. SHE'S GONNA LOVE US.
UM, MA'AM... WE, UH... GOT YOUR PURSE BACK FOR YOU AND—
OH, MY GOD!
HELLLLP!
YEAH, SHE LOVED US, ALL RIGHT.
PROBABLY COULDA THOUGHT THAT ONE OUT A LITTLE BETTER, HUH?
JUST A LITTLE.
AH, WELL, AIN'T THE FIRST TIME THAT HAPPENED. THERE'S A POLICE STATION NOT TOO FAR FROM HERE. WE CAN DROP IT OFF THERE THEN GO GET US SOME FOOD.

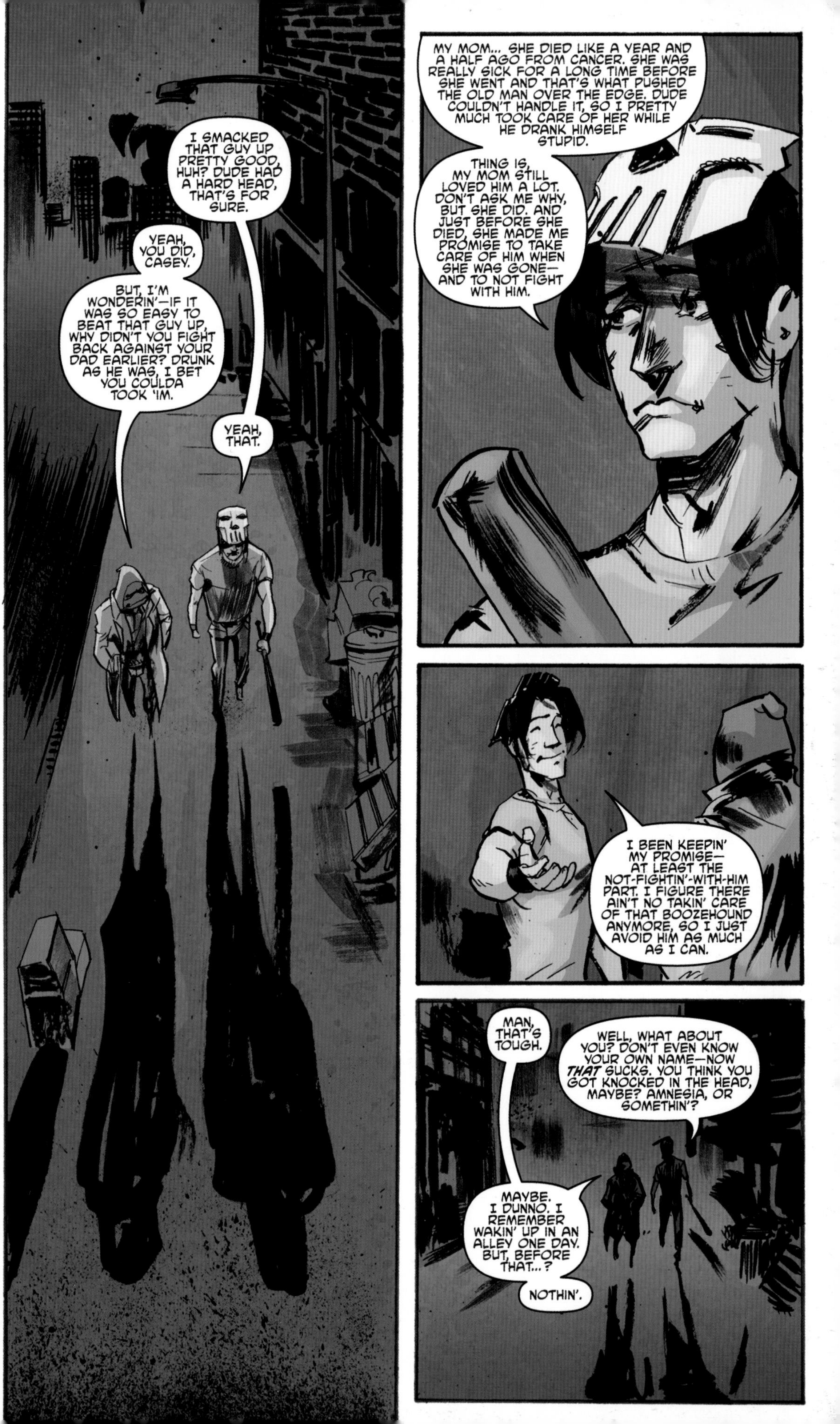
I SMACKED THAT GUY UP PRETTY GOOD, HUH? DUDE HAD A HARD HEAD, THAT'S FOR SURE.
YEAH, YOU DID, CASEY.
BUT, I'M WONDERIN'—IF IT WAS SO EASY TO BEAT THAT GUY UP, WHY DIDN'T YOU FIGHT BACK AGAINST YOUR DAD EARLIER? DRUNK AS HE WAS, I BET YOU COULDA TOOK 'IM.
YEAH, THAT.
MY MOM... SHE DIED LIKE A YEAR AND A HALF AGO FROM CANCER. SHE WAS REALLY SICK FOR A LONG TIME BEFORE SHE WENT AND THAT'S WHAT PUSHED THE OLD MAN OVER THE EDGE. DUDE COULDN'T HANDLE IT, SO I PRETTY MUCH TOOK CARE OF HER WHILE HE DRANK HIMSELF STUPID.
THING IS, MY MOM STILL LOVED HIM A LOT. DON'T ASK ME WHY, BUT SHE DID. AND JUST BEFORE SHE DIED, SHE MADE ME PROMISE TO TAKE CARE OF HIM WHEN SHE WAS GONE— AND TO NOT FIGHT WITH HIM.
I BEEN KEEPIN' MY PROMISE— AT LEAST THE NOT-FIGHTIN'-WITH-HIM PART. I FIGURE THERE AIN'T NO TAKIN' CARE OF THAT BOOZEHOUND ANYMORE, SO I JUST AVOID HIM AS MUCH AS I CAN.
MAN, THAT'S TOUGH.
WELL, WHAT ABOUT YOU? DON'T EVEN KNOW YOUR OWN NAME—NOW THAT SUCKS. YOU THINK YOU GOT KNOCKED IN THE HEAD, MAYBE? AMNESIA, OR SOMETHIN'?
MAYBE. I DUNNO. I REMEMBER WAKIN' UP IN AN ALLEY ONE DAY. BUT, BEFORE THAT...?
NOTHIN'.

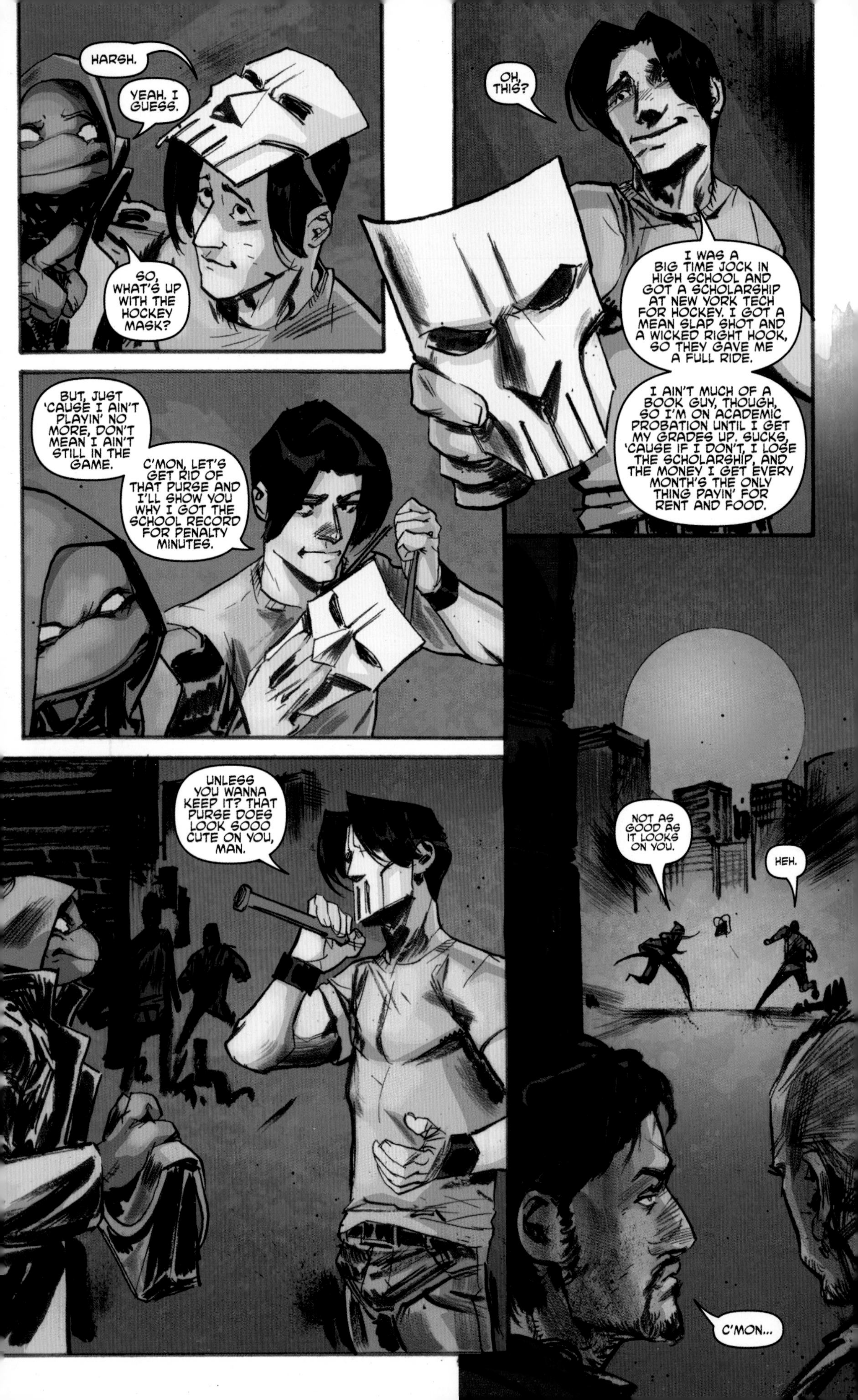
HARSH.
YEAH. I GUESS.
SO, WHAT'S UP WITH THE HOCKEY MASK?
OH, THIS?
I WAS A BIG TIME JOCK IN HIGH SCHOOL AND GOT A SCHOLARSHIP AT NEW YORK TECH FOR HOCKEY. I GOT A MEAN SLAP SHOT AND A WICKED RIGHT HOOK, SO THEY GAVE ME A FULL RIDE.
I AIN'T MUCH OF A BOOK GUY, THOUGH, SO I'M ON ACADEMIC PROBATION UNTIL I GET MY GRADES UP. SUCKS, 'CAUSE IF I DON'T, I LOSE THE SCHOLARSHIP, AND THE MONEY I GET EVERY MONTH'S THE ONLY THING PAYIN' FOR RENT AND FOOD.
BUT, JUST 'CAUSE I AIN'T PLAYIN' NO MORE, DON'T MEAN I AIN'T STILL IN THE GAME.
C'MON, LET'S GET RID OF THAT PURSE AND I'LL SHOW YOU WHY I GOT THE SCHOOL RECORD FOR PENALTY MINUTES.
UNLESS YOU WANNA KEEP IT? THAT PURSE DOES LOOK SOOO CUTE ON YOU, MAN.
NOT AS GOOD AS IT LOOKS ON YOU.
HEH.
C'MON...

"... WE GOTTA TELL HOB 'BOUT THIS."

HYAH!

WHOULF!

HA!

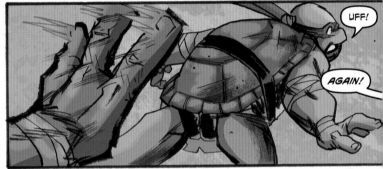

UFF!

AGAIN!

SHOW ME AGAIN, DONATELLO. AND THIS TIME, DO NOT LOSE FOCUS OF WHAT IS TRULY IMPORTANT.

INCAPACITATING LEONARDO IS WORTHLESS IF MICHELANGELO IS ABLE TO DO THE SAME TO YOU. YOU MUST STRIKE AND FORGET. THE PAST IS GONE AND ALL THAT MATTERS IS YOUR NEXT MOVE...

...TO CELEBRATE VICTORY PREMATURELY IS TO INVITE EARLY DEFEAT.

YES, SENSEI. I'M SORRY.

APOLOGIES ARE UNNECESSARY, MY SON. I ONLY ASK THAT YOU LEARN FROM YOUR MISTAKES AND STRIVE TO RECTIFY THAT WHICH IS WRONG. TRAINING IS EVERYTHING.

IF WE UNDERESTIMATE THE IMPORTANCE OF TRAINING, THEN WE UNDERESTIMATE THE FORMIDABILITY OF OUR ENEMIES.

UH, MASTER, SPEAKING OF ENEMIES, WHAT EXACTLY IS OLD HOB'S DEAL? I MEAN, WHY'S HE SO HOT TO GET AT US?

WHAT'D WE EVER DO TO HIM?

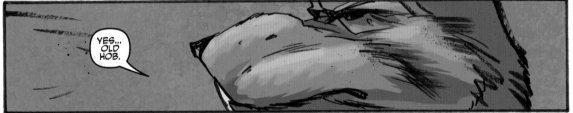

YES... OLD HOB.

YOU NEED NOT CONCERN YOURSELF WITH SUCH THINGS, MICHELANGELO—AS I SAID, YOU MUST FOCUS ON WHAT *IS*, NOT WHAT *WAS*.

IT IS SIMPLY ENOUGH FOR YOU TO UNDERSTAND...

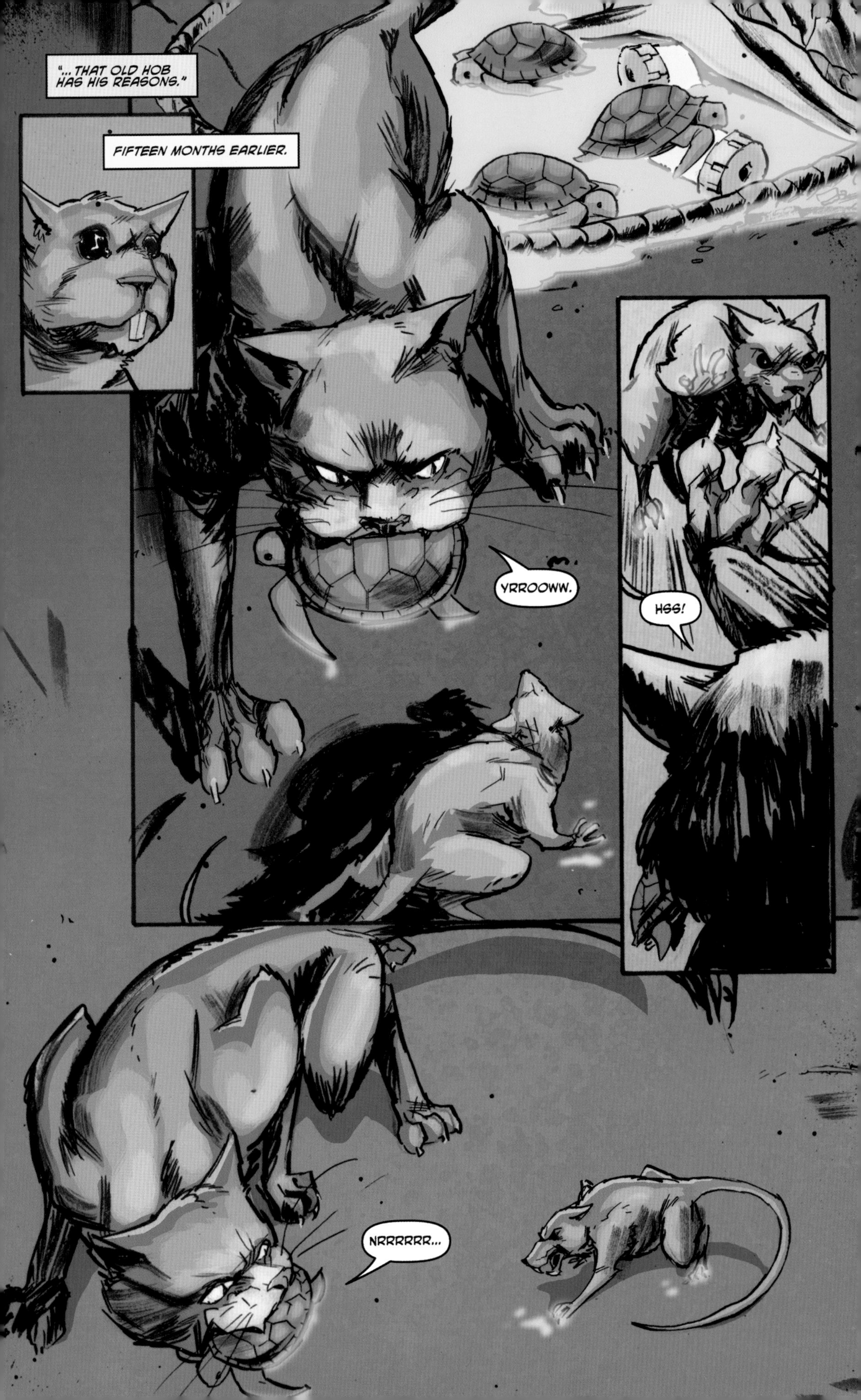
"...THAT OLD HOB HAS HIS REASONS."
FIFTEEN MONTHS EARLIER.
YRROOWW.
HSS!
NRRRRRR...

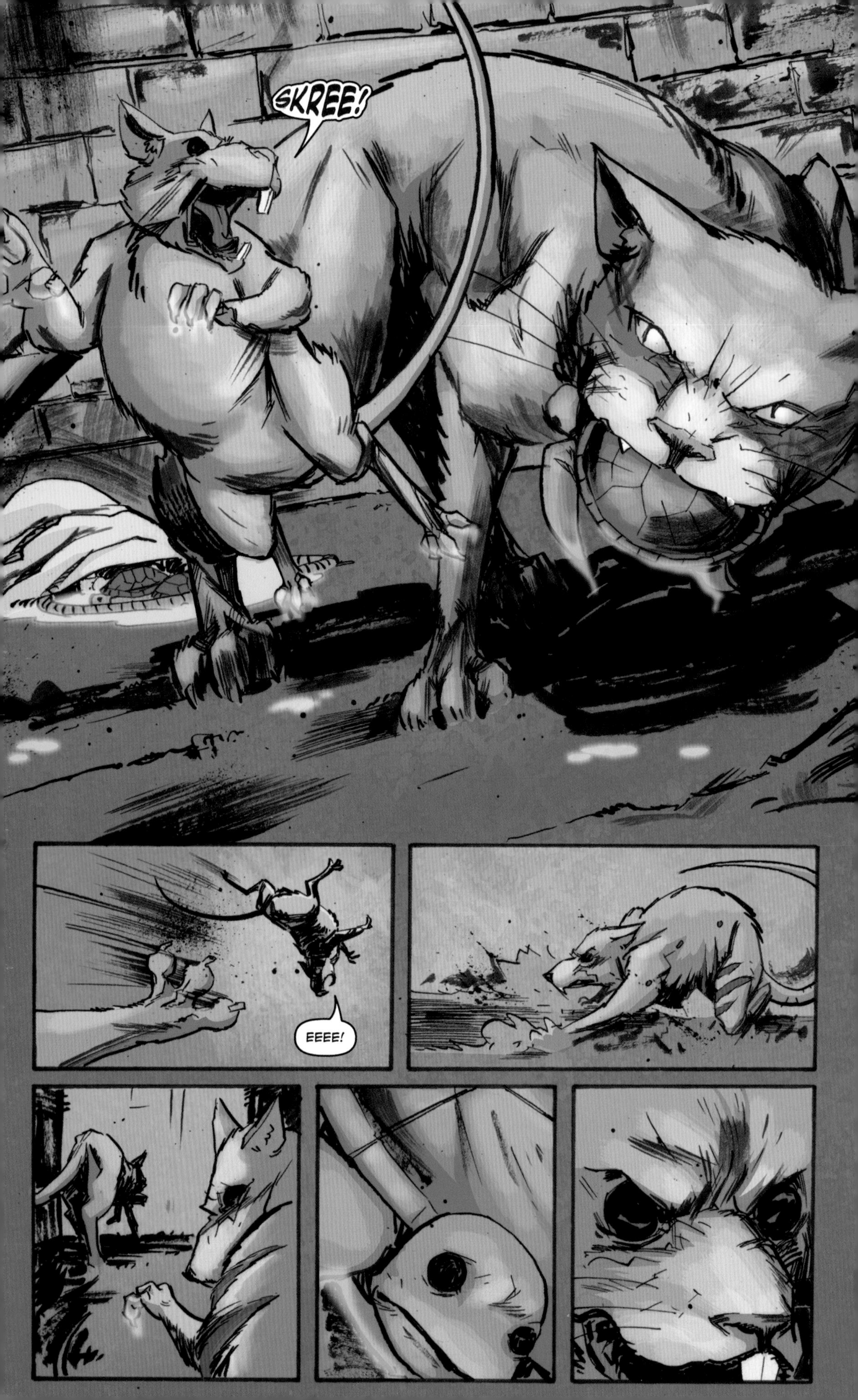
SKREE!
EEEE!

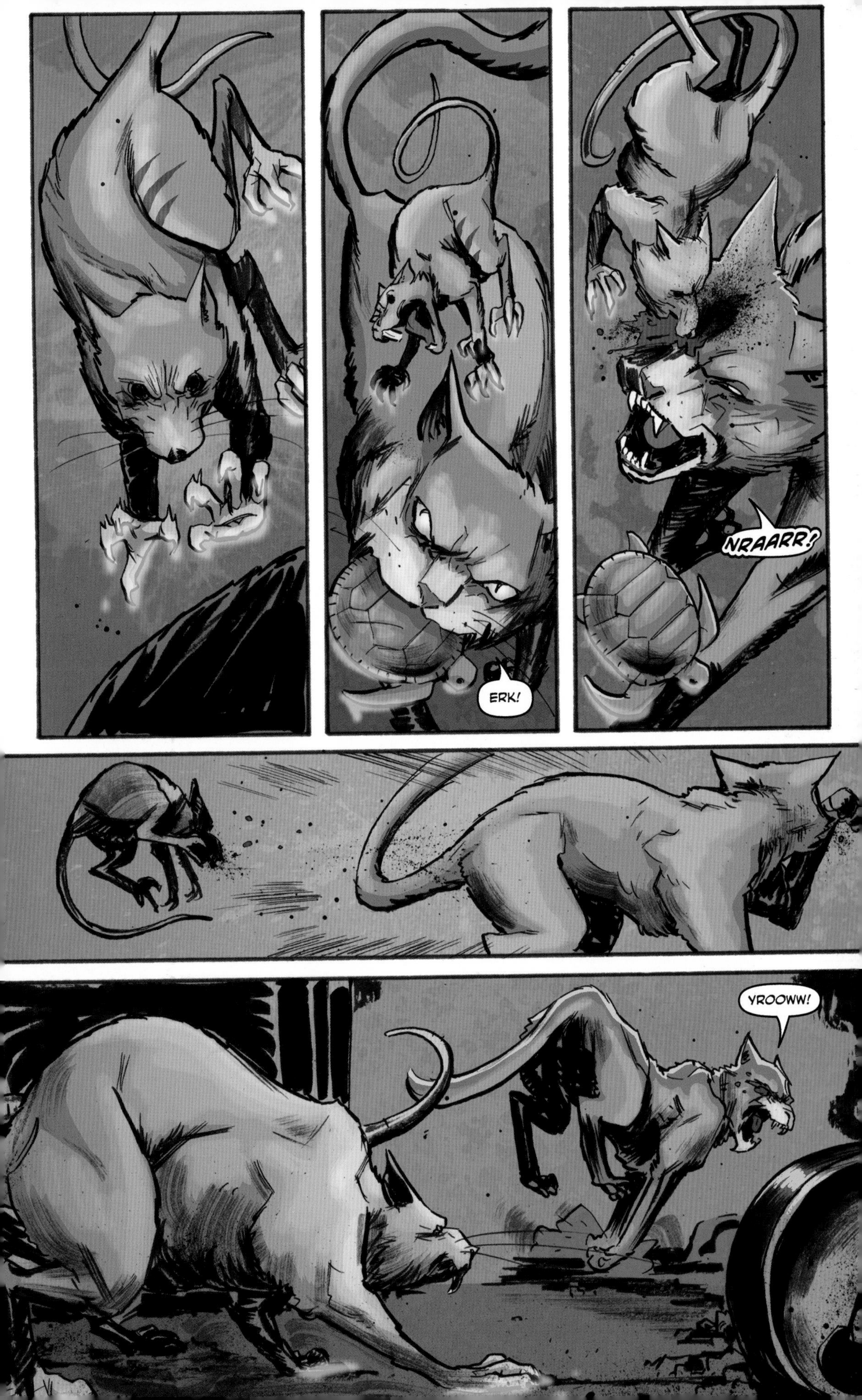
ERK!
NRAARR!
YROOWW!

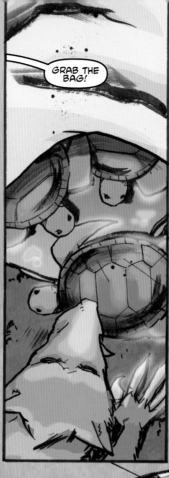

FWUMP

GRAB THE BAG!

THE RAT!

KILL IT!

XLANG

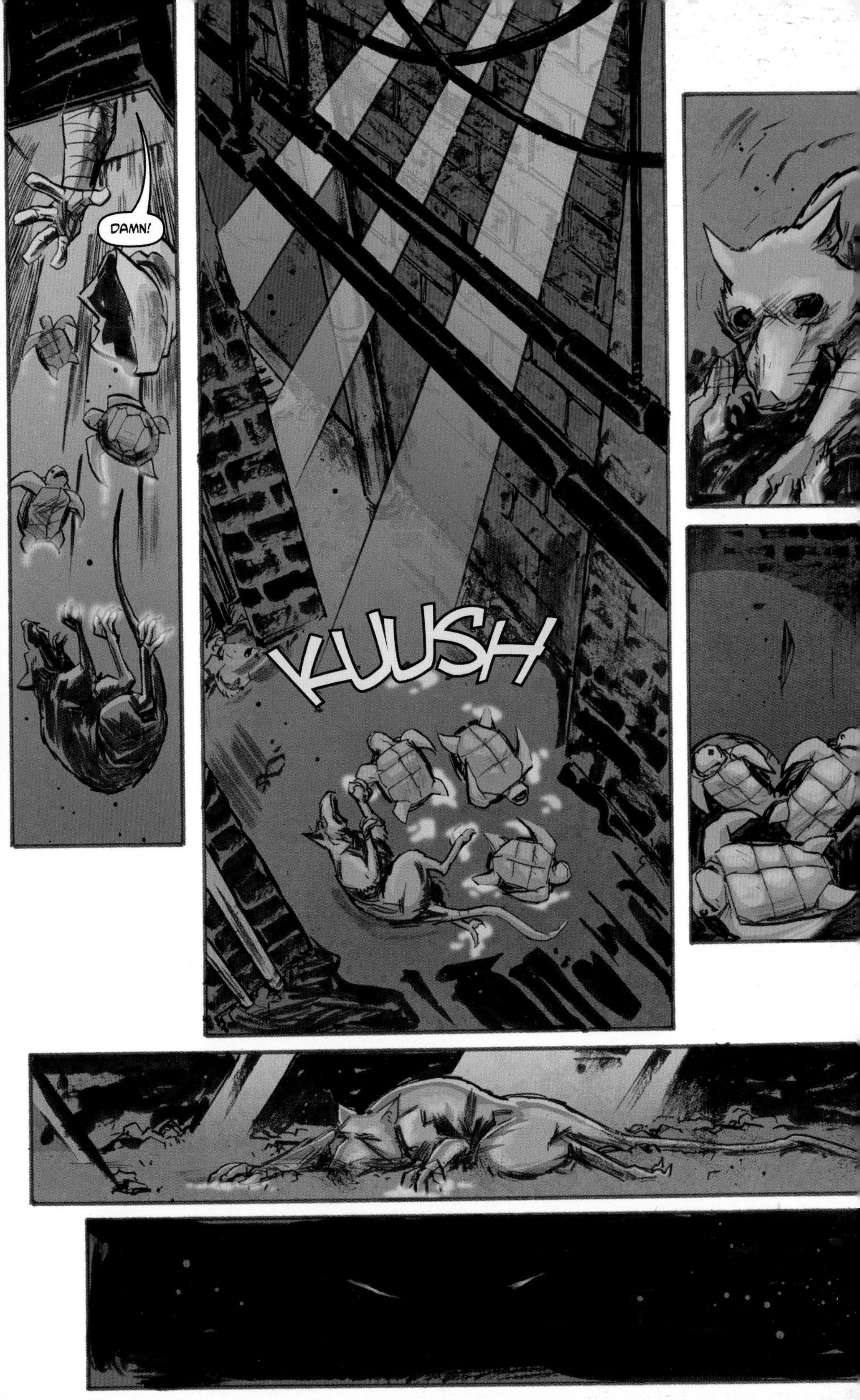
DAMN!
KUUSH

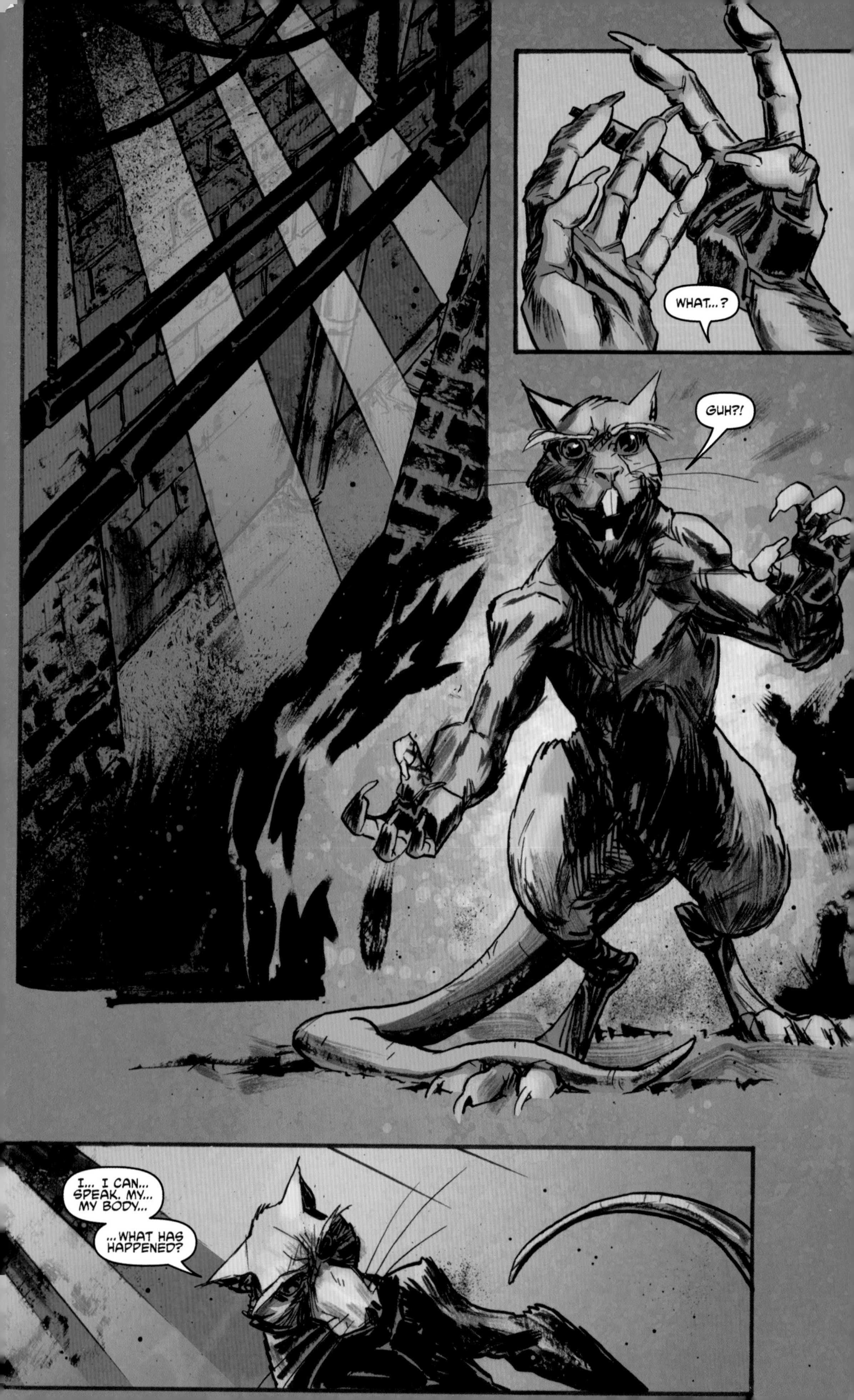
WHAT...?
GUH?!
I... I CAN... SPEAK. MY... MY BODY...
...WHAT HAS HAPPENED?

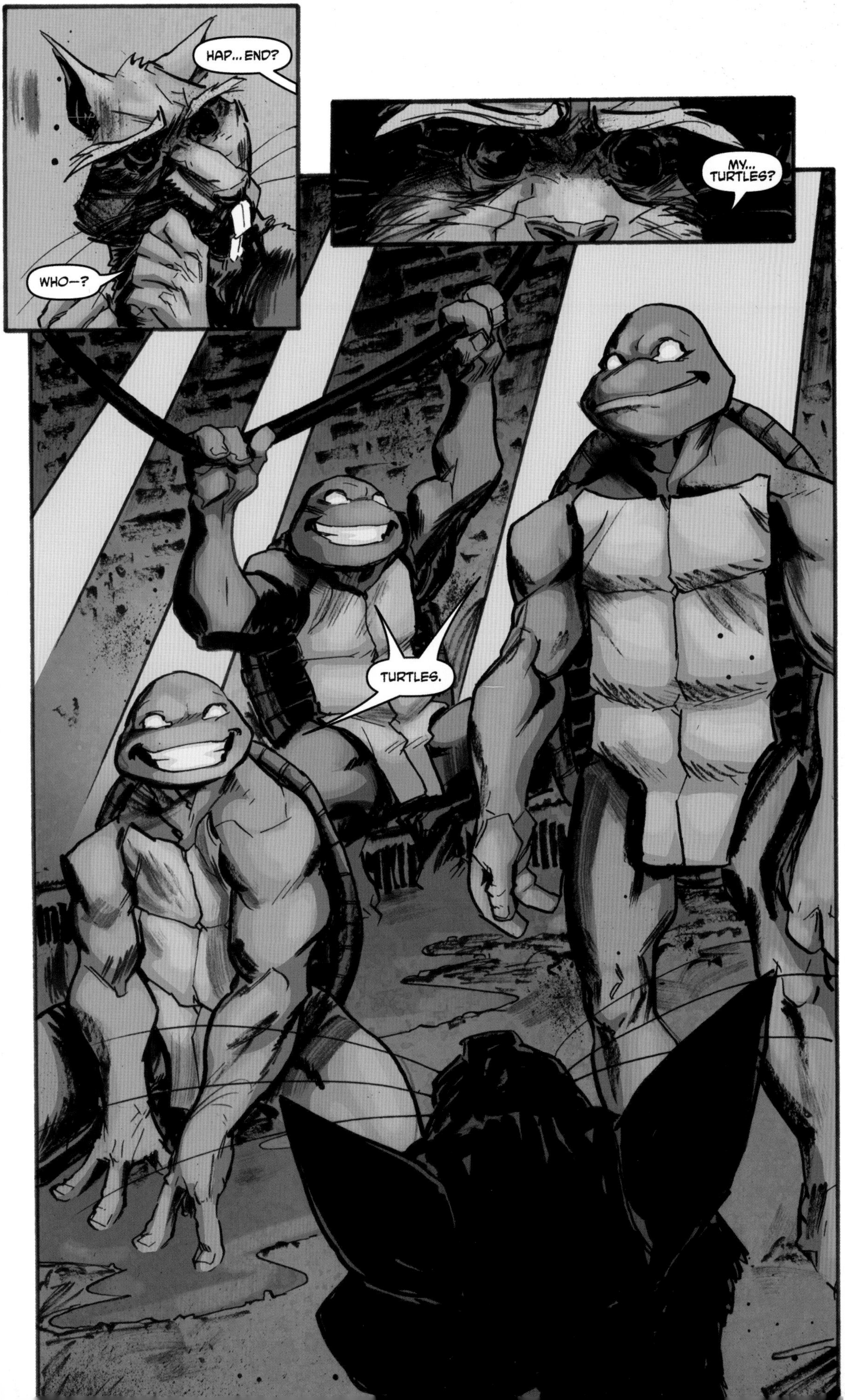
HAP... END?
WHO--?
MY... TURTLES?
TURTLES.

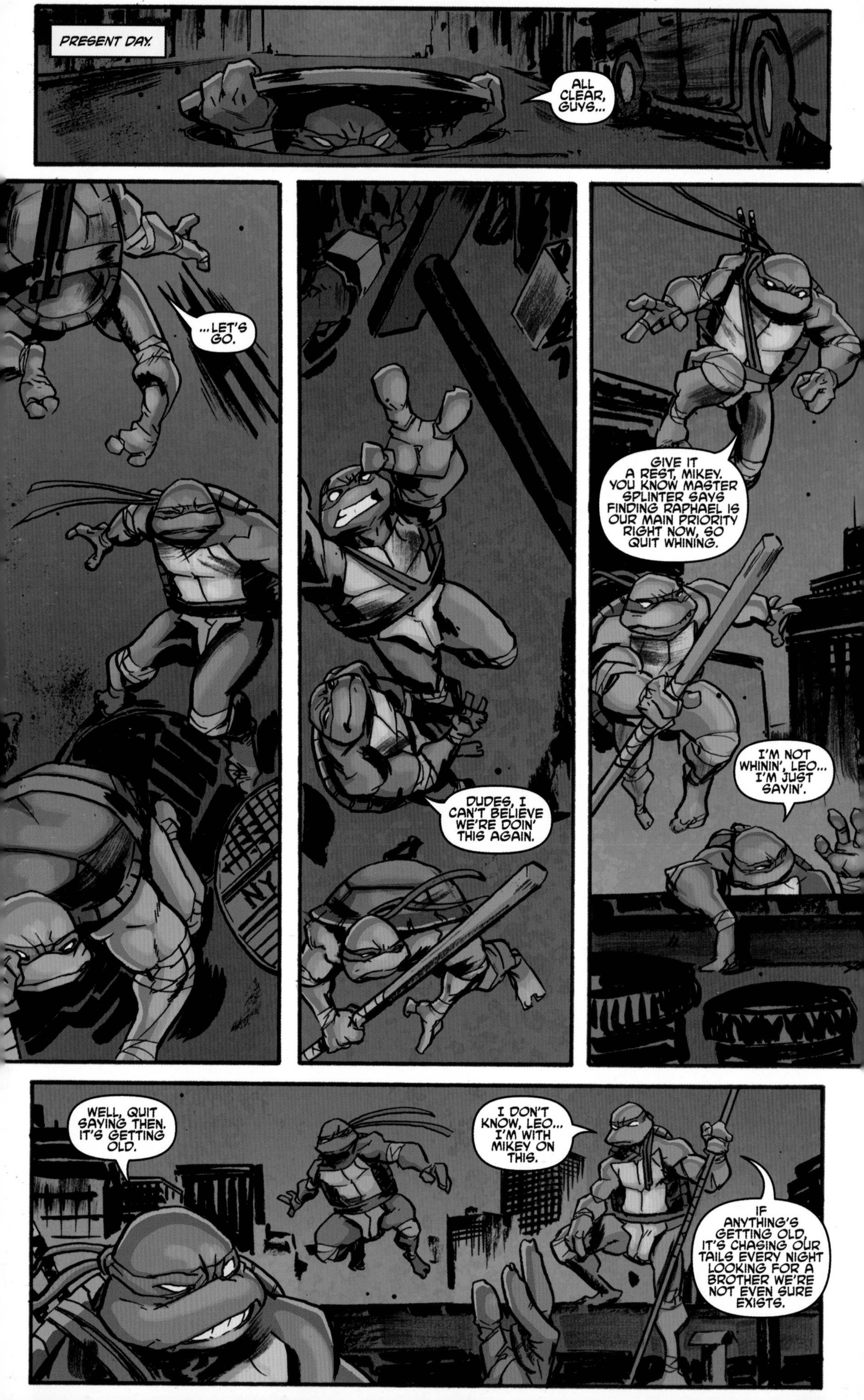
PRESENT DAY.
ALL CLEAR, GUYS...
...LET'S GO.
DUDES, I CAN'T BELIEVE WE'RE DOIN' THIS AGAIN.
GIVE IT A REST, MIKEY. YOU KNOW MASTER SPLINTER SAYS FINDING RAPHAEL IS OUR MAIN PRIORITY RIGHT NOW, SO QUIT WHINING.
I'M NOT WHININ', LEO... I'M JUST SAYIN'.
NY
WELL, QUIT SAYING THEN. IT'S GETTING OLD.
I DON'T KNOW, LEO... I'M WITH MIKEY ON THIS.
IF ANYTHING'S GETTING OLD, IT'S CHASING OUR TAILS EVERY NIGHT LOOKING FOR A BROTHER WE'RE NOT EVEN SURE EXISTS.

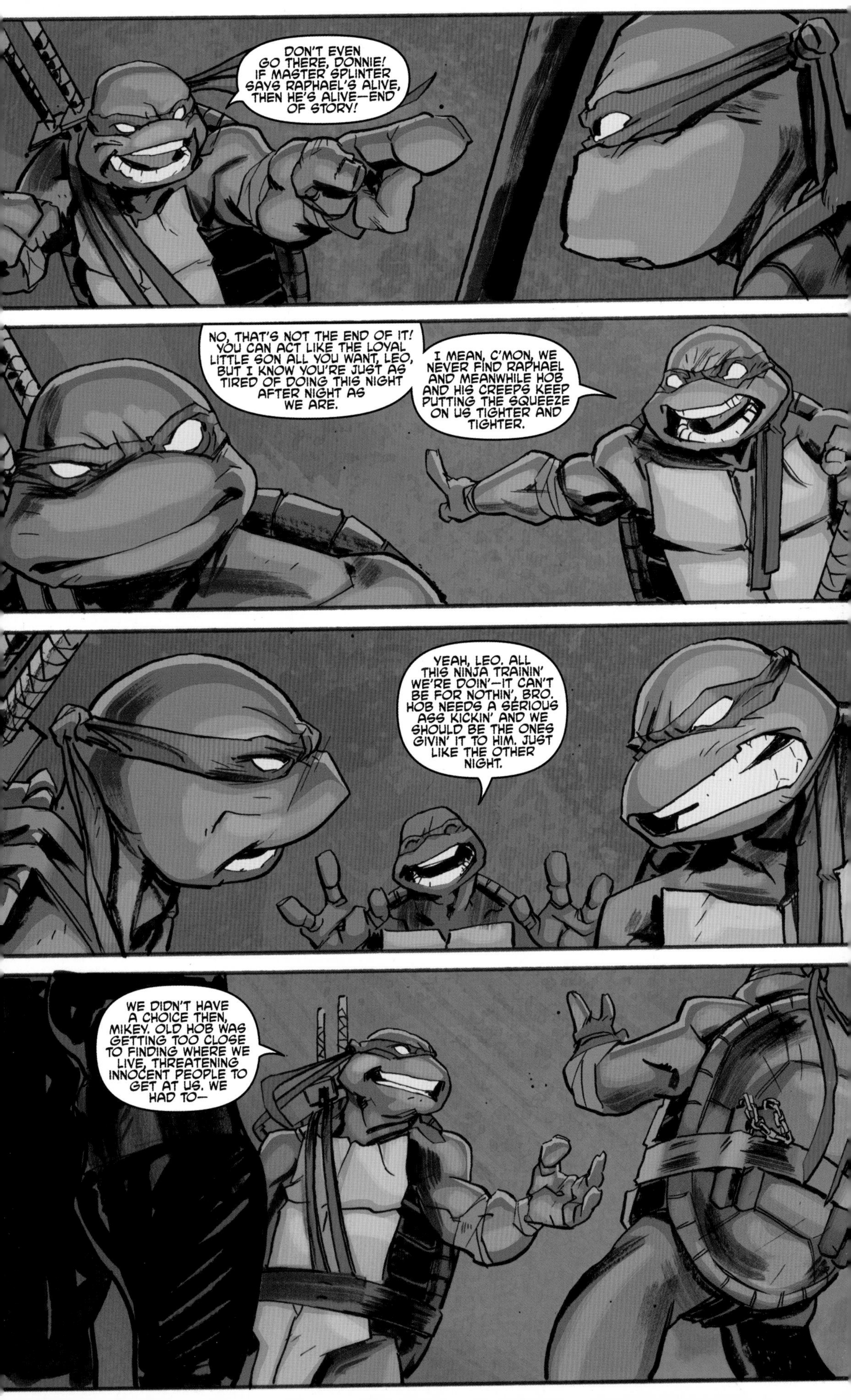
DON'T EVEN GO THERE, DONNIE! IF MASTER SPLINTER SAYS RAPHAEL'S ALIVE, THEN HE'S ALIVE—END OF STORY!
NO, THAT'S NOT THE END OF IT! YOU CAN ACT LIKE THE LOYAL LITTLE SON ALL YOU WANT, LEO, BUT I KNOW YOU'RE JUST AS TIRED OF DOING THIS NIGHT AFTER NIGHT AS WE ARE.
I MEAN, C'MON, WE NEVER FIND RAPHAEL AND MEANWHILE HOB AND HIS CREEPS KEEP PUTTING THE SQUEEZE ON US TIGHTER AND TIGHTER.
YEAH, LEO. ALL THIS NINJA TRAININ' WE'RE DOIN'—IT CAN'T BE FOR NOTHIN', BRO. HOB NEEDS A SERIOUS ASS KICKIN' AND WE SHOULD BE THE ONES GIVIN' IT TO HIM. JUST LIKE THE OTHER NIGHT.
WE DIDN'T HAVE A CHOICE THEN, MIKEY. OLD HOB WAS GETTING TOO CLOSE TO FINDING WHERE WE LIVE, THREATENING INNOCENT PEOPLE TO GET AT US. WE HAD TO—

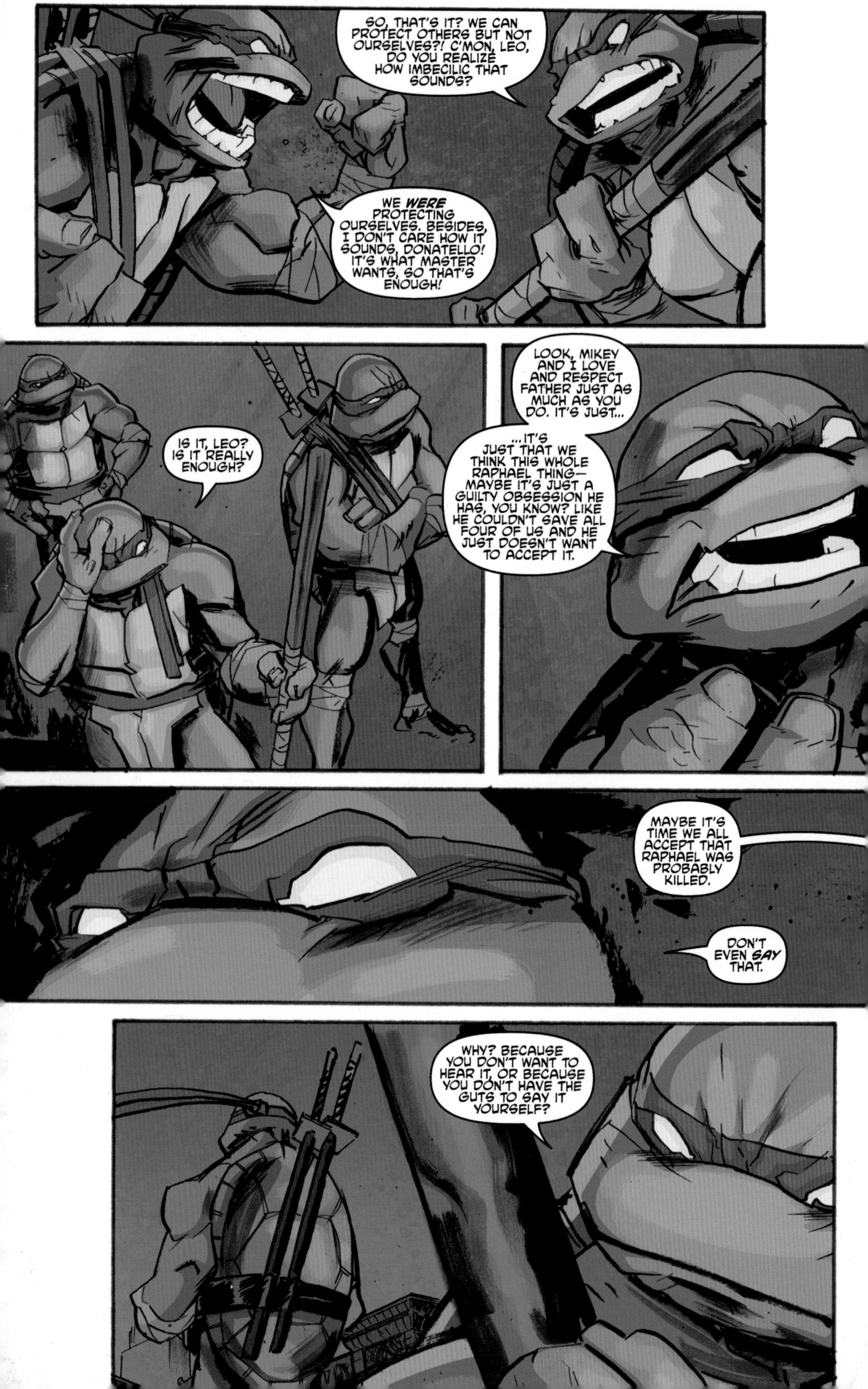
SO, THAT'S IT? WE CAN PROTECT OTHERS BUT NOT OURSELVES?! C'MON, LEO, DO YOU REALIZE HOW IMBECILIC THAT SOUNDS?
WE *WERE* PROTECTING OURSELVES. BESIDES, I DON'T CARE HOW IT SOUNDS, DONATELLO! IT'S WHAT MASTER WANTS, SO THAT'S ENOUGH!
IS IT, LEO? IS IT REALLY ENOUGH?
LOOK, MIKEY AND I LOVE AND RESPECT FATHER JUST AS MUCH AS YOU DO. IT'S JUST...
...IT'S JUST THAT WE THINK THIS WHOLE RAPHAEL THING— MAYBE IT'S JUST A GUILTY OBSESSION HE HAS, YOU KNOW? LIKE HE COULDN'T SAVE ALL FOUR OF US AND HE JUST DOESN'T WANT TO ACCEPT IT.
MAYBE IT'S TIME WE ALL ACCEPT THAT RAPHAEL WAS PROBABLY KILLED.
DON'T EVEN *SAY* THAT.
WHY? BECAUSE YOU DON'T WANT TO HEAR IT, OR BECAUSE YOU DON'T HAVE THE GUTS TO SAY IT YOURSELF?

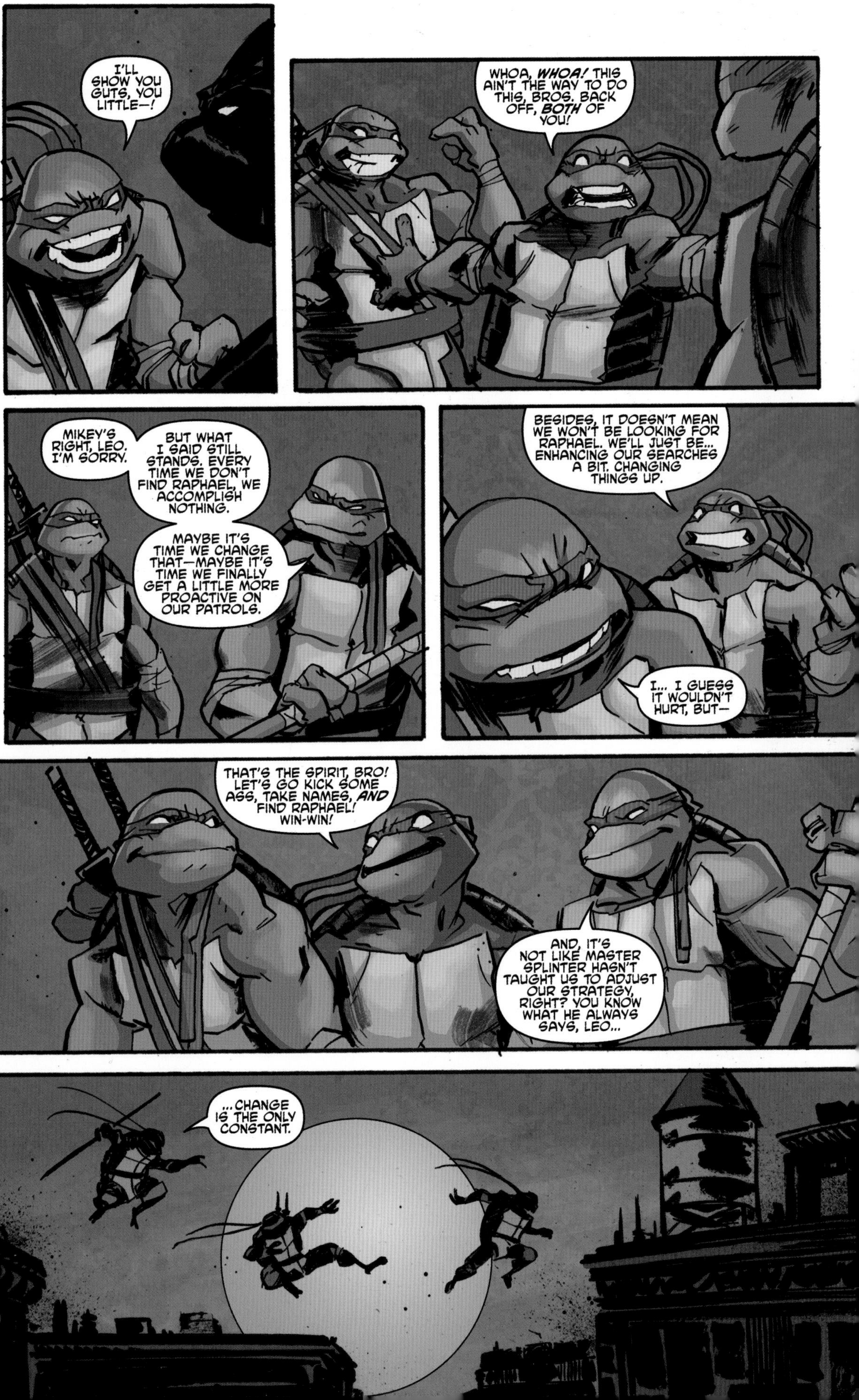

I'LL SHOW YOU GUTS, YOU LITTLE—!
WHOA, *WHOA!* THIS AIN'T THE WAY TO DO THIS, BROS. BACK OFF, *BOTH* OF YOU!
MIKEY'S RIGHT, LEO. I'M SORRY.
BUT WHAT I SAID STILL STANDS. EVERY TIME WE DON'T FIND RAPHAEL, WE ACCOMPLISH NOTHING.
MAYBE IT'S TIME WE CHANGE THAT—MAYBE IT'S TIME WE FINALLY GET A LITTLE MORE PROACTIVE ON OUR PATROLS.
BESIDES, IT DOESN'T MEAN WE WON'T BE LOOKING FOR RAPHAEL. WE'LL JUST BE... ENHANCING OUR SEARCHES A BIT. CHANGING THINGS UP.
I... I GUESS IT WOULDN'T HURT, BUT—
THAT'S THE SPIRIT, BRO! LET'S GO KICK SOME ASS, TAKE NAMES, *AND* FIND RAPHAEL! WIN-WIN!
AND, IT'S NOT LIKE MASTER SPLINTER HASN'T TAUGHT US TO ADJUST OUR STRATEGY, RIGHT? YOU KNOW WHAT HE ALWAYS SAYS, LEO...
...CHANGE IS THE ONLY CONSTANT.

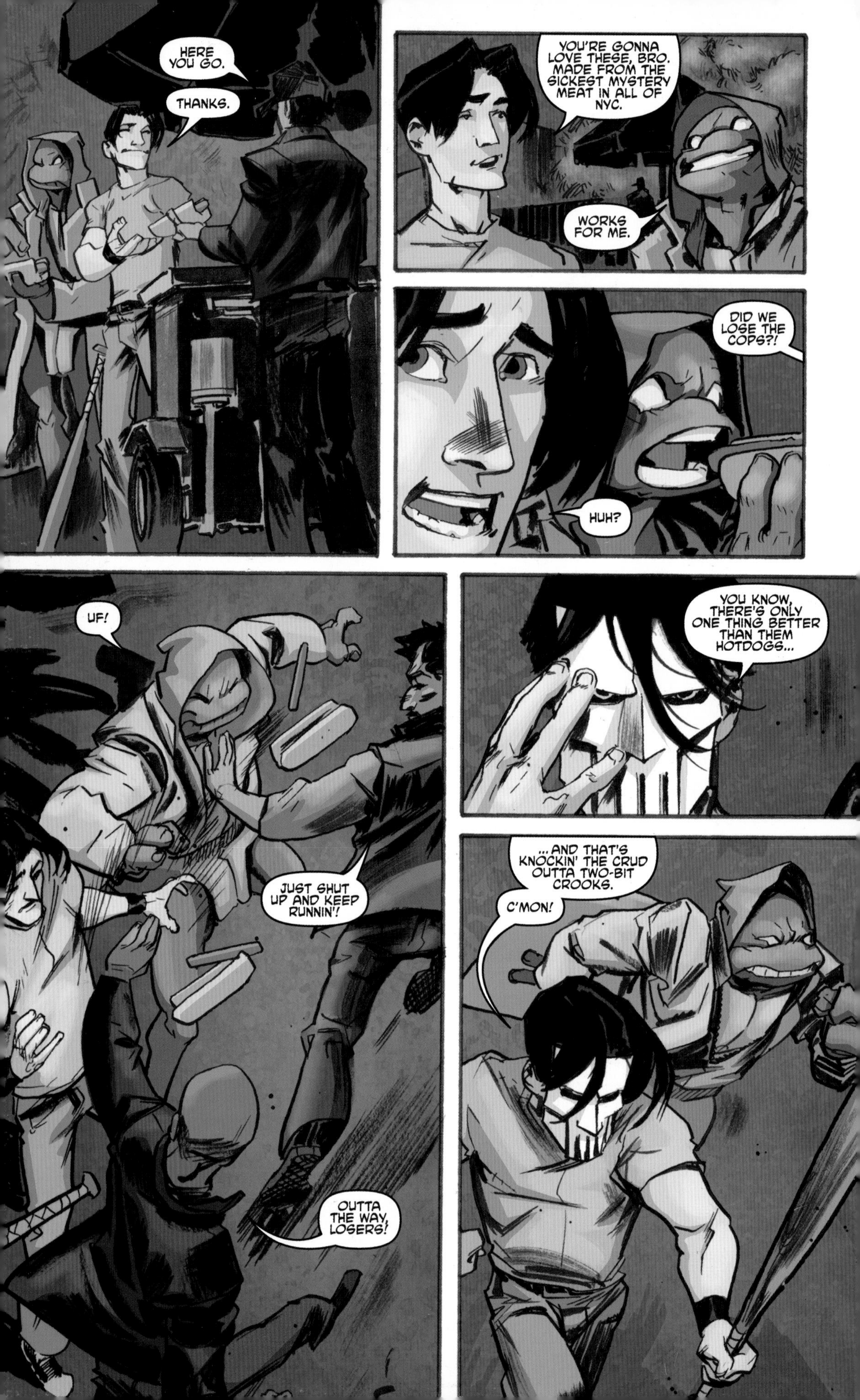
HERE YOU GO.
THANKS.
YOU'RE GONNA LOVE THESE, BRO. MADE FROM THE SICKEST MYSTERY MEAT IN ALL OF NYC.
WORKS FOR ME.
DID WE LOSE THE COPS?!
HUH?
UF!
JUST SHUT UP AND KEEP RUNNIN'!
OUTTA THE WAY, LOSERS!
YOU KNOW, THERE'S ONLY ONE THING BETTER THAN THEM HOTDOGS...
...AND THAT'S KNOCKIN' THE CRUD OUTTA TWO-BIT CROOKS.
C'MON!

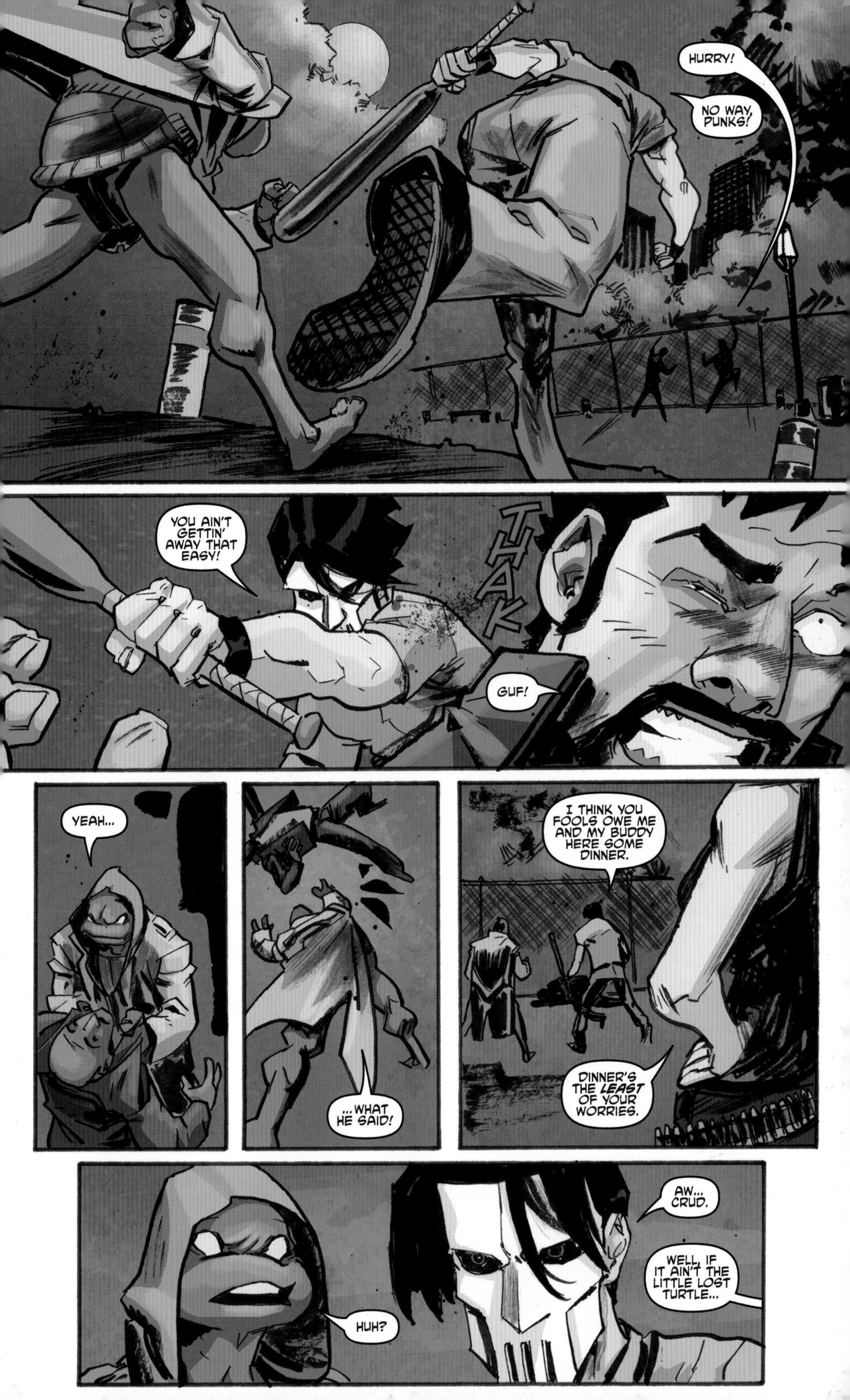
HURRY!
NO WAY, PUNKS!
YOU AIN'T GETTIN' AWAY THAT EASY!
THAK
GUF!
YEAH...
...WHAT HE SAID!
I THINK YOU FOOLS OWE ME AND MY BUDDY HERE SOME DINNER.
DINNER'S THE LEAST OF YOUR WORRIES.
AW... CRUD.
WELL, IF IT AIN'T THE LITTLE LOST TURTLE...
HUH?

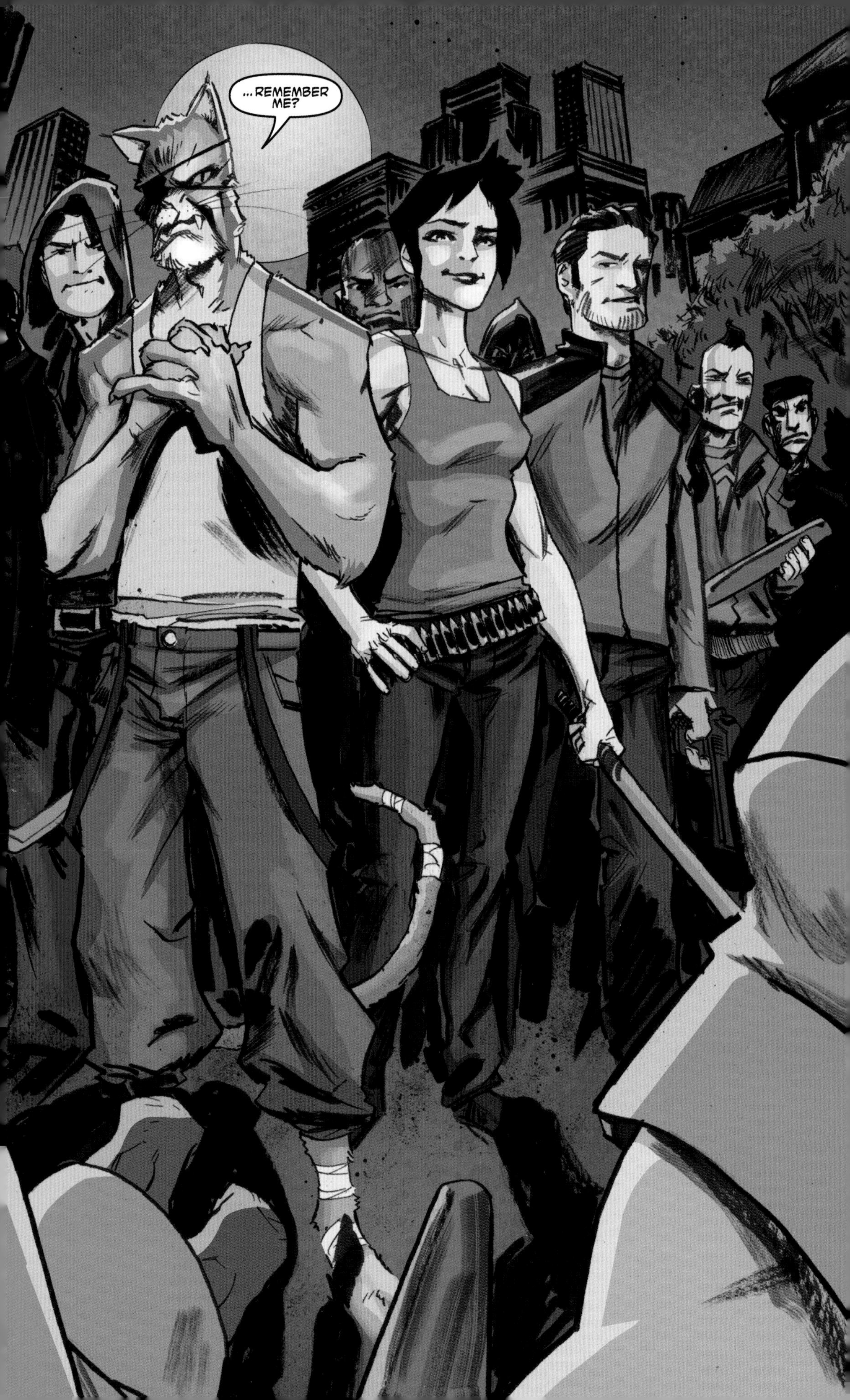
...REMEMBER ME?

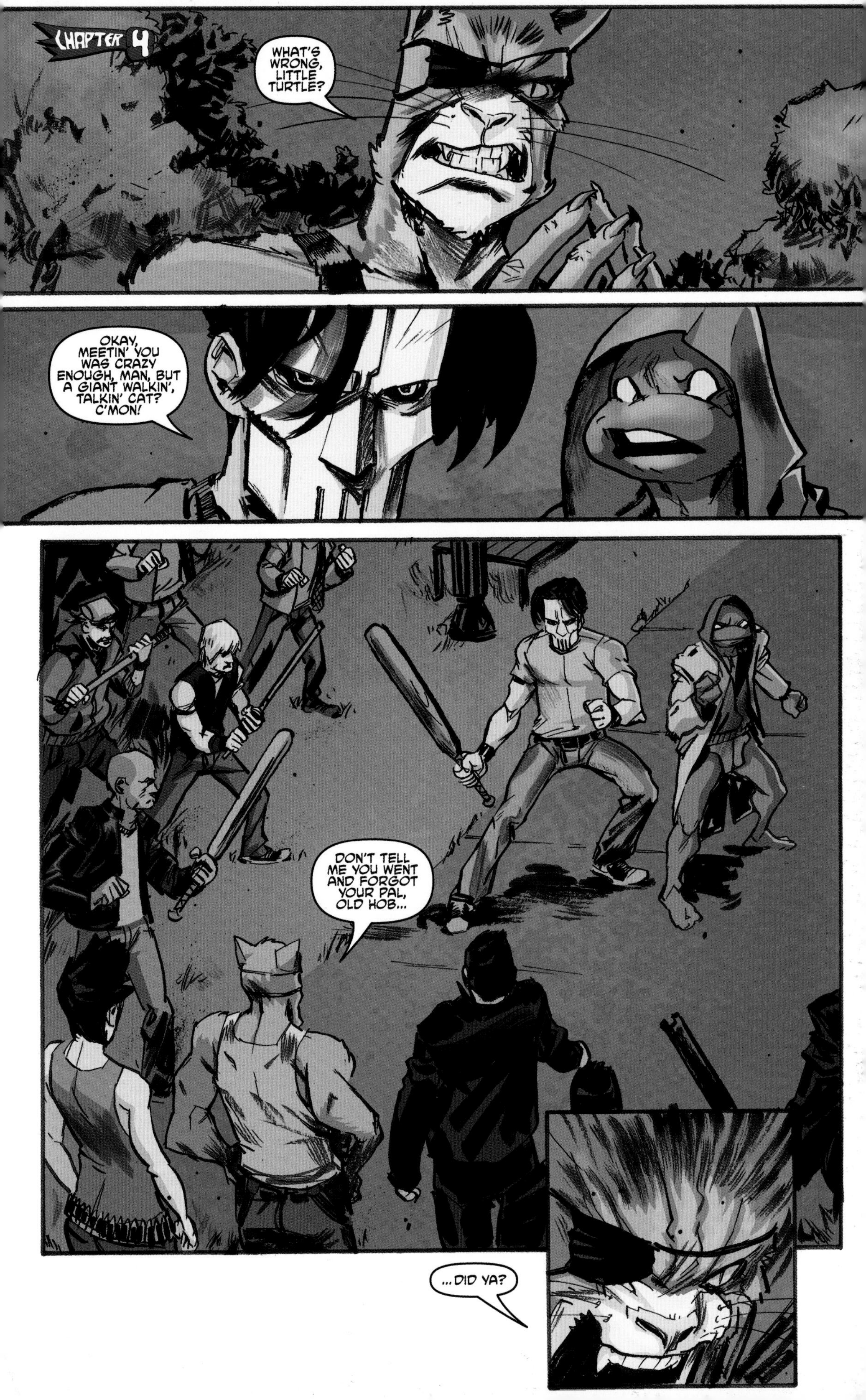
CHAPTER 4
WHAT'S WRONG, LITTLE TURTLE?
OKAY, MEETIN' YOU WAS CRAZY ENOUGH, MAN, BUT A GIANT WALKIN', TALKIN' CAT? C'MON!
DON'T TELL ME YOU WENT AND FORGOT YOUR PAL, OLD HOB...
...DID YA?

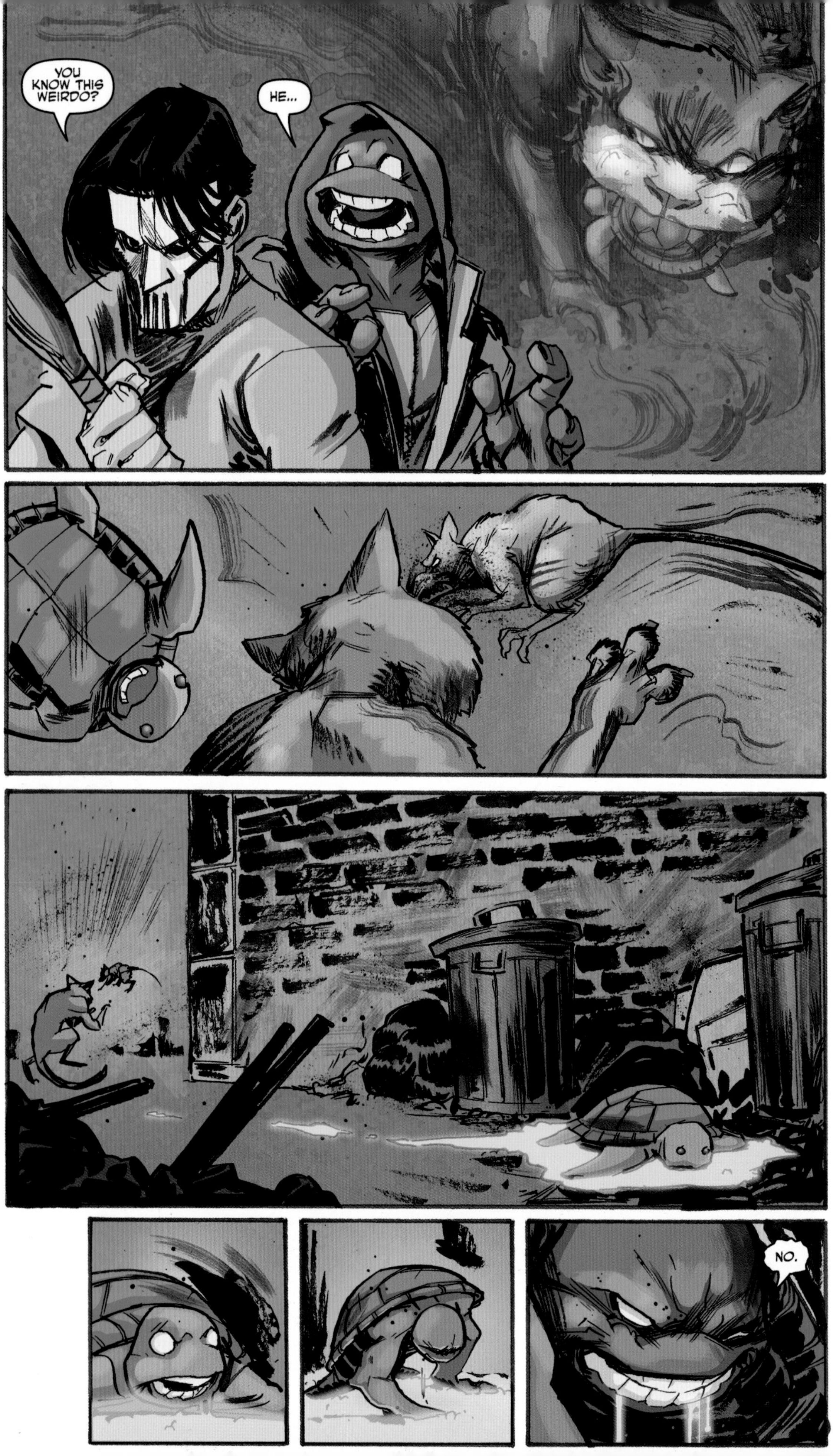
YOU KNOW THIS WEIRDO?
HE...
NO.

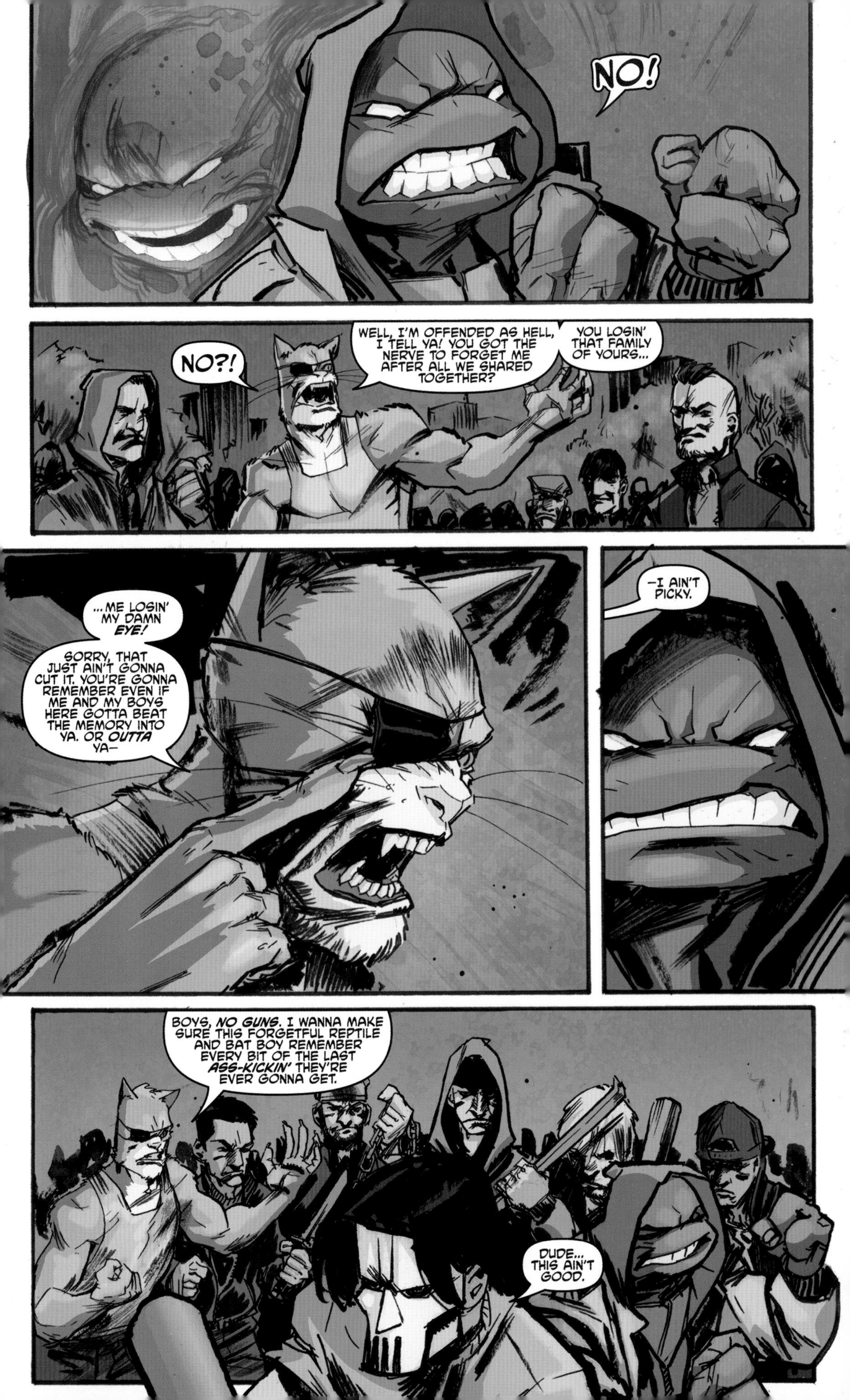
NO!
NO?!
WELL, I'M OFFENDED AS HELL, I TELL YA! YOU GOT THE NERVE TO FORGET ME AFTER ALL WE SHARED TOGETHER?
YOU LOSIN' THAT FAMILY OF YOURS...
...ME LOSIN' MY DAMN EYE!
SORRY, THAT JUST AIN'T GONNA CUT IT. YOU'RE GONNA REMEMBER EVEN IF ME AND MY BOYS HERE GOTTA BEAT THE MEMORY INTO YA. OR OUTTA YA—
—I AIN'T PICKY.
BOYS, NO GUNS. I WANNA MAKE SURE THIS FORGETFUL REPTILE AND BAT BOY REMEMBER EVERY BIT OF THE LAST ASS-KICKIN' THEY'RE EVER GONNA GET.
DUDE... THIS AIN'T GOOD.

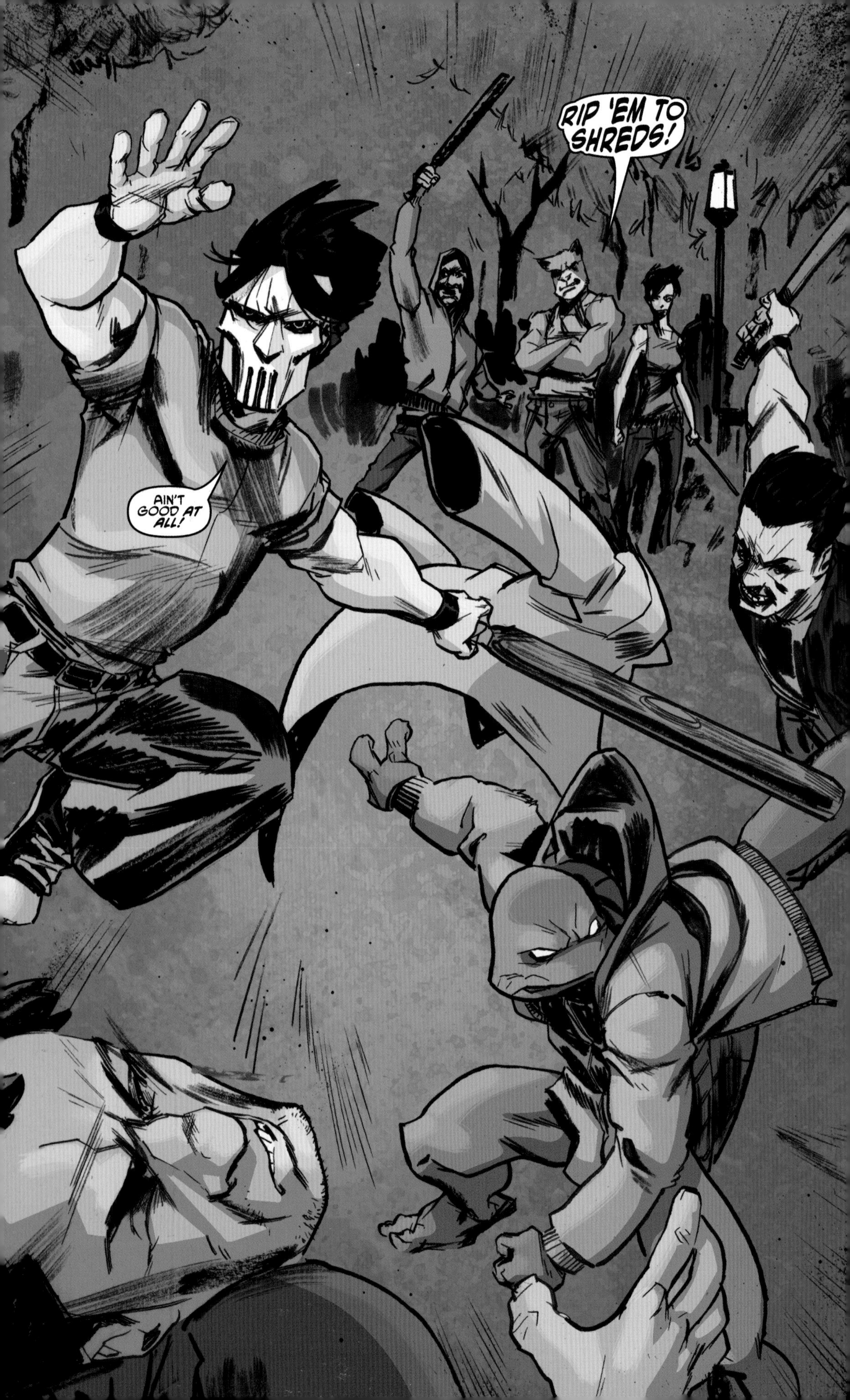
RIP 'EM TO SHREDS!
AIN'T GOOD AT ALL!

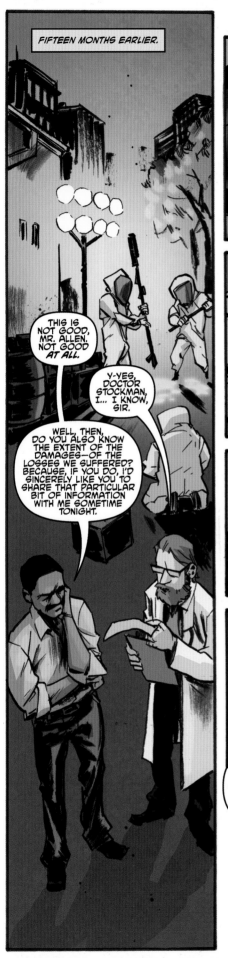

FIFTEEN MONTHS EARLIER.

THIS IS NOT GOOD, MR. ALLEN. NOT GOOD *AT ALL.*

Y-YES, DOCTOR STOCKMAN, I... I KNOW, SIR.

WELL, THEN, DO YOU ALSO KNOW THE EXTENT OF THE DAMAGES—OF THE LOSSES WE SUFFERED? BECAUSE, IF YOU DO, I'D SINCERELY LIKE YOU TO SHARE THAT PARTICULAR BIT OF INFORMATION WITH ME SOMETIME TONIGHT.

THAT IS, IF YOU DON'T MIND?

UM, YES, DOCTOR... UM, I M-MEAN, NO, SIR... I DON'T MIND.

WELL? I'M WAITING.

UM... OKAY, WELL, THE TERRAPIN EXO-ARMOR SAMPLES ARE INTACT FOR THE M-MOST PART, BUT THE PSYCHOTROPIC S-SERUM WAS A COMPLETE LOSS, AS WAS SPLINTER.

SPLINTER?

Y-YES... SPLINTER WAS THE, UM... RAT WE WERE USING TO T-TEST THE SERUM. WE LOST THE TURTLE SPECIMENS, TOO.

I SEE— QUITE THE TRAGEDY, THAT.

REMIND ME TO HAVE MY SECRETARY ALLOCATE THE FUNDS NECESSARY TO REPLACE THESE POOR LOST CREATURES. I'M GUESSING TWENTY DOLLARS AND A TRIP TO THE PET STORE SHOULD SUFFICE.

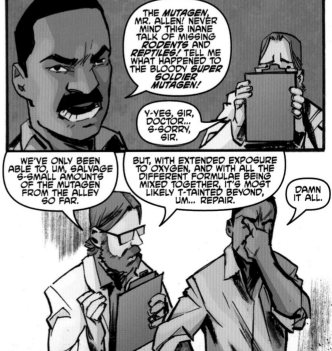

THE *MUTAGEN,* MR. ALLEN! NEVER MIND THIS INANE TALK OF MISSING *RODENTS* AND *REPTILES!* TELL ME WHAT HAPPENED TO THE BLOODY *SUPER SOLDIER MUTAGEN!*

Y-YES, SIR, DOCTOR... S-SORRY, SIR.

WE'VE ONLY BEEN ABLE TO, UM, SALVAGE S-SMALL AMOUNTS OF THE MUTAGEN FROM THE ALLEY SO FAR.

BUT, WITH EXTENDED EXPOSURE TO OXYGEN, AND WITH ALL THE DIFFERENT FORMULAE BEING MIXED TOGETHER, IT'S MOST LIKELY T-TAINTED BEYOND, UM... REPAIR.

DAMN IT ALL.

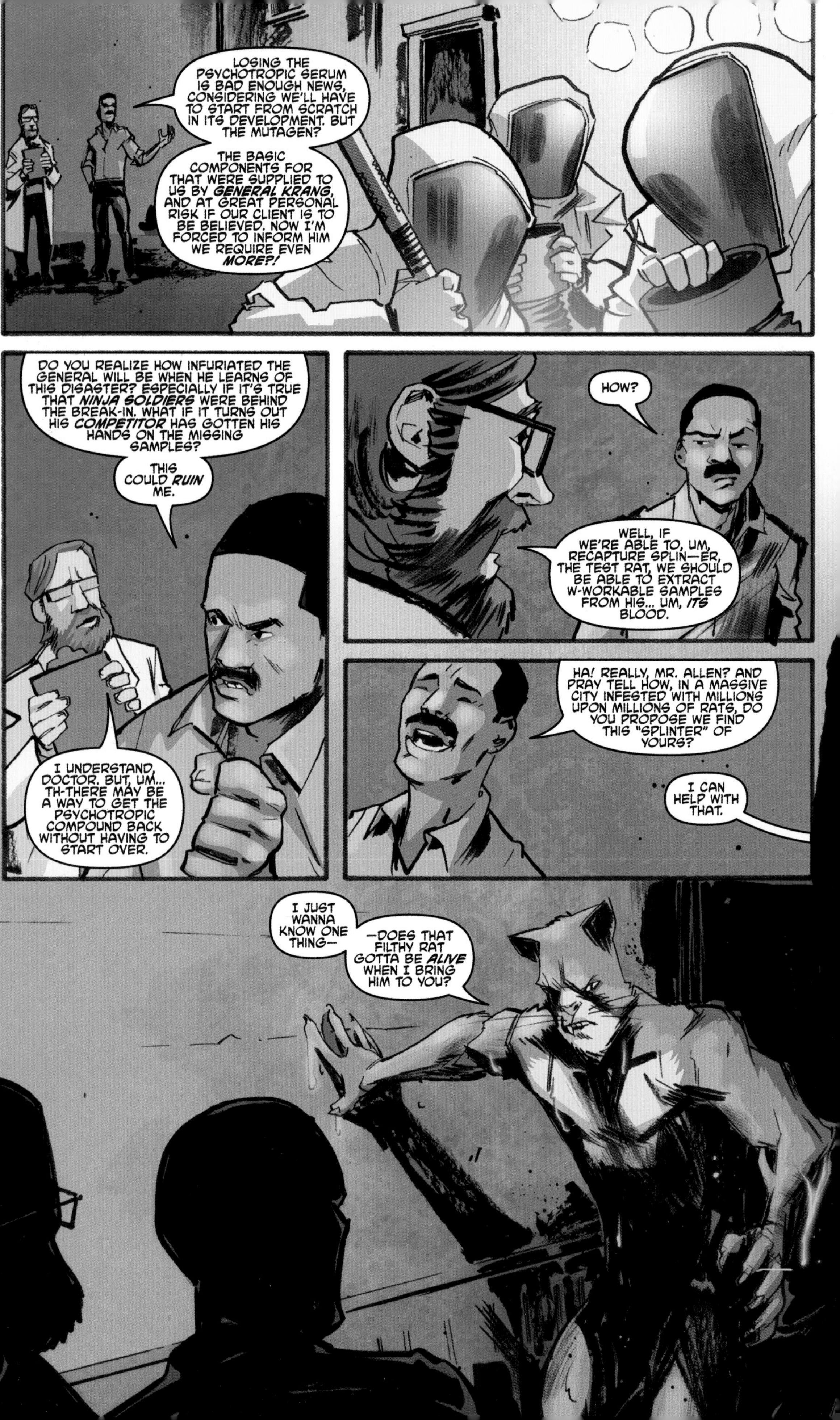
LOSING THE PSYCHOTROPIC SERUM IS BAD ENOUGH NEWS, CONSIDERING WE'LL HAVE TO START FROM SCRATCH IN ITS DEVELOPMENT. BUT THE MUTAGEN?
THE BASIC COMPONENTS FOR THAT WERE SUPPLIED TO US BY GENERAL KRANG, AND AT GREAT PERSONAL RISK IF OUR CLIENT IS TO BE BELIEVED. NOW I'M FORCED TO INFORM HIM WE REQUIRE EVEN MORE?!
DO YOU REALIZE HOW INFURIATED THE GENERAL WILL BE WHEN HE LEARNS OF THIS DISASTER? ESPECIALLY IF IT'S TRUE THAT NINJA SOLDIERS WERE BEHIND THE BREAK-IN. WHAT IF IT TURNS OUT HIS COMPETITOR HAS GOTTEN HIS HANDS ON THE MISSING SAMPLES?
THIS COULD RUIN ME.
I UNDERSTAND, DOCTOR. BUT, UM... TH-THERE MAY BE A WAY TO GET THE PSYCHOTROPIC COMPOUND BACK WITHOUT HAVING TO START OVER.
HOW?
WELL, IF WE'RE ABLE TO, UM, RECAPTURE SPLIN—ER, THE TEST RAT, WE SHOULD BE ABLE TO EXTRACT W-WORKABLE SAMPLES FROM HIS... UM, ITS BLOOD.
HA! REALLY, MR. ALLEN? AND PRAY TELL HOW, IN A MASSIVE CITY INFESTED WITH MILLIONS UPON MILLIONS OF RATS, DO YOU PROPOSE WE FIND THIS "SPLINTER" OF YOURS?
I CAN HELP WITH THAT.
I JUST WANNA KNOW ONE THING—
—DOES THAT FILTHY RAT GOTTA BE ALIVE WHEN I BRING HIM TO YOU?

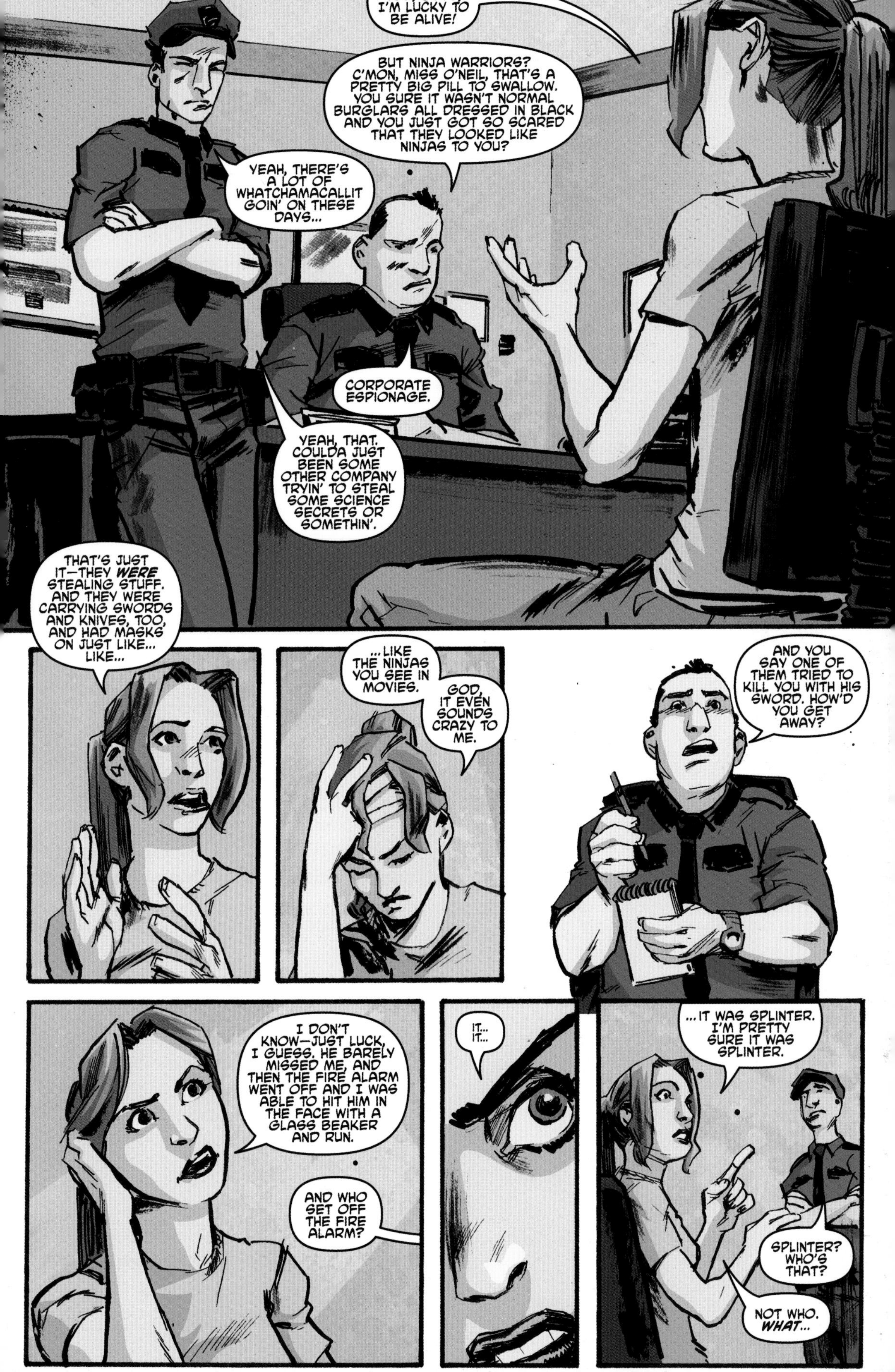
I'M TELLING YOU, GUYS, I'M LUCKY TO BE ALIVE!
BUT NINJA WARRIORS? C'MON, MISS O'NEIL, THAT'S A PRETTY BIG PILL TO SWALLOW. YOU SURE IT WASN'T NORMAL BURGLARS ALL DRESSED IN BLACK AND YOU JUST GOT SO SCARED THAT THEY LOOKED LIKE NINJAS TO YOU?
YEAH, THERE'S A LOT OF WHATCHAMACALLIT GOIN' ON THESE DAYS...
CORPORATE ESPIONAGE.
YEAH, THAT. COULDA JUST BEEN SOME OTHER COMPANY TRYIN' TO STEAL SOME SCIENCE SECRETS OR SOMETHIN'.
THAT'S JUST IT—THEY *WERE* STEALING STUFF. AND THEY WERE CARRYING SWORDS AND KNIVES, TOO, AND HAD MASKS ON JUST LIKE... LIKE...
...LIKE THE NINJAS YOU SEE IN MOVIES.
GOD, IT EVEN SOUNDS CRAZY TO ME.
AND YOU SAY ONE OF THEM TRIED TO KILL YOU WITH HIS SWORD. HOW'D YOU GET AWAY?
I DON'T KNOW—JUST LUCK, I GUESS. HE BARELY MISSED ME, AND THEN THE FIRE ALARM WENT OFF AND I WAS ABLE TO HIT HIM IN THE FACE WITH A GLASS BEAKER AND RUN.
AND WHO SET OFF THE FIRE ALARM?
IT... IT...
...IT WAS SPLINTER. I'M PRETTY SURE IT WAS SPLINTER.
SPLINTER? WHO'S THAT?
NOT WHO. *WHAT*...

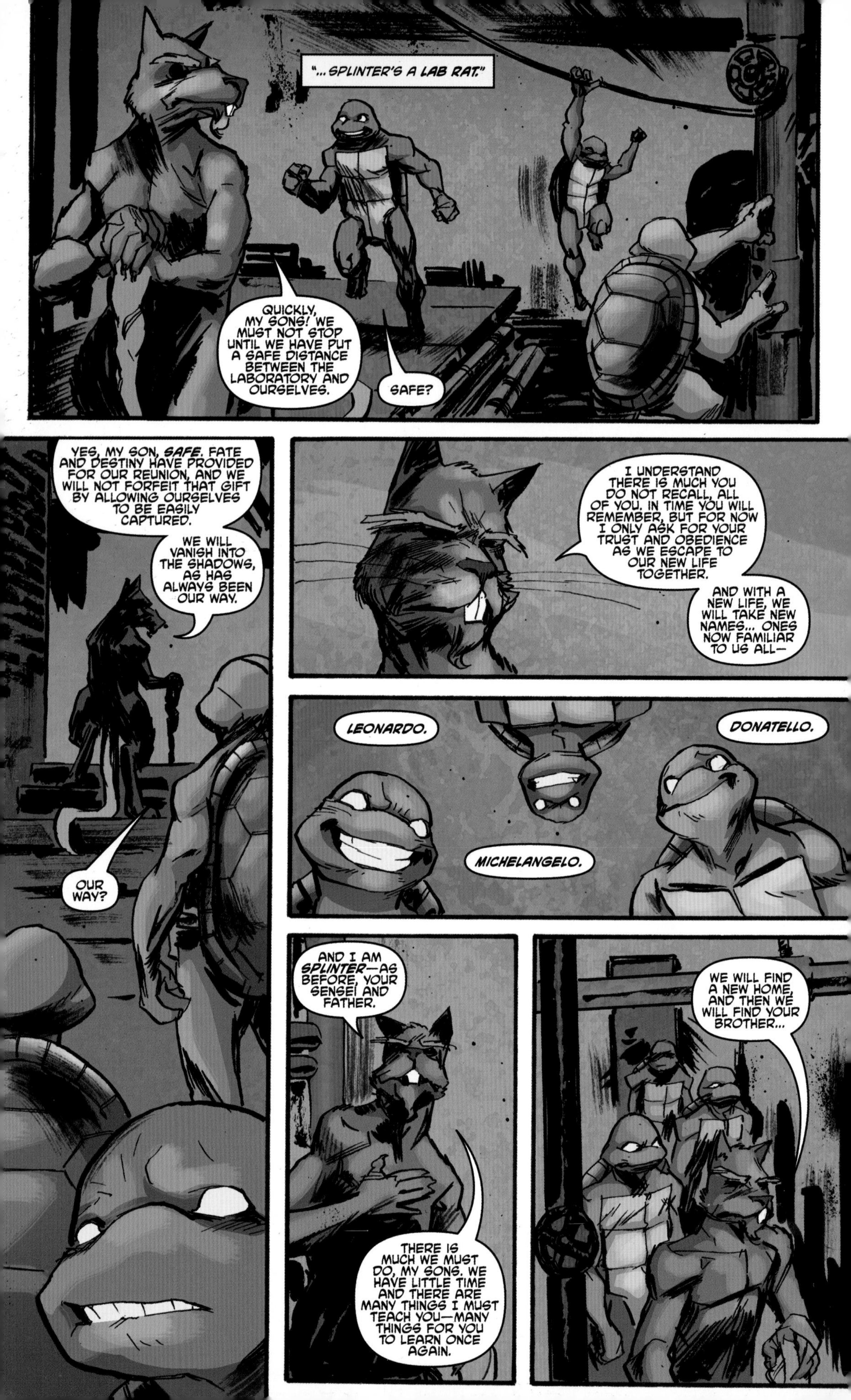
"...SPLINTER'S A LAB RAT."
QUICKLY, MY SONS! WE MUST NOT STOP UNTIL WE HAVE PUT A SAFE DISTANCE BETWEEN THE LABORATORY AND OURSELVES.
SAFE?
YES, MY SON, SAFE. FATE AND DESTINY HAVE PROVIDED FOR OUR REUNION, AND WE WILL NOT FORFEIT THAT GIFT BY ALLOWING OURSELVES TO BE EASILY CAPTURED.
WE WILL VANISH INTO THE SHADOWS, AS HAS ALWAYS BEEN OUR WAY.
OUR WAY?
I UNDERSTAND THERE IS MUCH YOU DO NOT RECALL, ALL OF YOU. IN TIME YOU WILL REMEMBER, BUT FOR NOW I ONLY ASK FOR YOUR TRUST AND OBEDIENCE AS WE ESCAPE TO OUR NEW LIFE TOGETHER.
AND WITH A NEW LIFE, WE WILL TAKE NEW NAMES... ONES NOW FAMILIAR TO US ALL—
LEONARDO.
DONATELLO.
MICHELANGELO.
AND I AM SPLINTER—AS BEFORE, YOUR SENSEI AND FATHER.
THERE IS MUCH WE MUST DO, MY SONS. WE HAVE LITTLE TIME AND THERE ARE MANY THINGS I MUST TEACH YOU—MANY THINGS FOR YOU TO LEARN ONCE AGAIN.
WE WILL FIND A NEW HOME, AND THEN WE WILL FIND YOUR BROTHER...

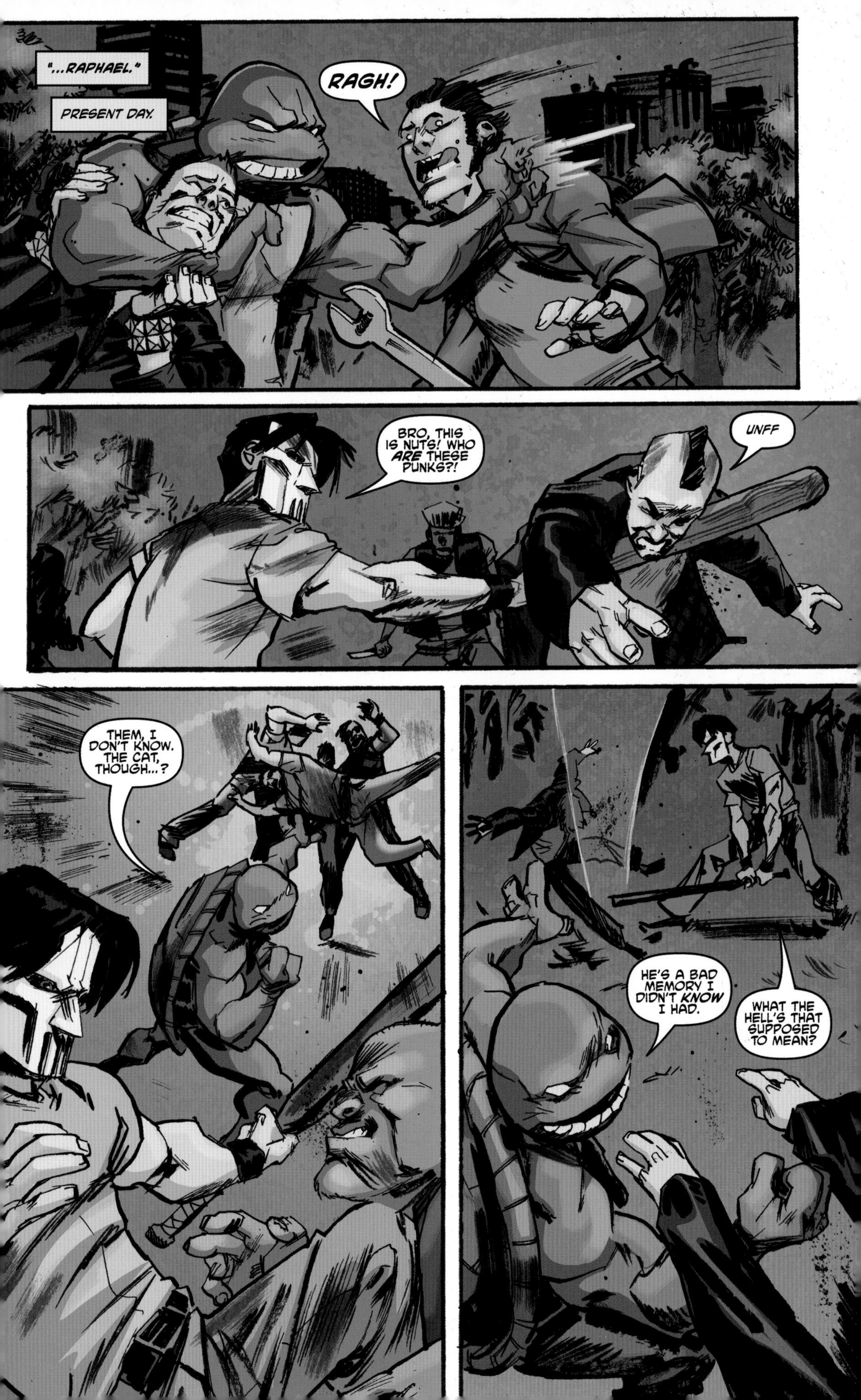
"...RAPHAEL."
PRESENT DAY.
RAGH!
BRO, THIS IS NUTS! WHO ARE THESE PUNKS?!
UNFF
THEM, I DON'T KNOW. THE CAT, THOUGH...?
HE'S A BAD MEMORY I DIDN'T KNOW I HAD.
WHAT THE HELL'S THAT SUPPOSED TO MEAN?

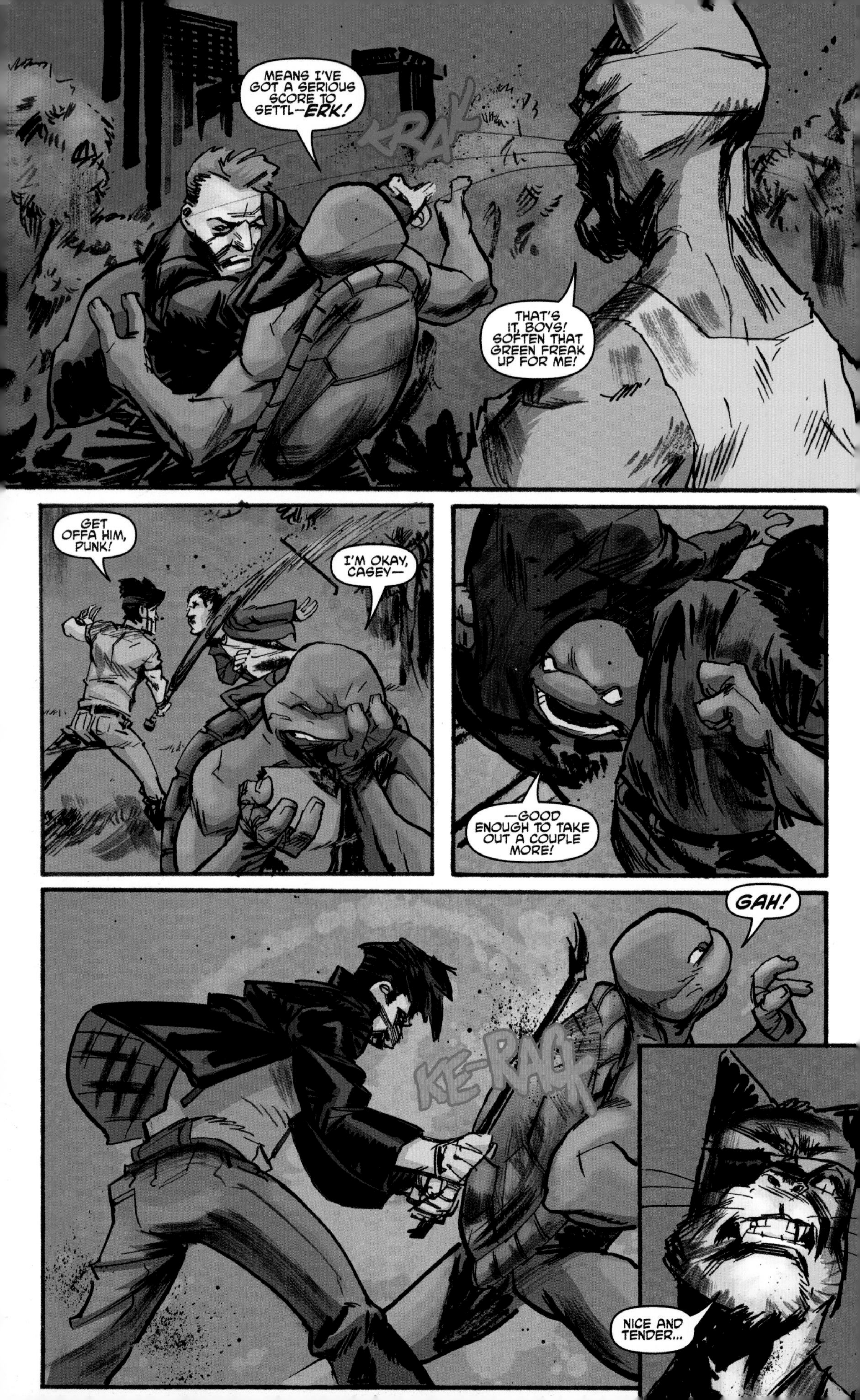

MEANS I'VE GOT A SERIOUS SCORE TO SETTL—ERK!
KRAK
THAT'S IT, BOYS! SOFTEN THAT GREEN FREAK UP FOR ME!
GET OFFA HIM, PUNK!
I'M OKAY, CASEY—
—GOOD ENOUGH TO TAKE OUT A COUPLE MORE!
GAH!
KE-RACK
NICE AND TENDER...

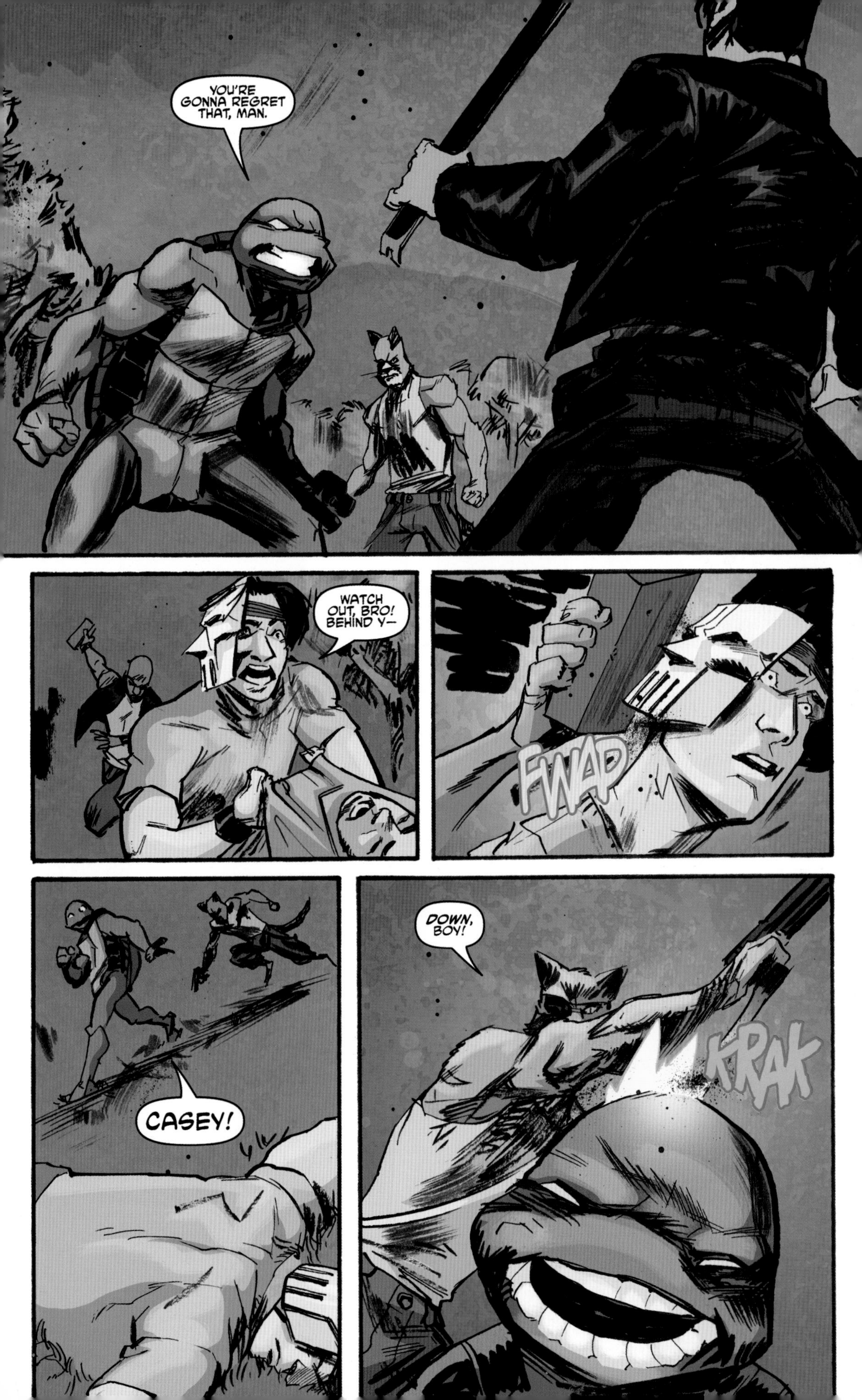
YOU'RE GONNA REGRET THAT, MAN.
WATCH OUT, BRO! BEHIND Y--
FWAP
CASEY!
DOWN, BOY!
KRAK

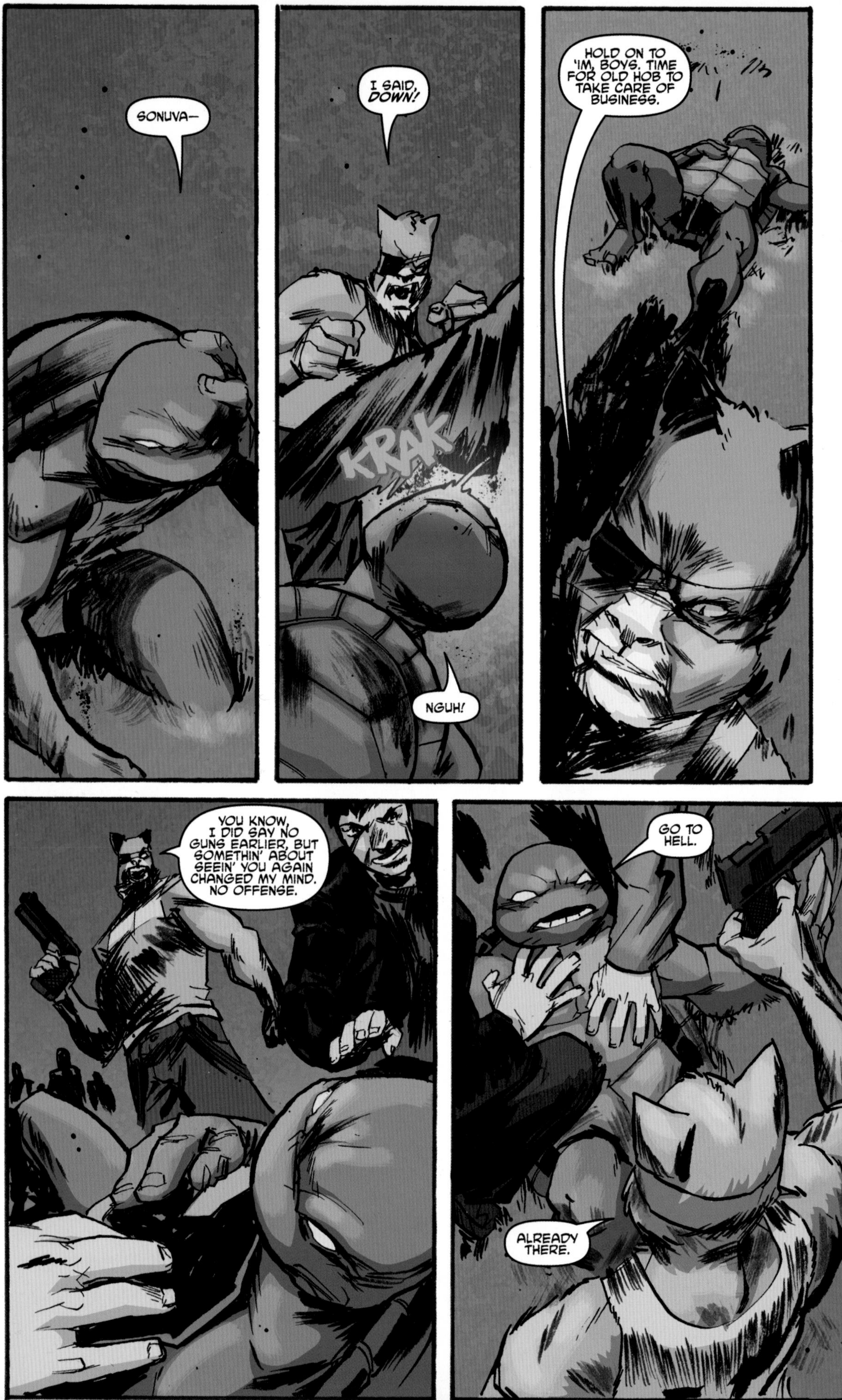
SONUVA—
I SAID, DOWN!
KRAK
NGUH!
HOLD ON TO 'IM, BOYS. TIME FOR OLD HOB TO TAKE CARE OF BUSINESS.
YOU KNOW, I DID SAY NO GUNS EARLIER, BUT SOMETHIN' ABOUT SEEIN' YOU AGAIN CHANGED MY MIND. NO OFFENSE.
GO TO HELL.
ALREADY THERE.

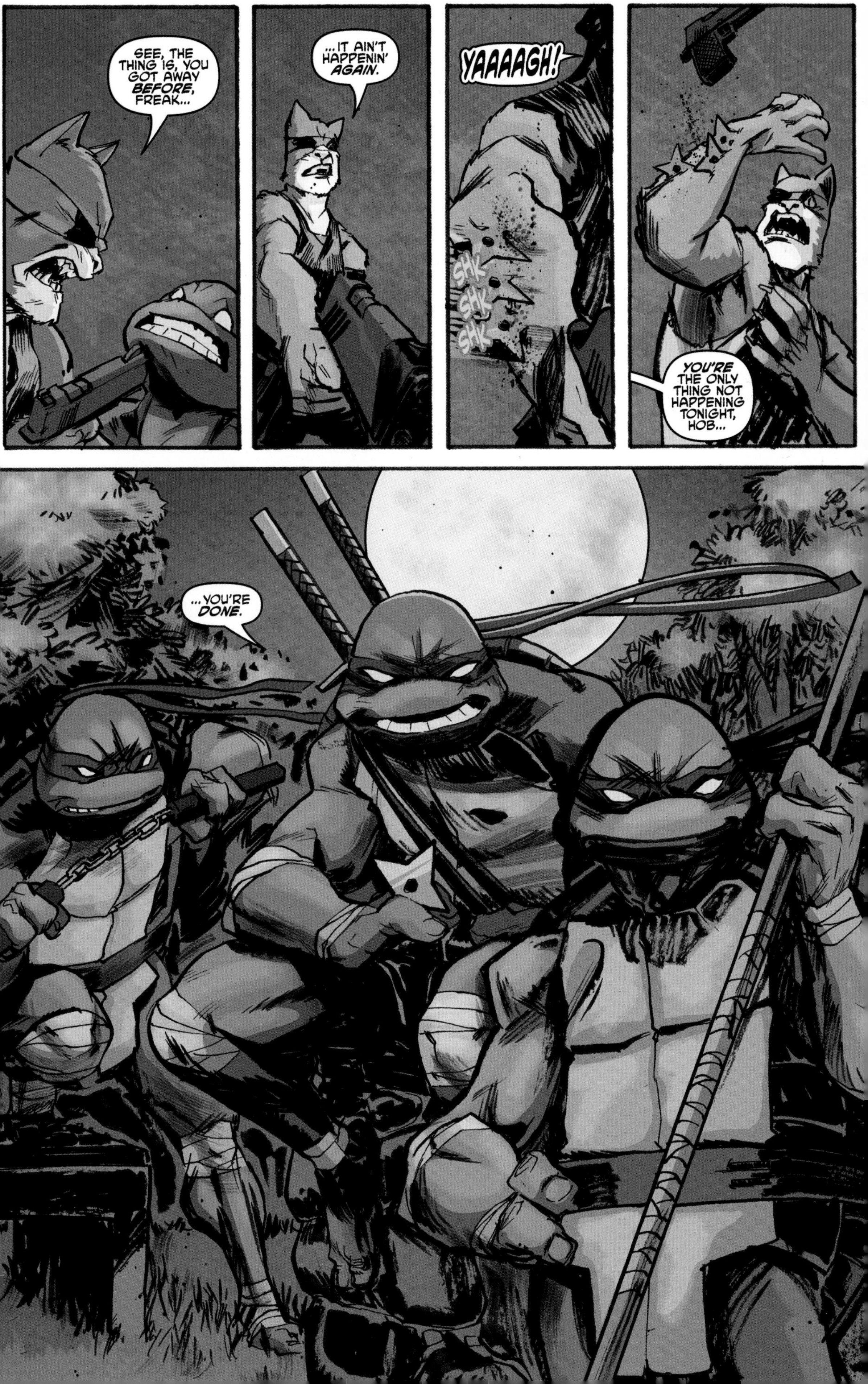
SEE, THE THING IS, YOU GOT AWAY *BEFORE*, FREAK...
...IT AIN'T HAPPENIN' *AGAIN*.
YAAAAGH!
SHK
SHK
SHK
YOU'RE THE ONLY THING NOT HAPPENING TONIGHT, HOB...
...YOU'RE *DONE*.

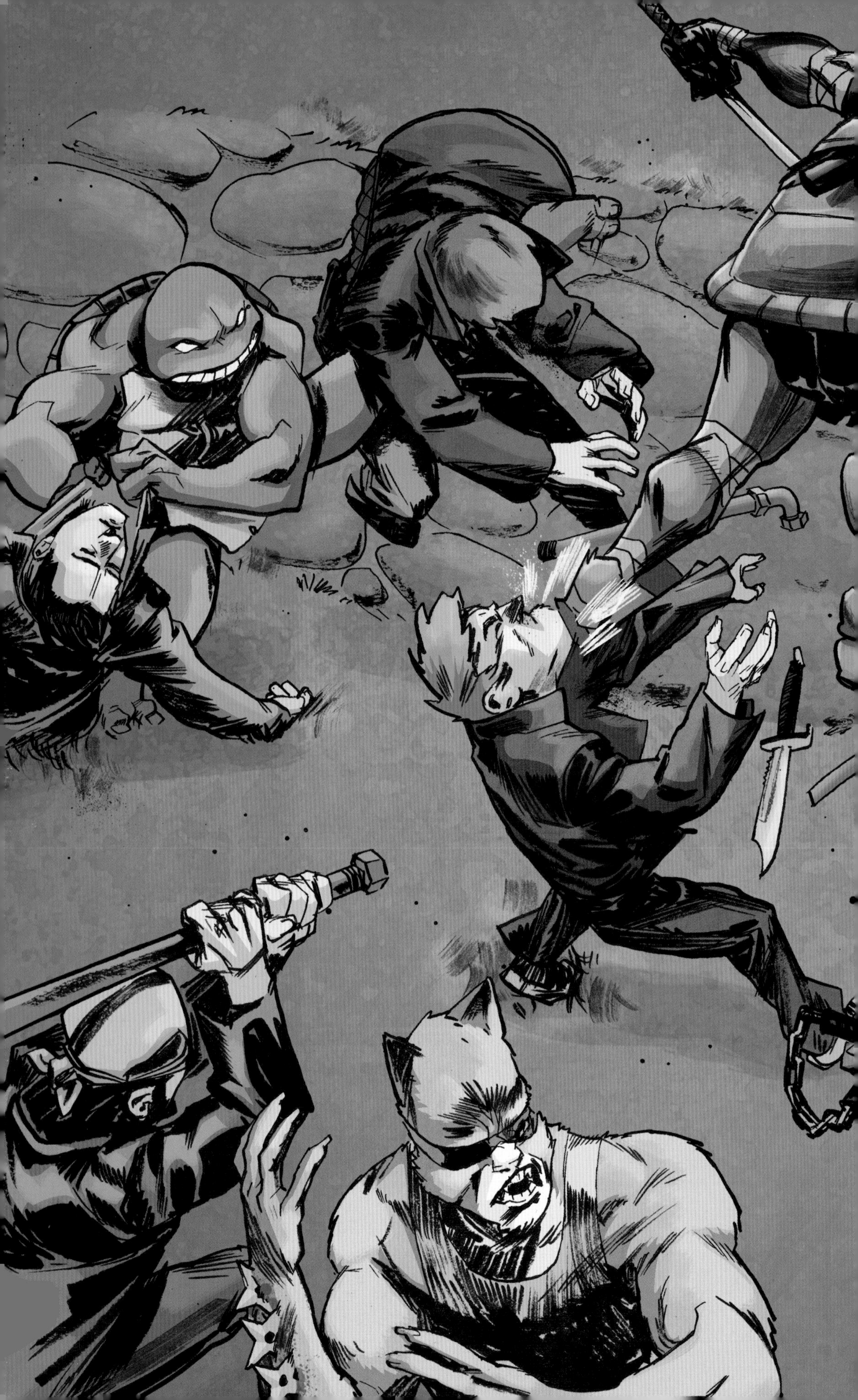

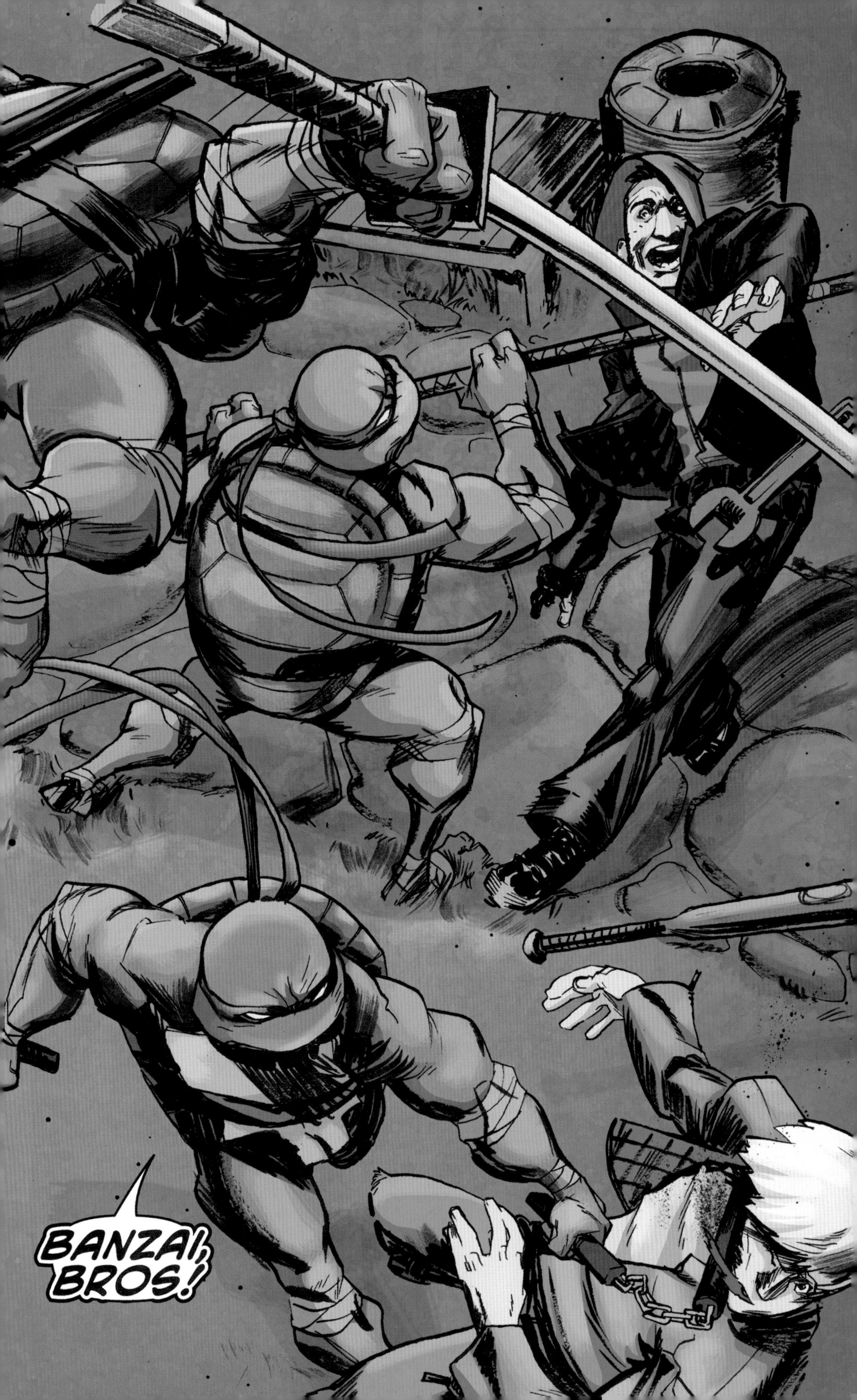
BANZAI, BROS!

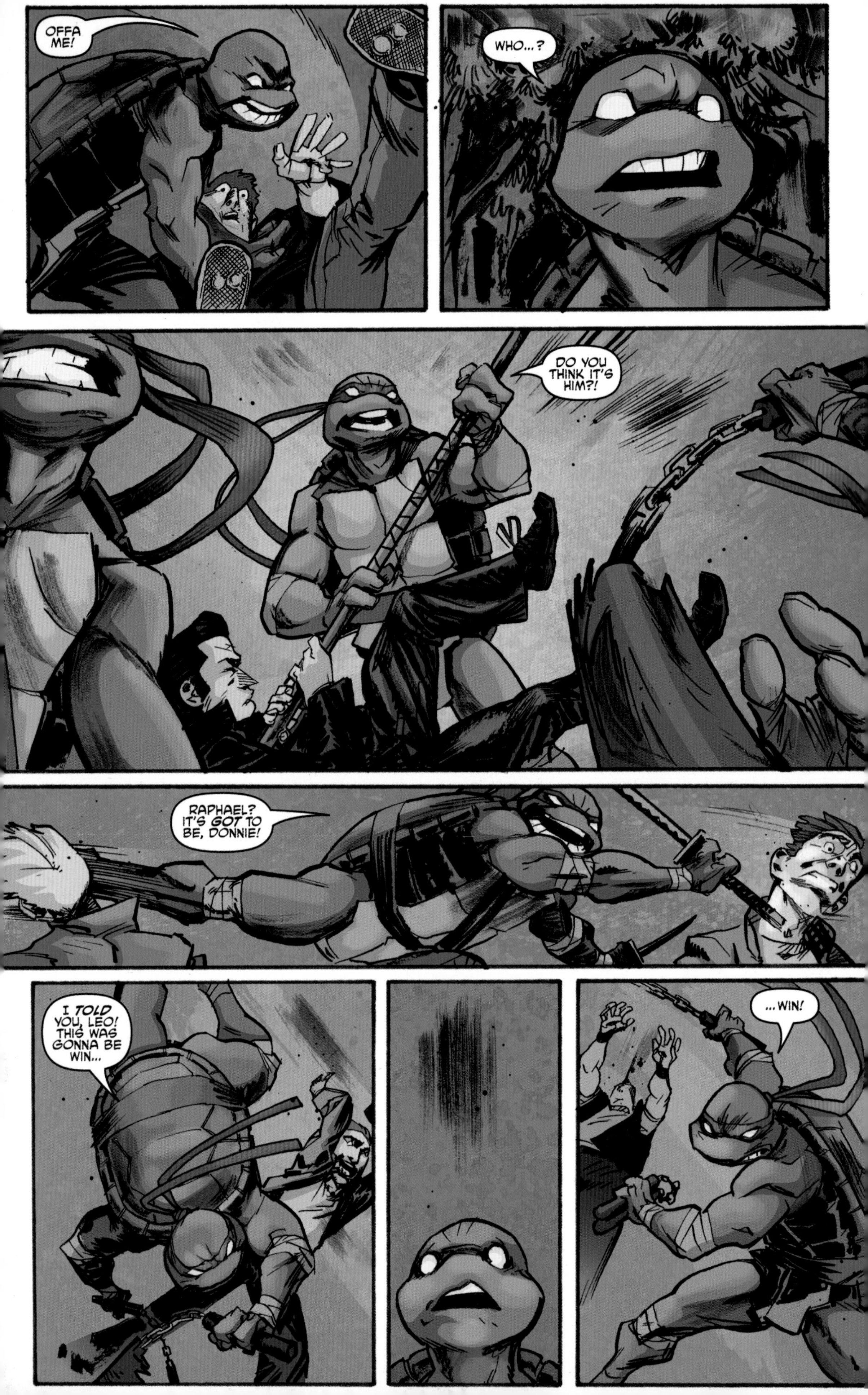
OFFA ME!
WHO...?
DO YOU THINK IT'S HIM?!
RAPHAEL? IT'S *GOT* TO BE, DONNIE!
I *TOLD* YOU, LEO! THIS WAS GONNA BE WIN...
...WIN!

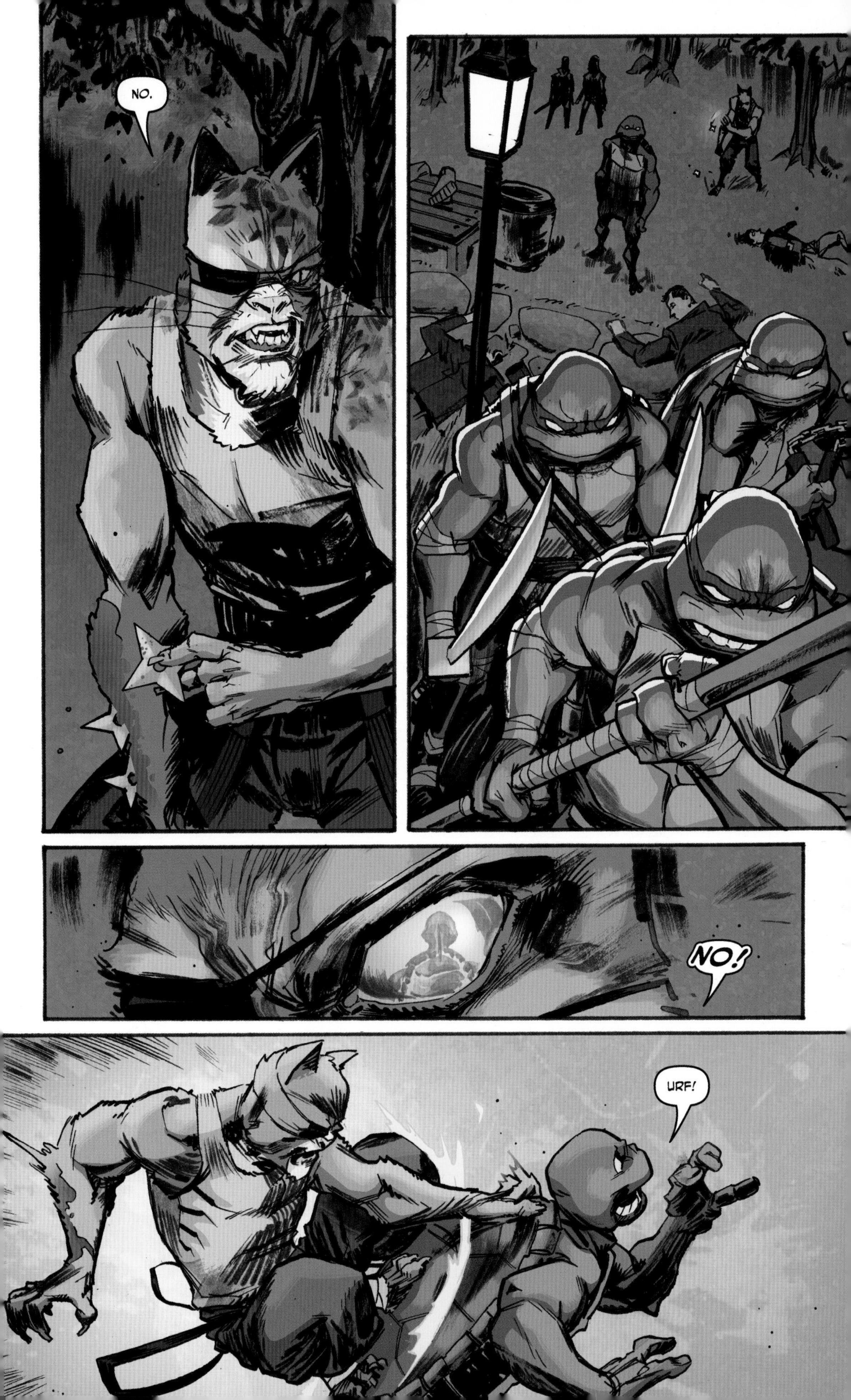
NO.
NO!
URF!

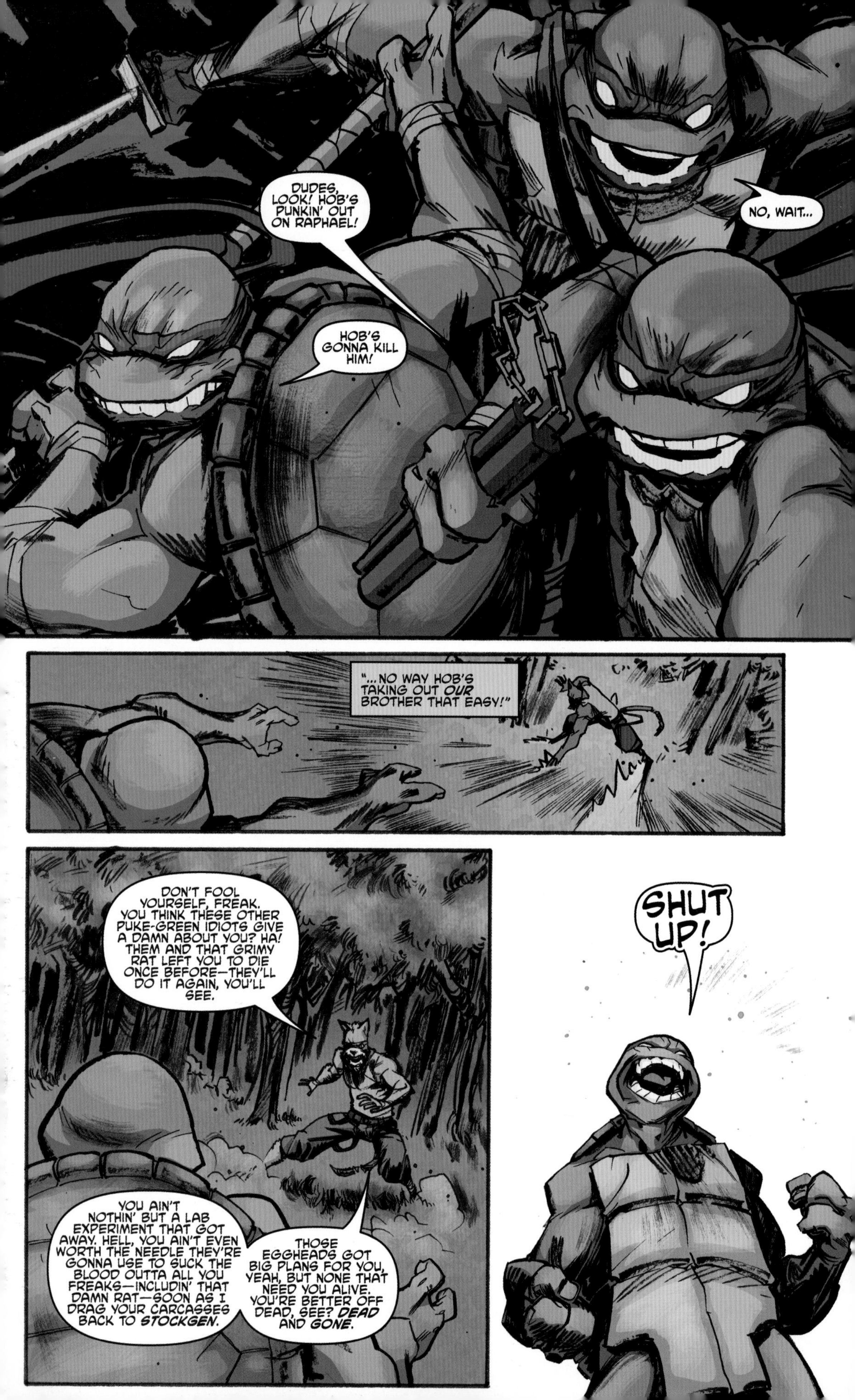
DUDES, LOOK! HOB'S PUNKIN' OUT ON RAPHAEL!
NO, WAIT...
HOB'S GONNA KILL HIM!
"...NO WAY HOB'S TAKING OUT *OUR* BROTHER THAT EASY!"
DON'T FOOL YOURSELF, FREAK. YOU THINK THESE OTHER PUKE-GREEN IDIOTS GIVE A DAMN ABOUT YOU? HA! THEM AND THAT GRIMY RAT LEFT YOU TO DIE ONCE BEFORE—THEY'LL DO IT AGAIN, YOU'LL SEE.
YOU AIN'T NOTHIN' BUT A LAB EXPERIMENT THAT GOT AWAY. HELL, YOU AIN'T EVEN WORTH THE NEEDLE THEY'RE GONNA USE TO SUCK THE BLOOD OUTTA ALL YOU FREAKS—INCLUDIN' THAT DAMN RAT—SOON AS I DRAG YOUR CARCASSES BACK TO ***STOCKGEN***.
THOSE EGGHEADS GOT BIG PLANS FOR YOU, YEAH, BUT NONE THAT NEED YOU ALIVE. YOU'RE BETTER OFF DEAD, SEE? ***DEAD*** AND ***GONE***.
SHUT UP!

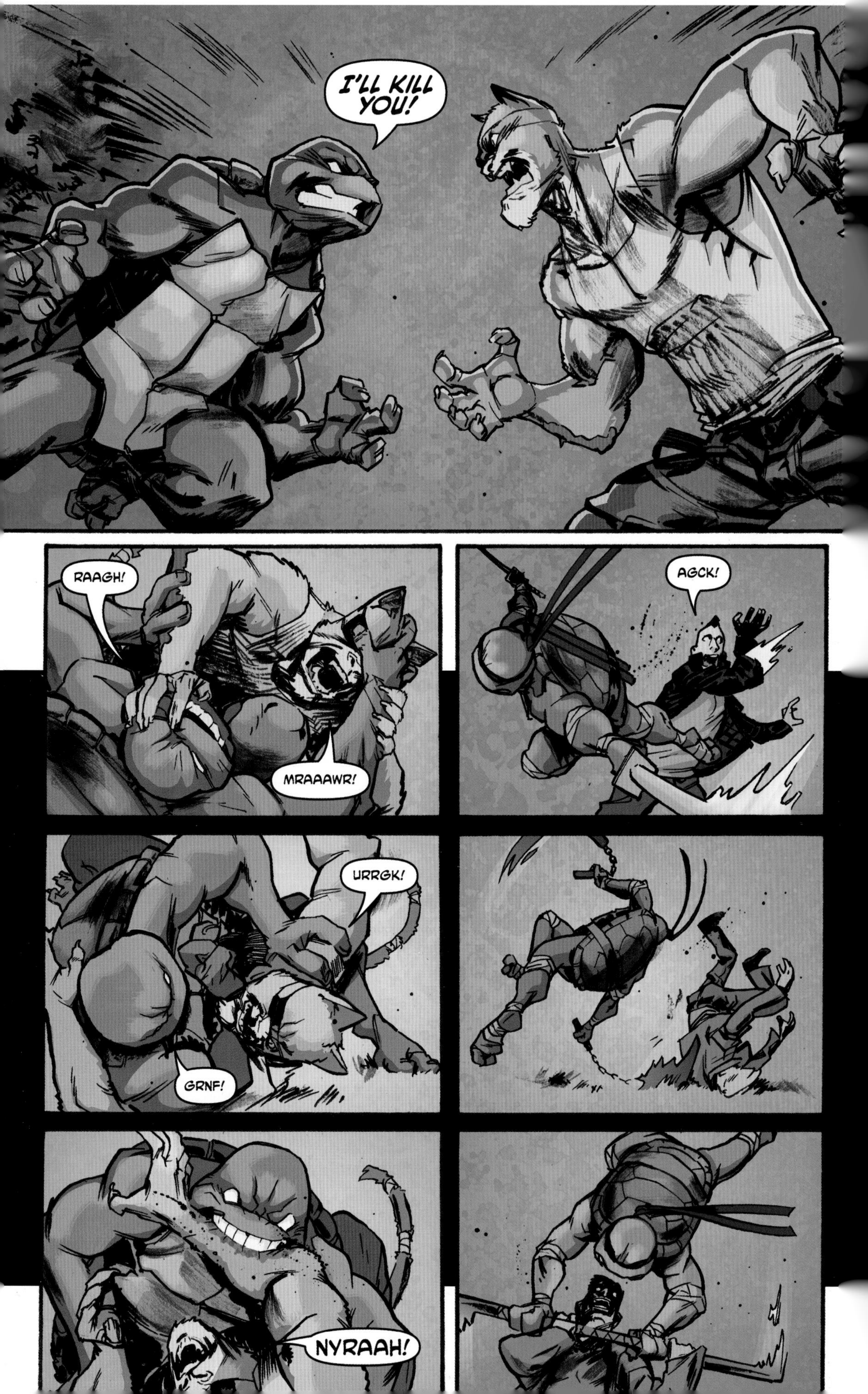
I'LL KILL YOU!
RAAGH!
MRAAAWR!
AGCK!
URRGK!
GRNF!
NYRAAH!

NO MORE!

KRAK

I WANT YOU *DEAD*!

DO YOU *HEAR* ME?!

D—!

NO, RAPHAEL...

...NOT LIKE THAT. HE'S BEATEN. LET IT GO, MAN.

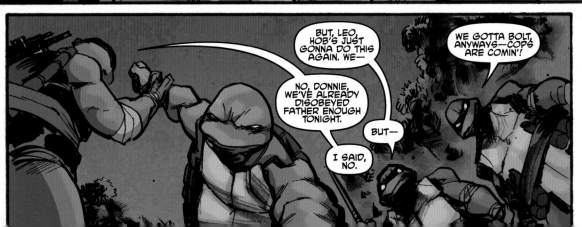
BUT, LEO, HOB'S JUST GONNA DO THIS AGAIN. WE—

WE GOTTA BOLT, ANYWAYS—COPS ARE COMIN'!

NO, DONNIE, WE'VE ALREADY DISOBEYED FATHER ENOUGH TONIGHT.

BUT—

I SAID, NO.

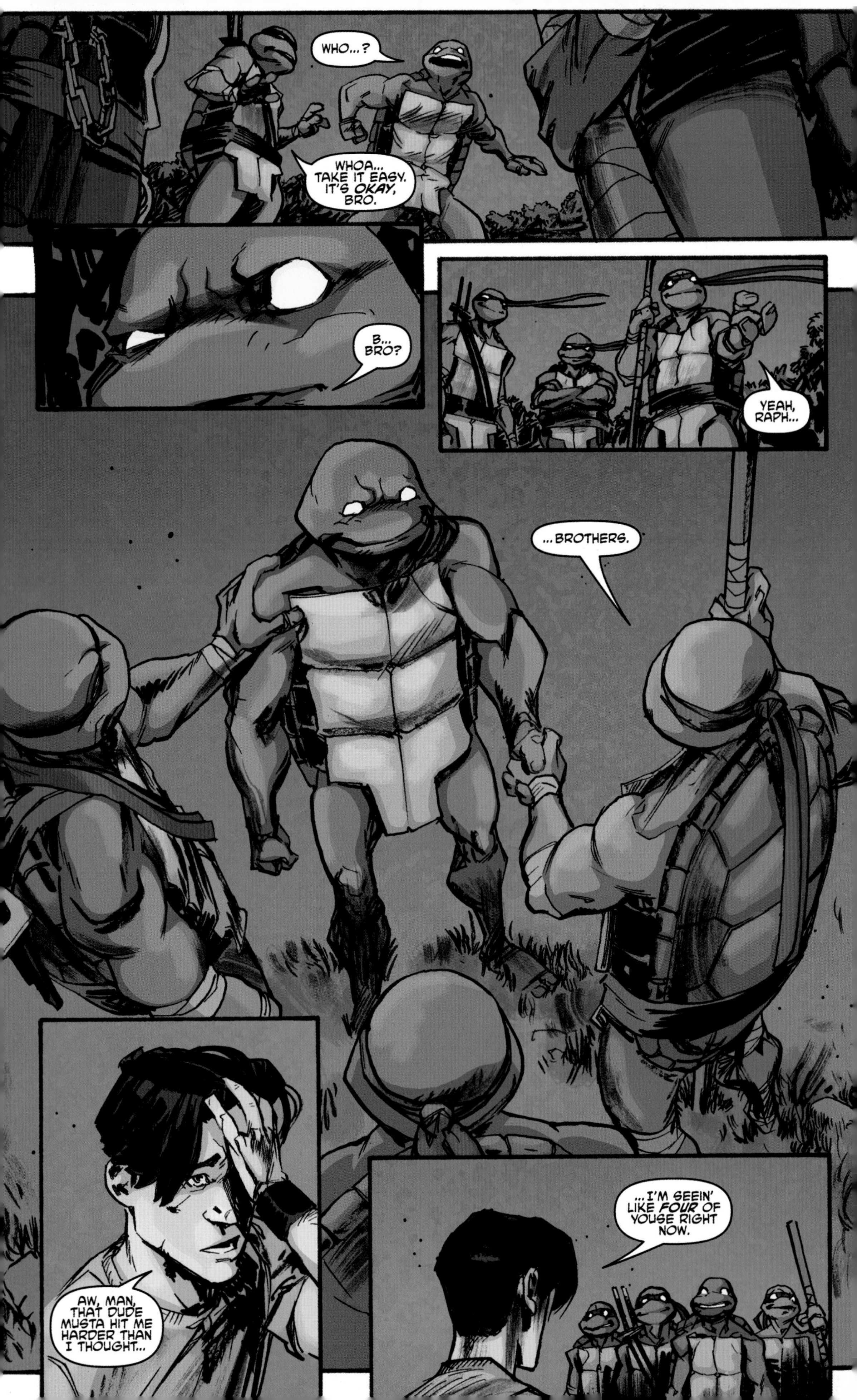
WHO...?
WHOA... TAKE IT EASY. IT'S *OKAY,* BRO.
B... BRO?
YEAH, RAPH...
...BROTHERS.
AW, MAN, THAT DUDE MUSTA HIT ME HARDER THAN I THOUGHT...
...I'M SEEIN' LIKE *FOUR* OF YOUSE RIGHT NOW.

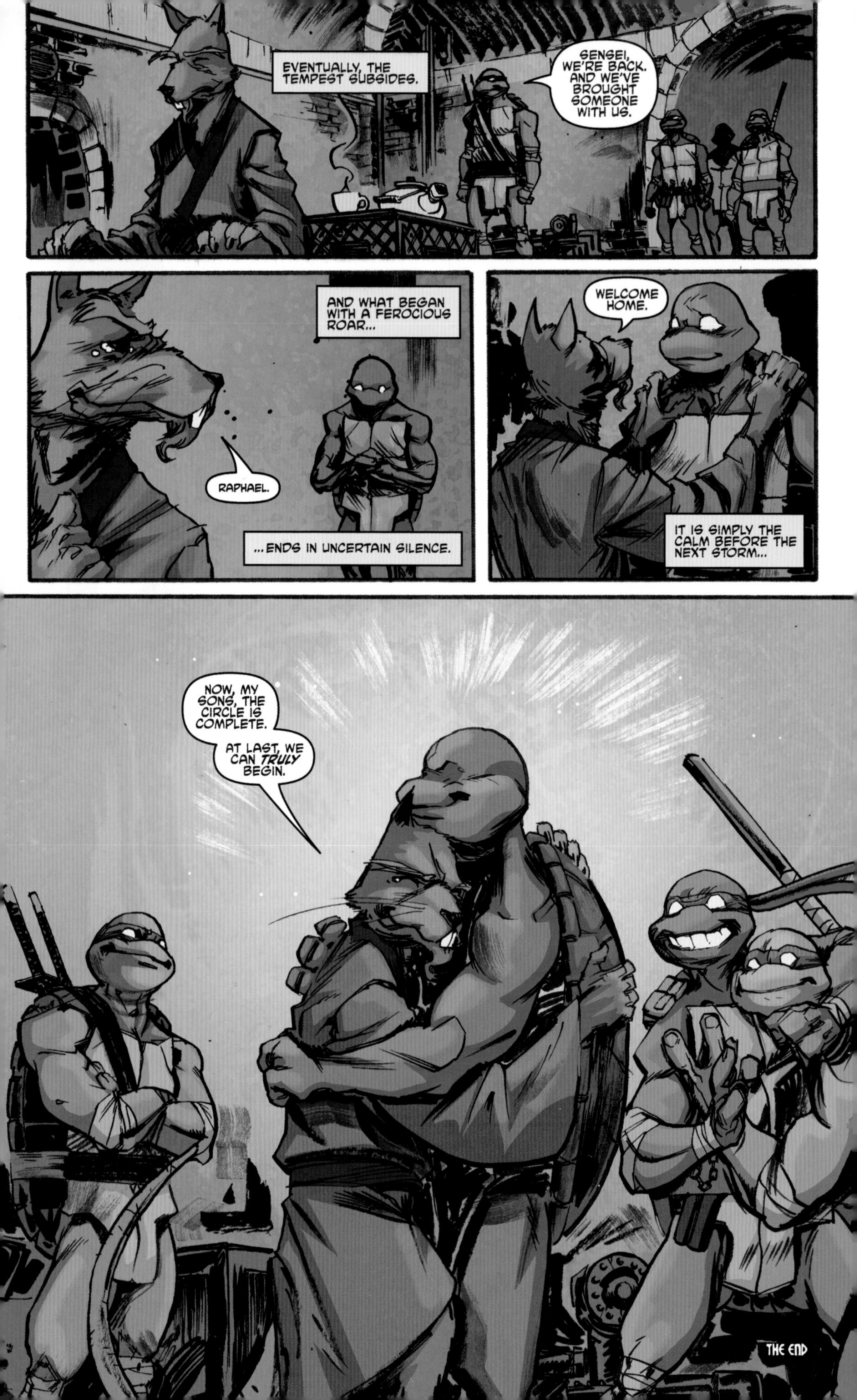
EVENTUALLY, THE TEMPEST SUBSIDES.
SENSEI, WE'RE BACK. AND WE'VE BROUGHT SOMEONE WITH US.
AND WHAT BEGAN WITH A FEROCIOUS ROAR...
RAPHAEL.
...ENDS IN UNCERTAIN SILENCE.
WELCOME HOME.
IT IS SIMPLY THE CALM BEFORE THE NEXT STORM...
NOW, MY SONS, THE CIRCLE IS COMPLETE.
AT LAST, WE CAN *TRULY* BEGIN.
THE END

ART GALLERY

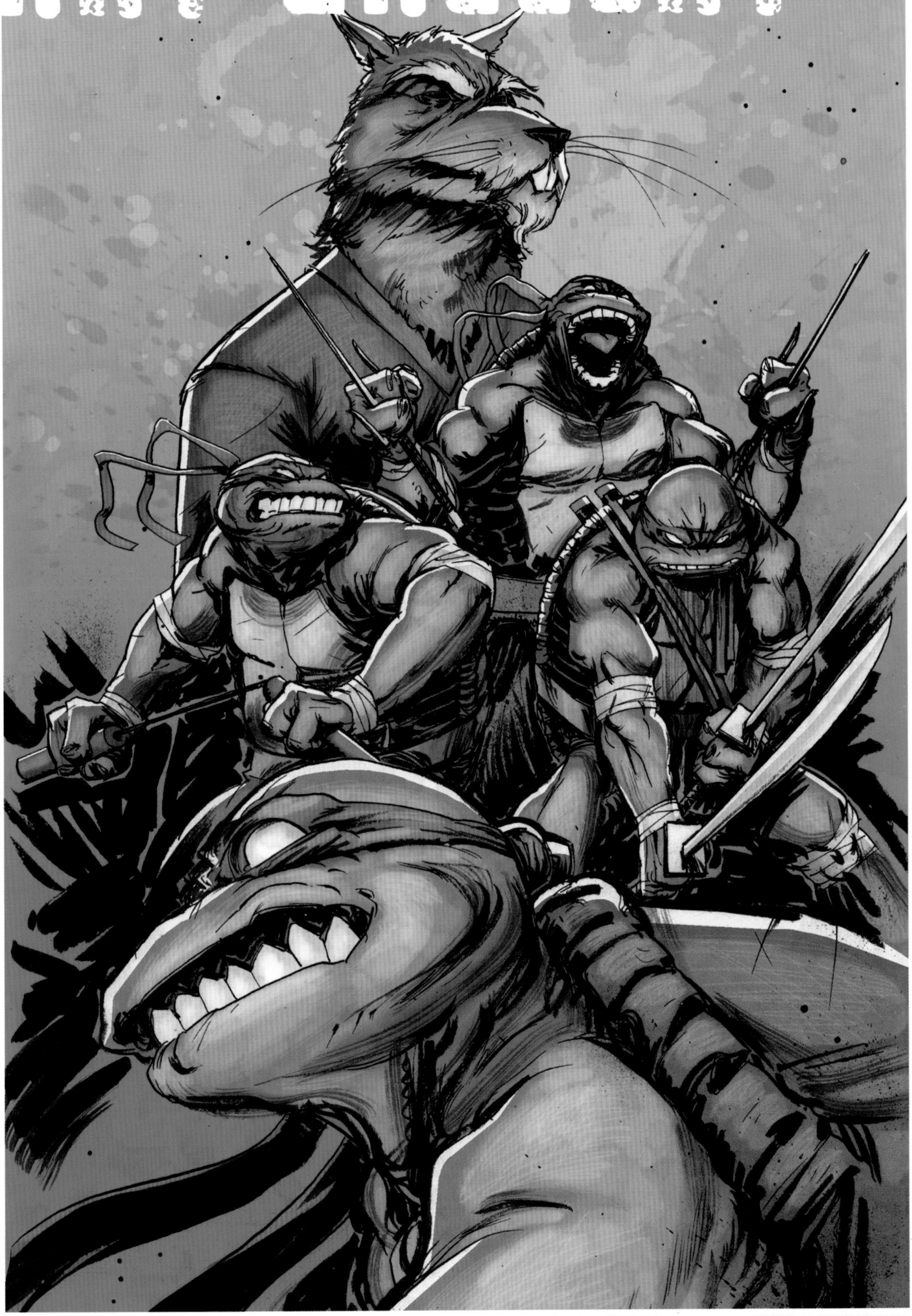

ART BY DAN DUNCAN · COLORS BY RONDA PATTISON

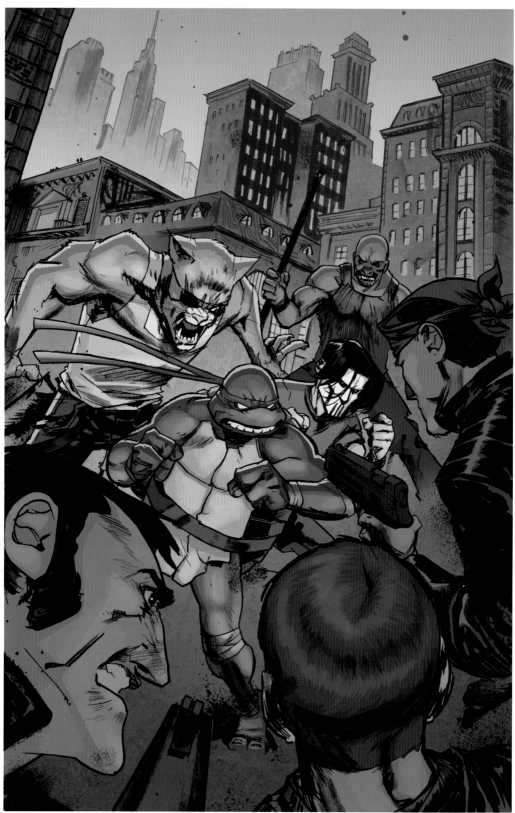

THIS PAGE: ART BY DAN DUNCAN · COLORS BY RONDA PATTISON

OPPOSITE PAGE: ART BY WALTER SIMONSON · COLORS BY RONDA PATTISON

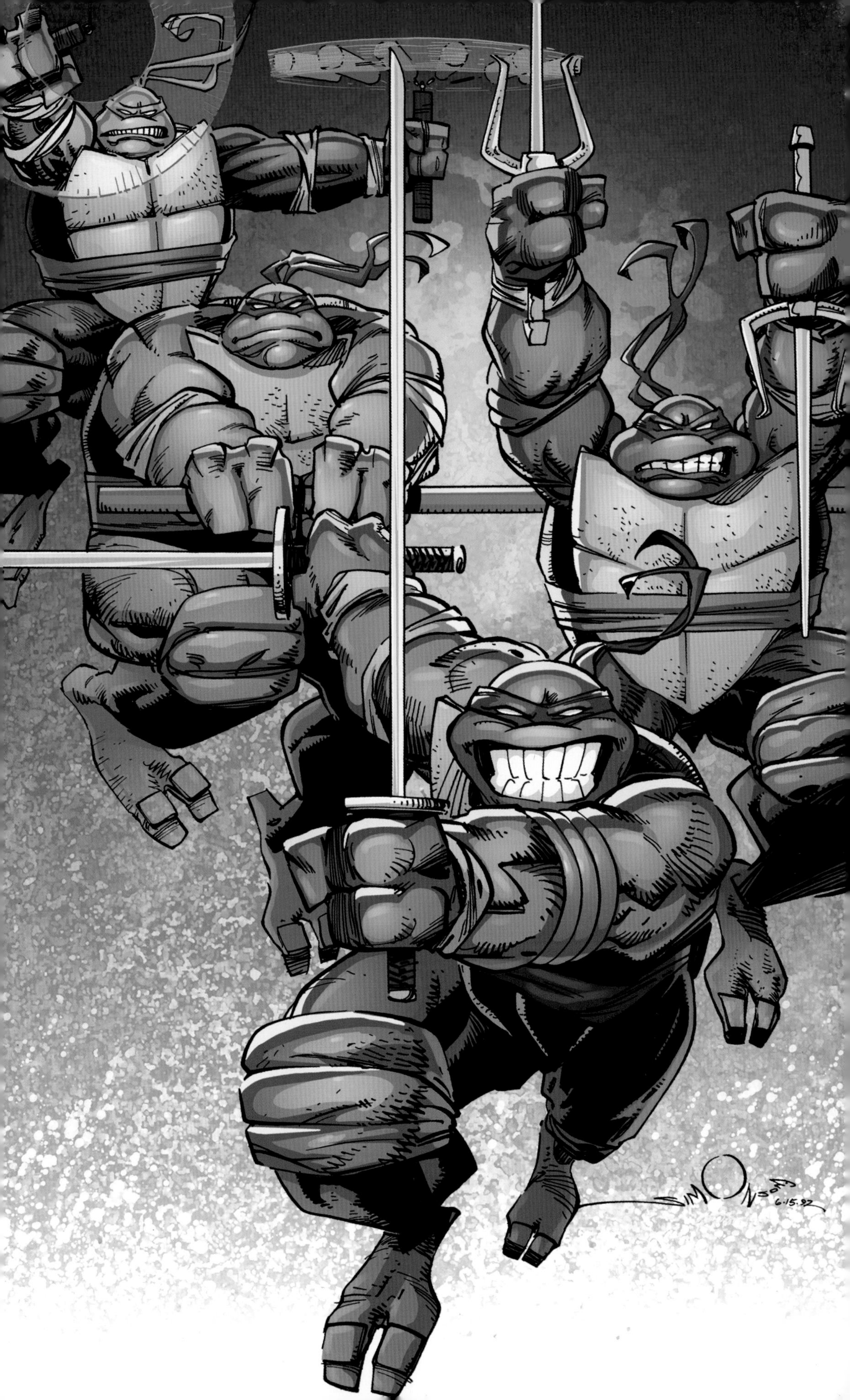
SIMONSON
6.15.92

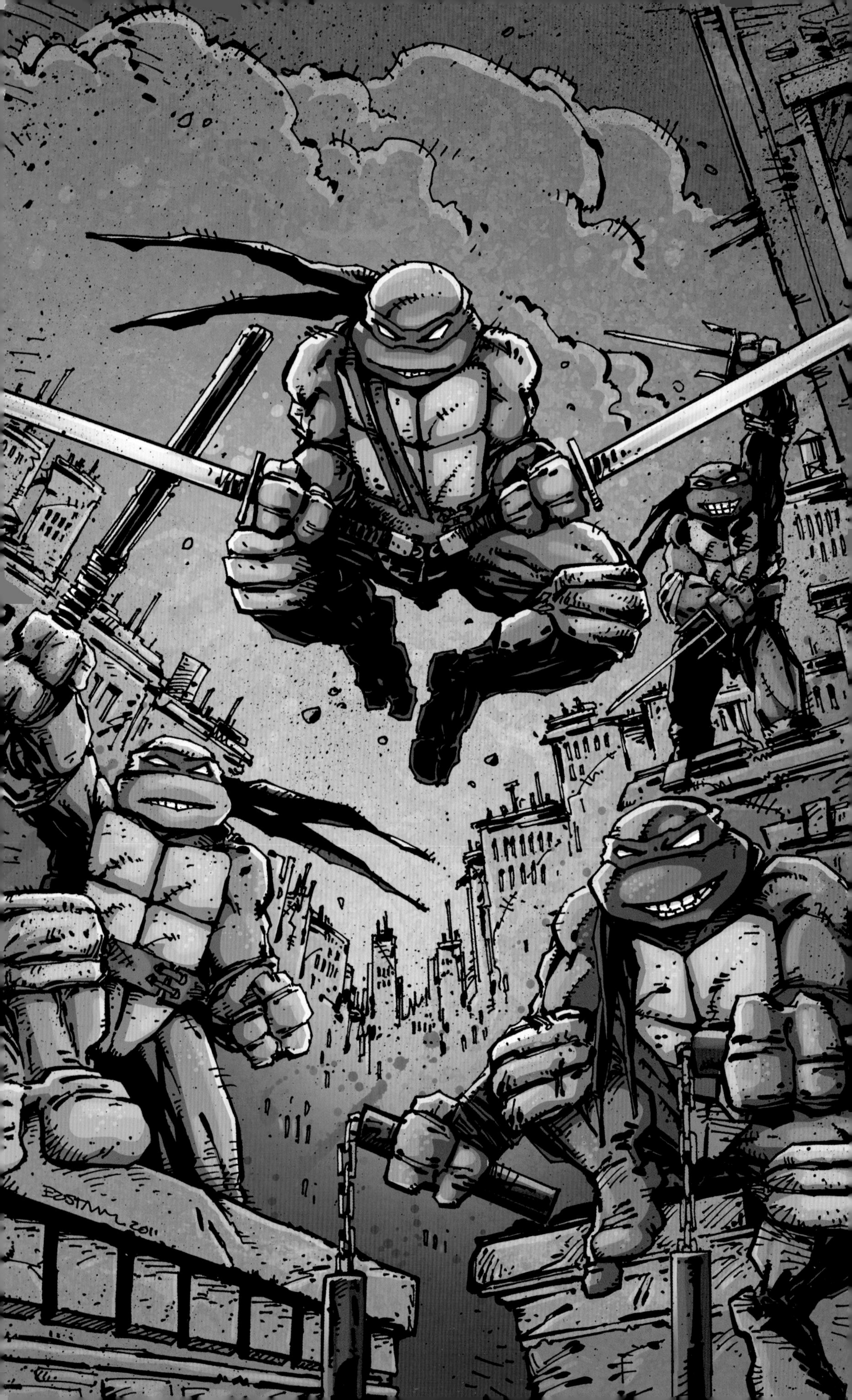

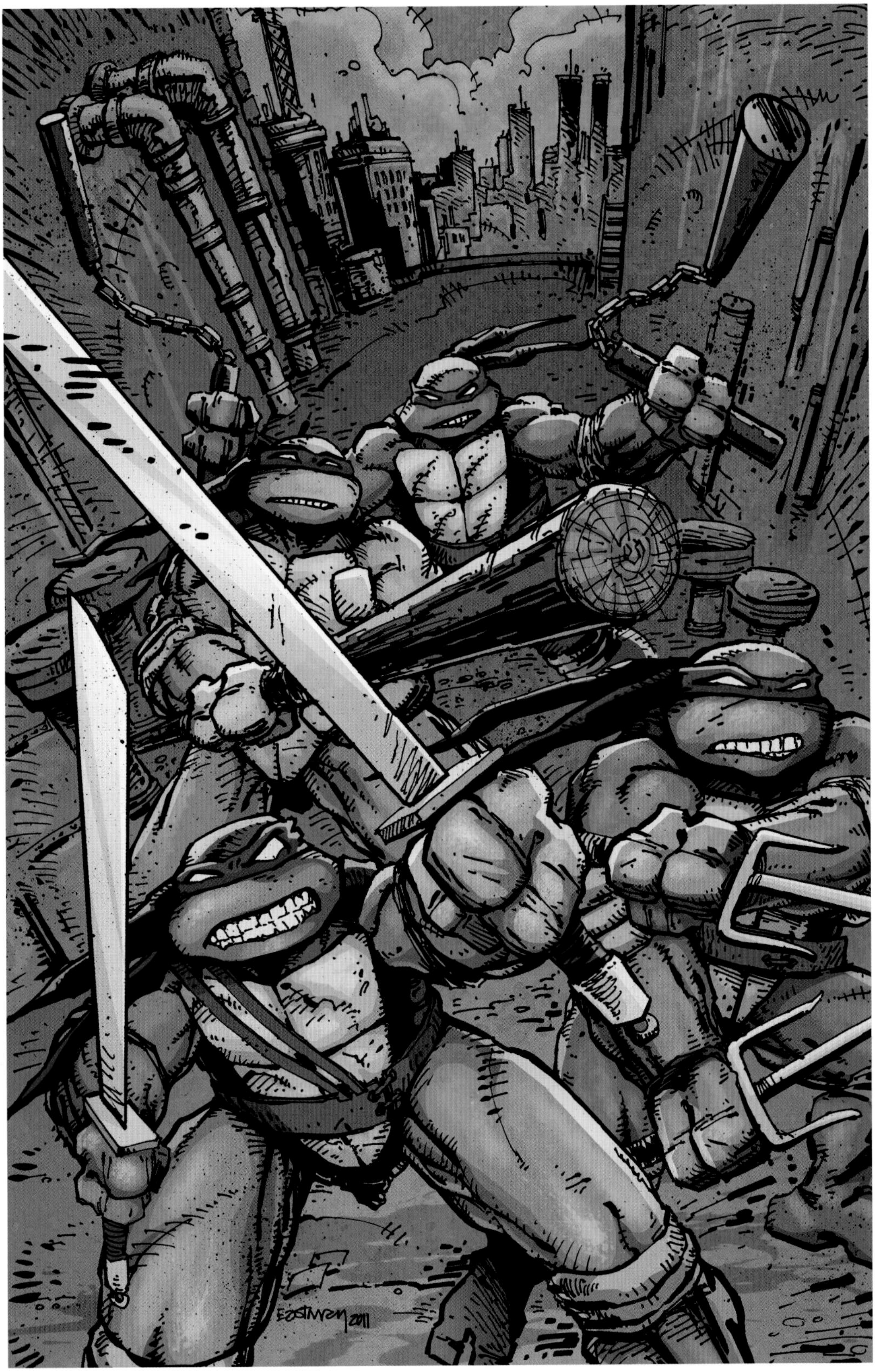

OPPOSITE AND THIS PAGE: ART BY KEVIN EASTMAN · COLORS BY RONDA PATTISON

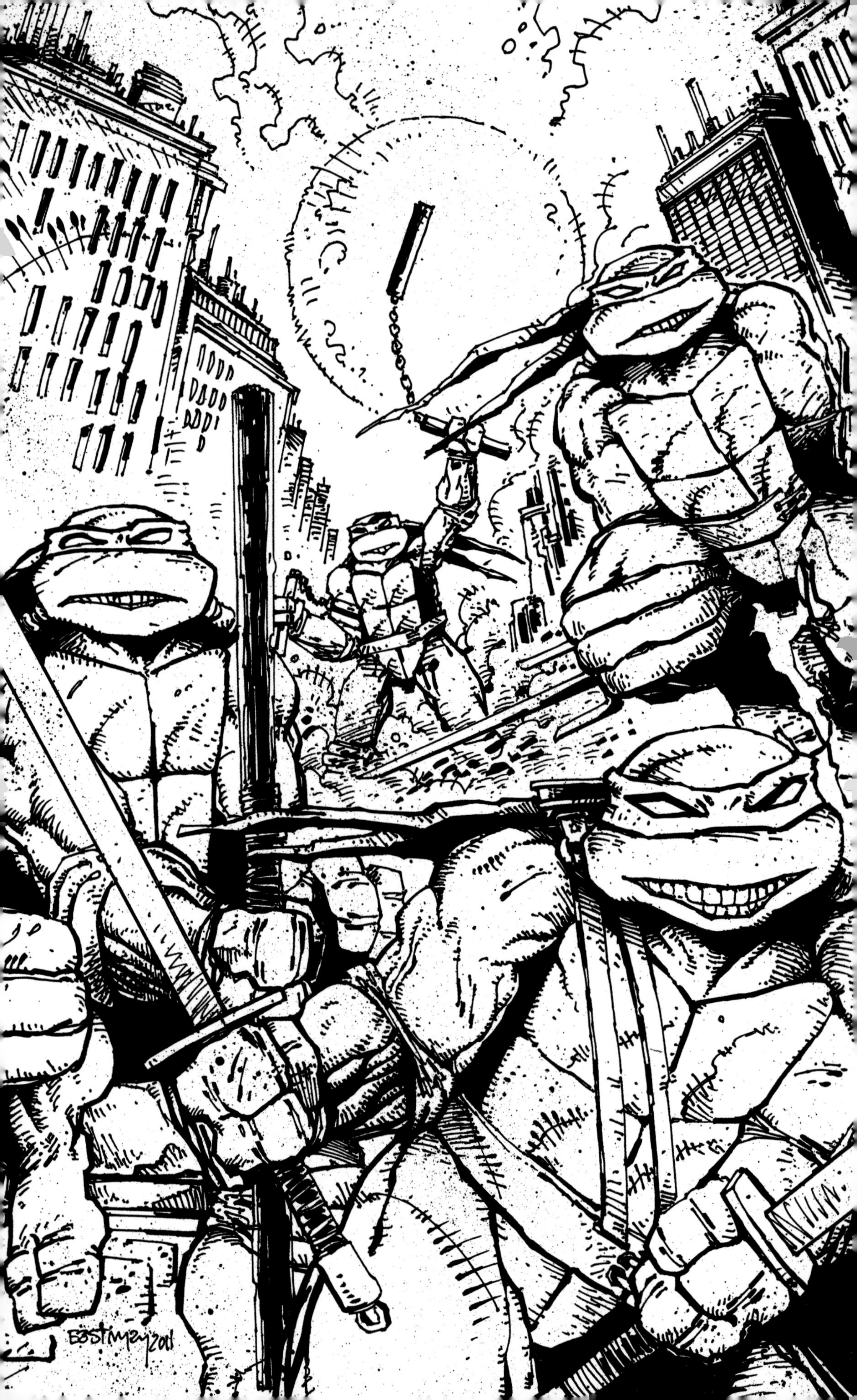
EASTMAN 2011

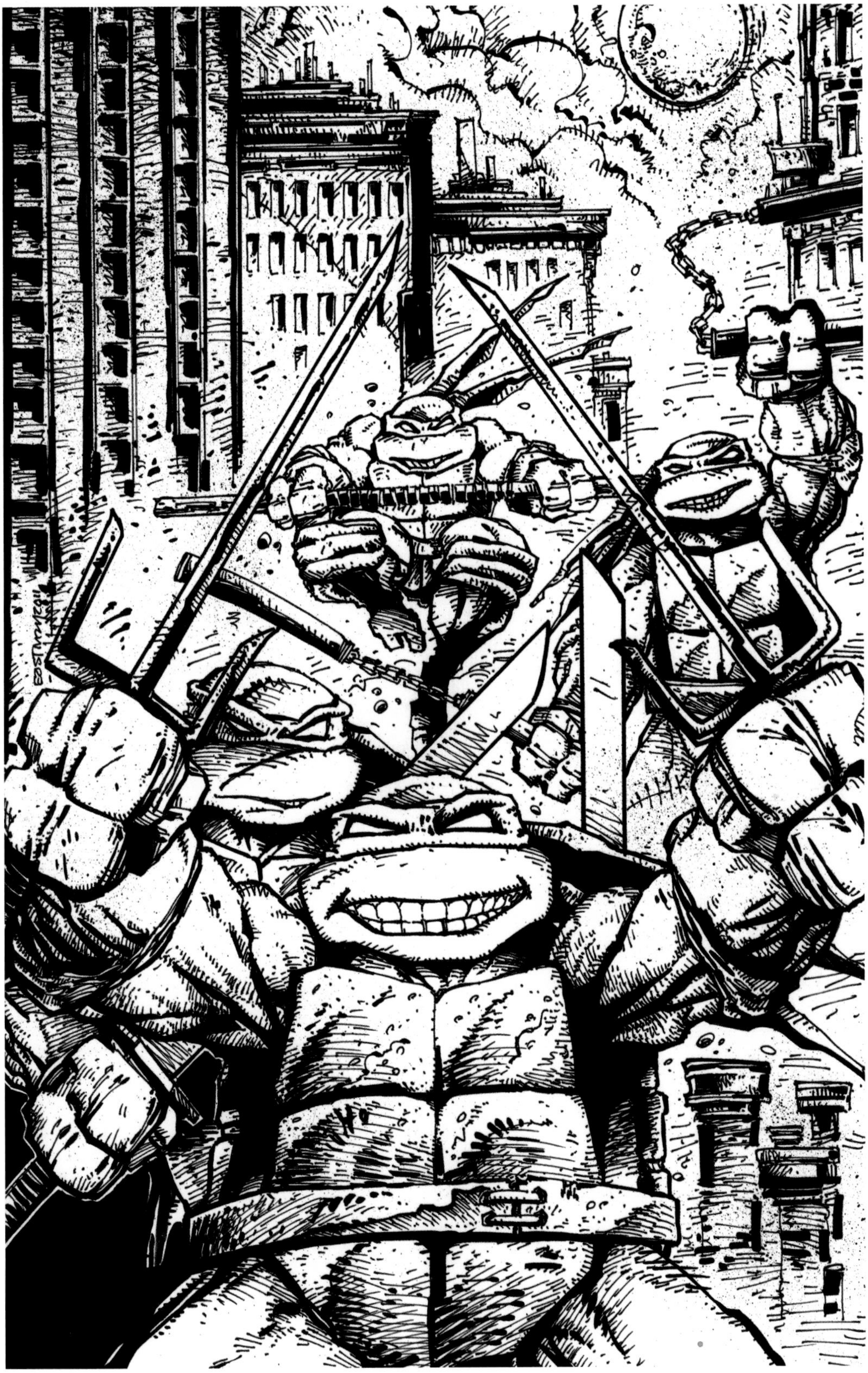

OPPOSITE AND THIS PAGE: ART BY **KEVIN EASTMAN**

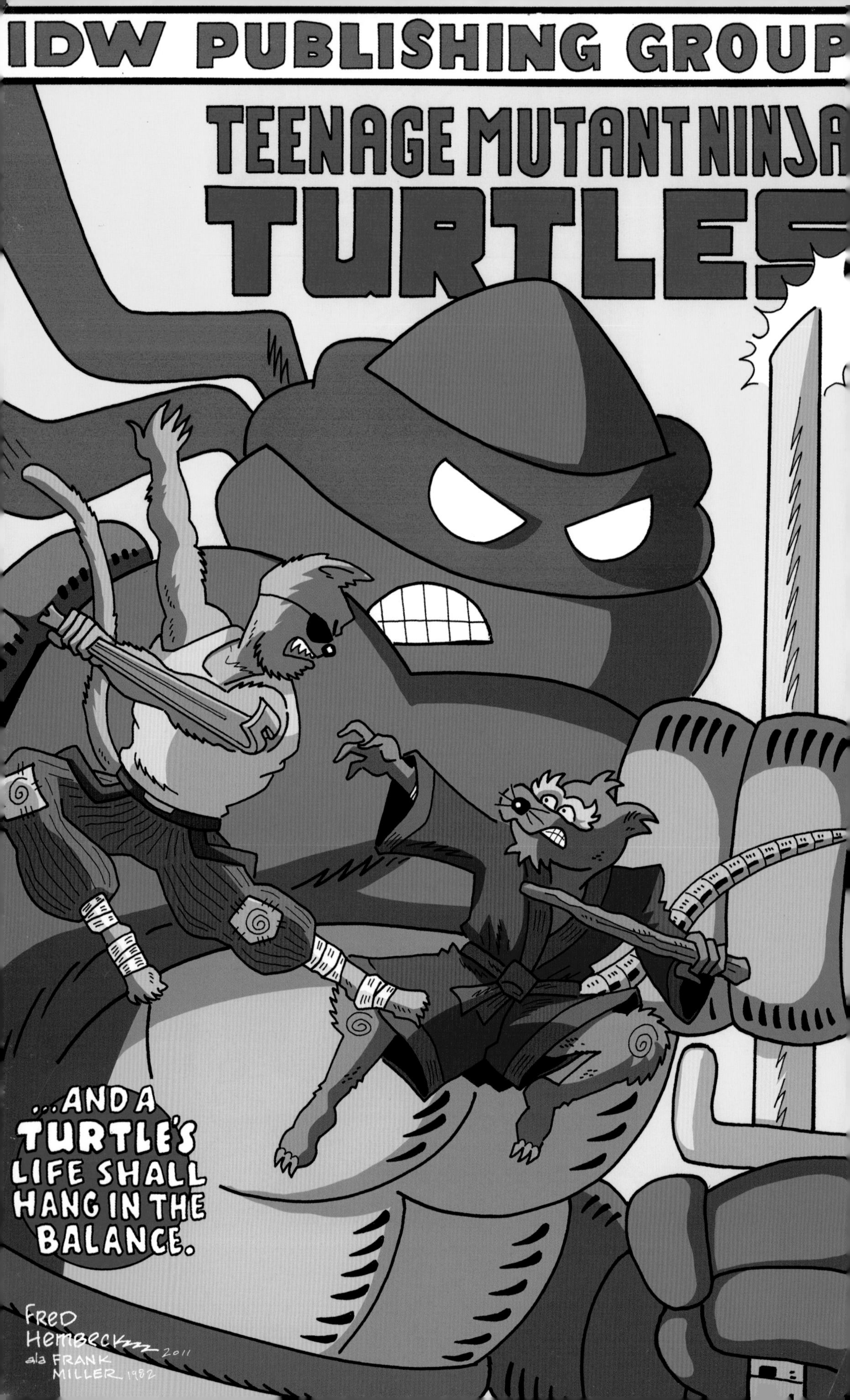
IDW PUBLISHING GROUP
TEENAGE MUTANT NINJA
TURTLES
...AND A TURTLE'S LIFE SHALL HANG IN THE BALANCE.
FRED HEMBECK 2011 ala FRANK MILLER 1982

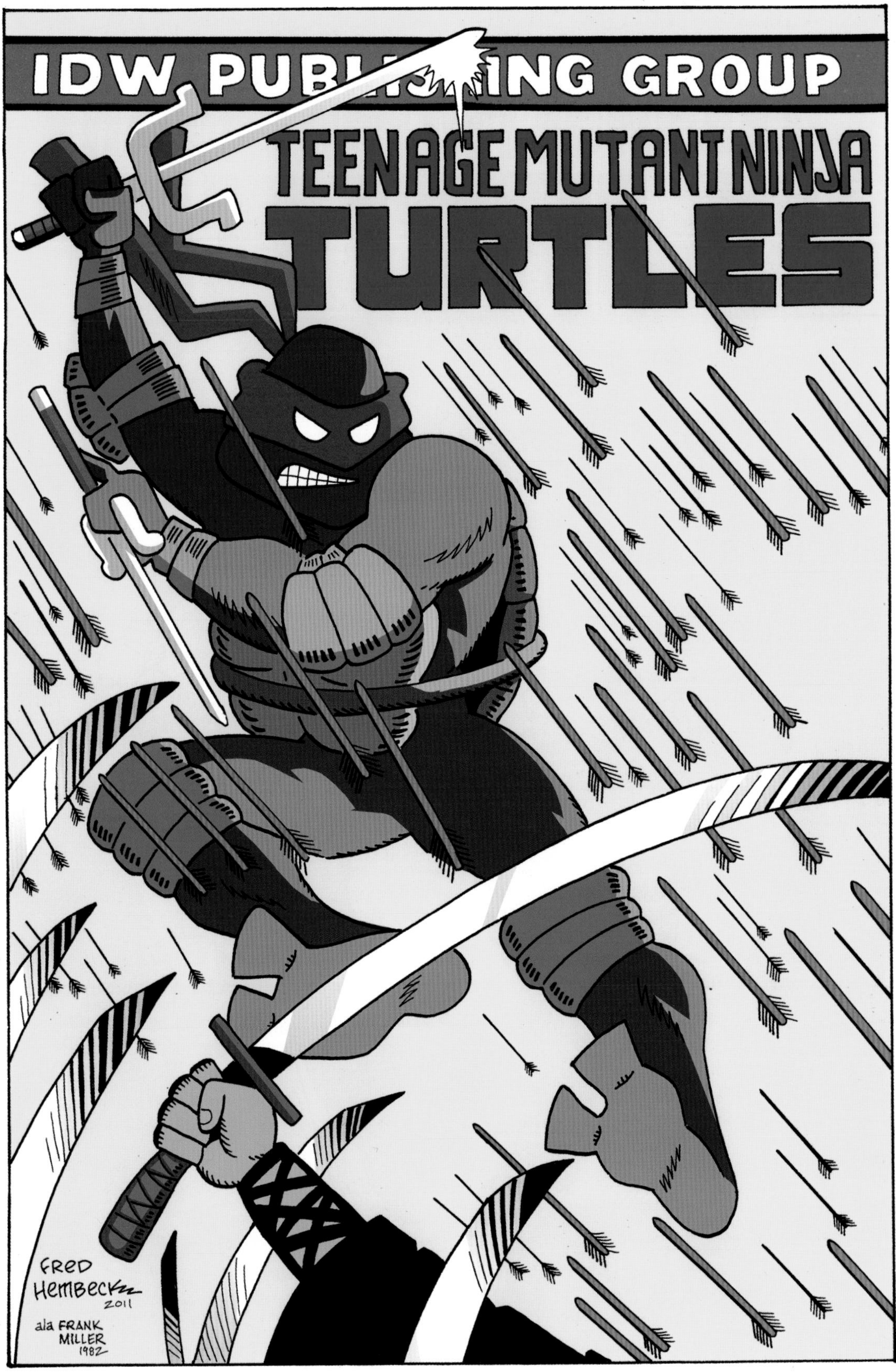
IDW PUBLISHING GROUP
TEENAGE MUTANT NINJA
TURTLES
FRED HEMBECK 2011
ala FRANK MILLER 1982

OPPOSITE AND THIS PAGE: ART BY FRED HEMBECK · COLORS BY RONDA PATTISON

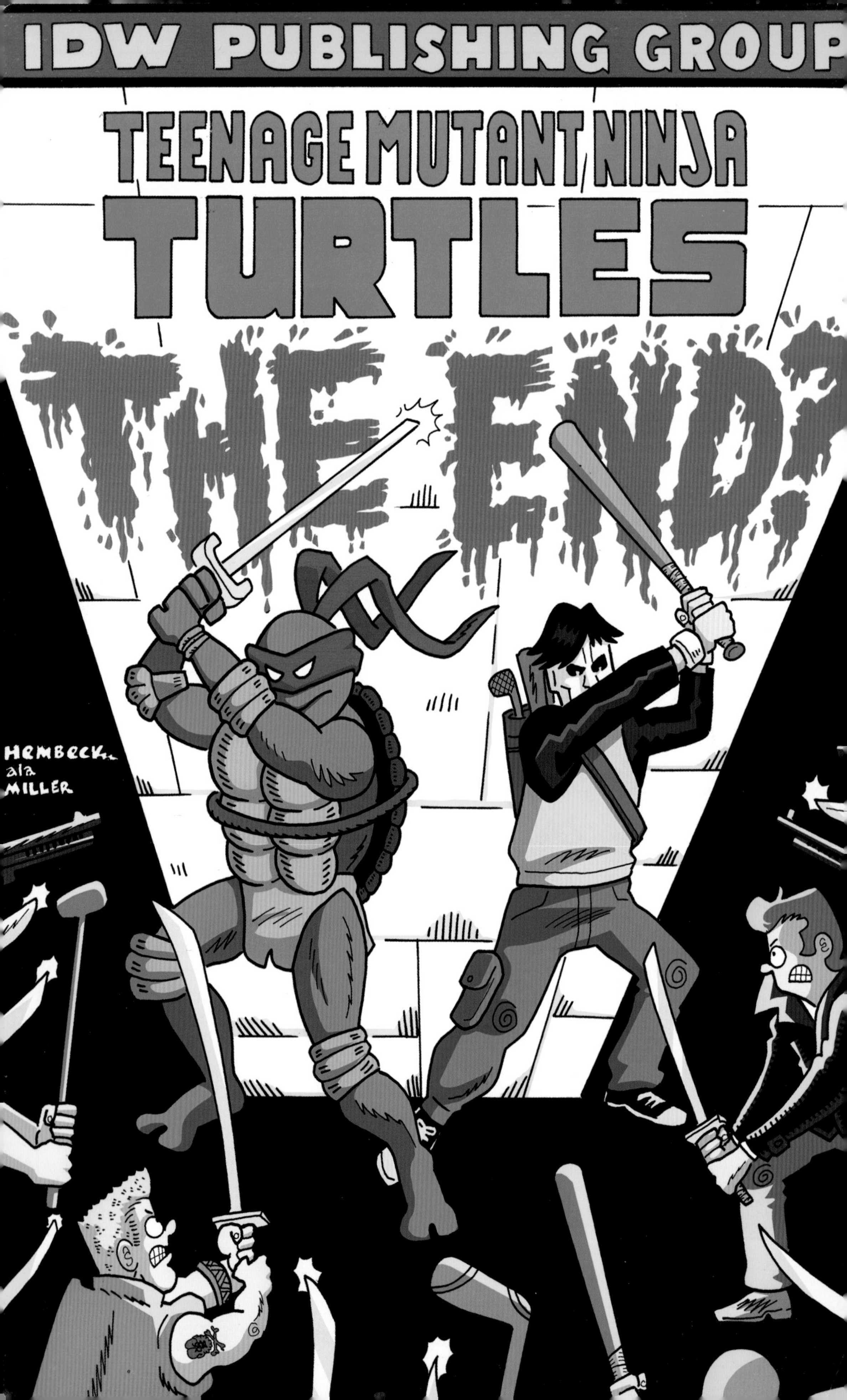
IDW PUBLISHING GROUP
TEENAGE MUTANT NINJA
TURTLES
THE END?
HEMBECK ala MILLER

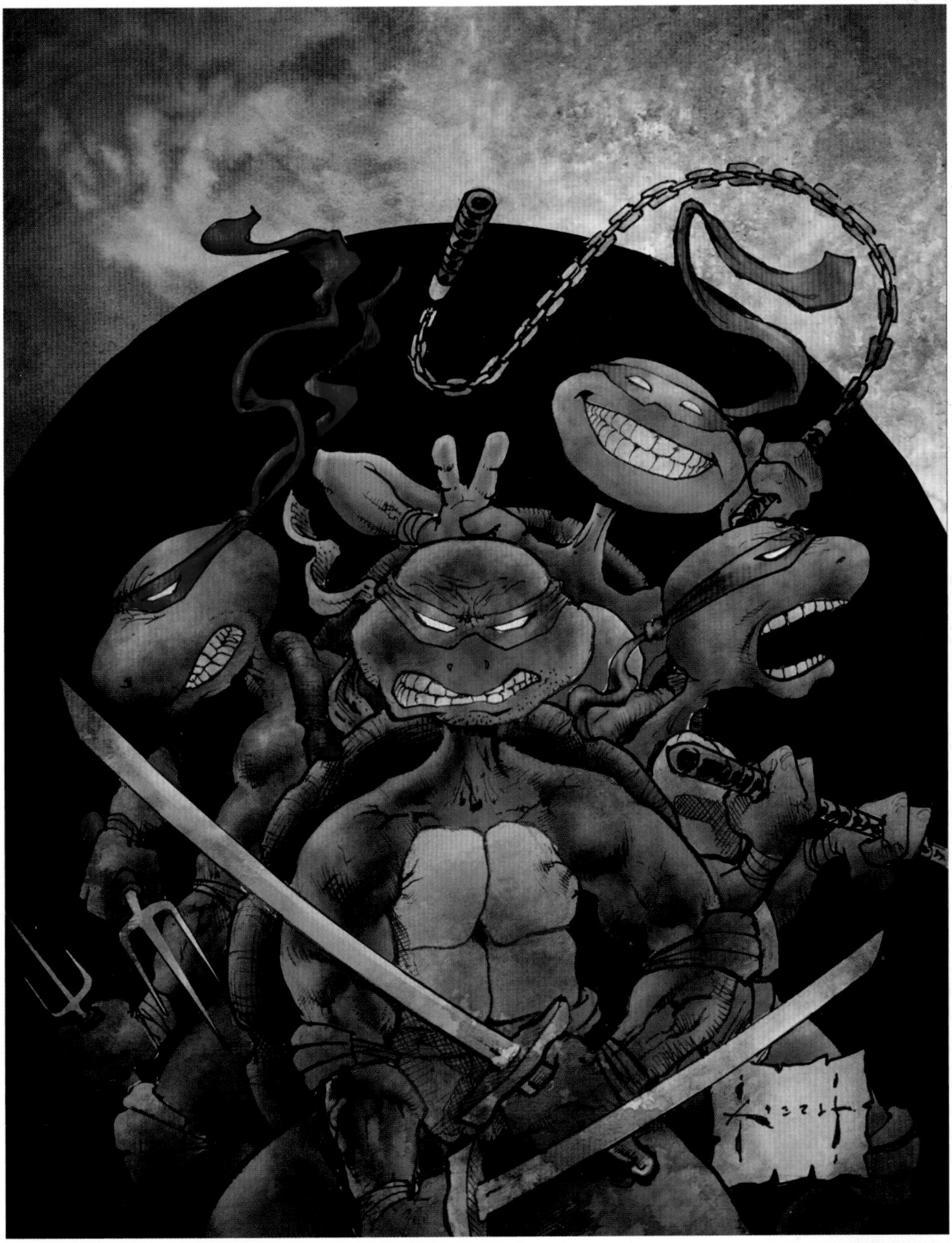

ART BY SAM KIETH

OPPOSITE PAGE: ART BY FRED HEMBECK · COLORS BY RONDA PATTISON